P9-CJR-498

The Courtesans

Joanna Richardson

The Courtesans

The demi-monde
in nineteenth-century France

THE WORLD PUBLISHING COMPANY
CLEVELAND AND NEW YORK

Copyright © 1967 by Joanna Richardson
Published by The World Publishing Company
2231 West 110th Street, Cleveland, Ohio 44102

FIRST EDITION

Library of Congress Catalog Card Number: 67–24363
All rights reserved. No part of this book may be reproduced
in any form without written permission from the publisher,
except for brief passages included in a review appearing in a
newspaper or magazine.

Printed in Great Britain GBWP 567

Que le lecteur ne se scandalise pas de cette gravité dans le frivole.

Baudelaire

Contents

Contents

Illustrations

Illustrations

View of Baden-Baden; from a stereoscopic photograph (*Sirot*)

Landing-stage on the Seine; from a stereoscopic photograph (*Sirot*)

More than half-seas over: un anglais qui ne peut plus. Musée Carnavalet

Route de Monaco, by Draner, from *Voyages et Voyageurs*. Musée Carnavalet

Caricature by Lavrate (*Sirot*)

Souper fin, c. 1860 (*Yvan Christ*)

Rue de la Paix (*Sirot*)

Cora Pearl; photo Anatole Pougnet (*Sirot*)

Moeurs Parisiennes – La Sortie de l'Opéra; engraving by Dumont after Emile Bayard. Bibliothèque de l'Opéra (*Archives Photographiques*)

Cora Pearl; photo Disdéri (*Mander and Mitchenson Theatre Collection*)

The Prince of Orange; photo Disdéri (*Sirot*)

Prince Napoleon; photo Charles D. Fredericks & Co (*Sirot*)

Charles-Auguste-Louis-Joseph, Duc de Morny, *c.* 1857; photo Nadar (*Archives Photographiques*)

Interior of Prince Napoleon's *Palais pompéien*; photo Richebourg (*Sirot*)

Alfred Stevens, *The Bath*, Musée de Luxembourg. (*Archives Photographiques*)

Constantin Guys, *Scene at the Races*. Petit Palais (*Bulloz*)

Gladiateur winning the Grand Prix de Paris at Longchamp, 1865 (*Radio Times Hulton Picture Library*)

Gustave Doré, *La Grande Avenue des Champs-Elysées*; from Desforges, *Chroniques Anecdotiques*. Bibliothèque Historique de la Ville de Paris

Winning horse with jockey and owner (*Sirot*)

Horse with an English groom (*Sirot*)

An Amazon (*Sirot*)

Alfred Stevens, *Désespérée*. Musée Royal des Beaux-Arts, Antwerp (*Copyright ACL*)

ESTHER GUIMOND AND LA PAÏVA   67

North side of the boulevard des Italiens (*Françoise Foliot*)

Le café Tortoni; from J. Castelnau, *En remontant les grands Boulevards*

Bal de l'Opéra; engraving by Provost (*Collection Viollet*)

Emile de Girardin, *c.* 1846; from Count Maurice Fleury and Louis Sonolet, *La Société du Second Empire*, 1911. Bibliothèque Nationale

General Cavaignac; from Horace de Viel-Castel, *Mémoires sur le Règne de Napoléon III*, 1883–4. British Museum

Les Fêtes d'Hiver – Une soirée chez Arsène Houssaye; from Arsène Houssaye, *Les Confessions*, 1885–91. Bibliothèque Nationale

François Guizot; from Horace de Viel-Castel, *op. cit.* British Museum

Louis-Philippe and Marie-Amélie; from Horace de Viel-Castel, *op. cit.* British Museum

La Païva (*Collection Viollet*)

View of Bad Ems (*Sirot*)

Henri Herz; photo Gaston, Mathieu & Cie (*Sirot*)

Onyx staircase in the Hôtel Païva; from Arsène Houssaye, *Un Hôtel célèbre sous le Second Empire* (*Sirot*)

Richard Wagner, *c.* 1867; photo Pierre Petit (*Sirot*)

Emile de Girardin, *c.* 1867; photo Pierre Petit (*Sirot*)

Illustrations

Paul de Saint-Victor. Musée Carnavalet

Théophile Gautier, *Portrait of Cydalise*; from Arsène Houssaye, *Les Confessions*, 1885–91. Bibliothèque Nationale

Ceiling in the *grand salon* of the Hôtel Païva painted by Paul Baudry; from Arsène Houssaye, *Un Hôtel célèbre sous le Second Empire* (*Sirot*)

La Païva's bed (*Collection Viollet*)

Arsène Houssaye; photo Pierre Petit & Trinquart (*Sirot*)

The Goncourt Brothers; from a sketch by Gavarni (*Author*)

Marquis de Païva. Bibliothèque Nationale

Alexandre Dumas *fils*, *c.* 1868; photo Frank (*Yvan Christ*)

Guido Henckel von Donnersmarck; caricature by Sem. Musée Carnavalet

Emile de Girardin (*Sirot*)

Prussian troops in the Place de la Concorde, 1 March 1871 (*Yvan Christ*)

CAROLINE LETESSIER, MADEMOISELLE MAXIMUM AND MARGUERITE BELLANGER 107

Young woman at her dressing-table; from a stereoscopic photograph (*Sirot*)

Féerie-revue (*Sirot*)

Caroline Letessier. Bibliothèque Nationale

Theatrical scene (*Sirot*)

Caroline Letessier in sailor's costume. Bibliothèque Nationale

Dinner-party in the 1860s; from a stereoscopic photograph (*Sirot*)

Léonide Leblanc; photo Disdéri (*Sirot*)

Georges Clemenceau, *c.* 1867; photo Etienne Carjat (*Sirot*)

Henri d'Orléans, Duc d'Aumale; photo A. Liébert (*Sirot*)

Léonide Leblanc (*Mander and Mitchenson Theatre Collection*)

Jean-Baptiste Carpeaux, *Bal costumé aux Tuileries*, 1867. Louvre (*Archives Photographiques*)

Marguerite Bellanger (*Sirot*)

Soldiers of the *Cent Gardes* (*Sirot*)

Ces petites dames; lithograph after Jules Pelcoq. Musée Carnavalet

Place de la Bourse, 1866; photo Ch. Marville (*Sirot*)

Marguerite Bellanger in male dress; from Pierre de Lano, *L'Amour à Paris sous le Second Empire*, 1896. Bibliothèque Nationale

Jean-Baptiste Carpeaux, bust of Marguerite Bellanger; from Hector Fleischmann, *Napoléon III et les Femmes*, 1913. Bibliothèque Historique de la Ville de Paris

Marguerite Bellanger with her carriage and horses; from Pierre de Lano, *op. cit.*

Marguerite Bellanger crowned with marguerites (*Radio Times Hulton Picture Library*)

View of Baden-Baden (*Sirot*)

Napoleon III, 20 April 1858; photo MM. Mayer frères et Pierson, imperial photographers (*Sirot*)

Empress Eugénie; photo Nadar (*Sirot*)

Marguerite Bellanger with her son (*Sirot*)

The Emperor's châlet at Vichy; from Hector Fleischmann, *op. cit.*

Woman and her maid at the dressing-table; from a stereoscopic photograph (*Sirot*)

Trying on a crinoline; from a stereoscopic photograph (*Sirot*)

Scene at a ball; from a stereoscopic photograph (*Sirot*)

'*Cocotte en délire*'. Musée Carnavalet

Tableau of diners at a restaurant; from a stereoscopic photograph (*Sirot*)
'*Vive la joie!*'. Musée Carnavalet
Frontispiece of *Les Cocodés par une cocodette*. Bibliothèque Historique de la Ville de Paris
Title-page of *Confessions de Marguerite Bellanger*, 1862. British Museum

ALICE OZY   139

Portrait of Alice Ozy, 1842, by Vincent Vidal. Bibliothèque Nationale
La Maison d'Or; after the lithograph by Provost, from Louis Barron, *Paris Pittoresque,*
    1800–1900, 1899. Bibliothèque Historique de la Ville de Paris
Café des Algériennes; lithograph by D. Alex (*Sirot*)
Alice Ozy's châlet on Lake Enghien; from Emile de Girardin etc., *Les Eaux Illustrées.*
    Enghien et ses Environs, 1862. British Museum
The Duc d'Aumale, 1840; after the portrait by Winterhalter, from J.-L. Vaudoyer,
    Alice Ozy ou l'Aspasie moderne (*Trémois*). Bibliothèque Nationale
Edmond About; from Arsène Houssaye, *Les Confessions*, 1885–91. Bibliothèque Nationale
Bohemian gathering. Bibliothèque Nationale
Gustave Doré (*Author*)
Théodore Chassériau; engraving after a self-portrait. Musée Carnavalet
Théophile Gautier, 1849; from a sketch by Chassériau, from J.-L. Vaudoyer, *op. cit.*
Chassériau, *Alice Ozy in a Gandoura*, 1849. Musée Carnavalet (*Archives Photographiques*)
Chassériau, *Baigneuse endormie*, 1850. Musée Calvet, Avignon (*Archives Photographiques*)
Victor Hugo with his sons (*Bulloz*)
Madame Pilloy. Bibliothèque Nationale

LA DAME AUX CAMÉLIAS   155

Marie Duplessis, anonymous miniature. Comédie-Française
Foyer de danse at the Opéra; engraving by Staines. Bibliothèque de l'Opéra (*Archives
    Photographiques*)
Arcade in the Palais-Royal; from Desforges, *Chroniques Anecdotiques*. Bibliothèque
    Historique de la Ville de Paris
Ranelagh Gardens, August 1846 (*Collection Viollet*)
Alexandre Dumas *fils, c.* 1850; photo Nadar (*Sirot*)
Title-page and illustrations of Marguerite Gautier and Armand Duval from Alexandre
    Dumas (*fils*), *La Dame aux camélias*, 1858, *édition illustrée par Gavarni*. British Museum
Franz Liszt, portrait by Lehmann. Musée Carnavalet (*Bulloz*)
Jules Janin; from Arsène Houssaye, *Les Confessions*, 1885–91. Bibliothèque Nationale
A box at the Théâtre des Italiens; from Jules Janin, *L'Eté à Paris*, 1843. British Museum
Camille Roqueplan, *Marie Duplessis at the Theatre*, 1845. Musée Carnavalet
The old passage de l'Opéra; from Louis Cheronnet, *Paris tel qu'il fut*. Bibliothèque
    Historique de la Ville de Paris

LA PRÉSIDENTE   187

Jean-Baptiste Clésinger, bust of Mme Sabatier, 1847. Louvre (*Archives Photographiques*)

Illustrations

ACKNOWLEDGMENTS

The author and publishers would like to thank the institutions and photographers
mentioned above for kind permission to use their photographs, and, in particular,
Georges Sirot, who made his unique collection of photographs available, and Françoise
Foliot, who photographed all the items in Paris museums and libraries and gave in-
valuable help in the preparation of this book.

Picture Research by Georgia Tennant

Layout of illustrations by Jane Mackay

Introduction

A courtesan is less than a mistress, and more than a prostitute. She is less than a mistress because she sells her love for material benefits; she is more than a prostitute because she chooses her lovers. The courtesan is, in fact, a woman whose profession is love, and whose clients may be more or less distinguished. She may have been a respectable woman, cast by some unhappy affair into the demi-monde; she may be a woman of humble birth, whose only hope of fortune seemed to be her physical attraction. She may be an actress who willingly abandoned her inadequate hopes in the theatre; she may simply be a careerist, set on a life of adventure. But whatever her origins and purpose, whatever her other accomplishments may be, the courtesan's profession is to sell her favours well, to practise her particular arts with skill. Her profession is hard; by a certain age she will either be rich and respectably, even triumphantly, married, or she will be prematurely old, alone, and with no means of earning her living. The courtesan's profession may give her a life well beyond her dreams, or it may finally break her.

The profession she follows may be the oldest in the world; but in nineteenth-century France it proved itself to be a profession of distinction. Perhaps one might suggest some reasons why. French society has always given a generous place to women. It has always been an ambiance in which a woman felt delightedly feminine. 'A woman's first duty,' wrote Théophile Gautier, 'is to be beautiful;' and if nature sometimes failed to make her so – as it did with Mme de Maintenon – her intelligence and intellect and her quality of character were recognised. The English concept of the club could never have been widely accepted in France. In the nineteenth century there were certain clubs in Paris which conferred a cachet on their members (Parisian solicitors used to say that membership of the Jockey Club meant another two hundred thousand francs in a dowry). But Parisian clubs could never become a welcome escape from life, a masculine haven from the domestic world. The Frenchman has never found it enough to show civility, gallantry and *empressement*, and to escape to his club for conversation. He naturally prefers mixed society.

But while his character has remained constant (at least in this respect), the nineteenth century gave the courtesan all the opportunities of a golden age. In 1815, the fall of Napoleon ended an era of warfare which had stretched back over generations. For the first time for decades, indeed for centuries, French youth was not summoned to expend its chief energies on the battlefield and at sea. The House of Bourbon was restored, under the aegis of the Allied Powers. France was free to practise the arts and enjoy the pleasures of peace. Nor was there only vast relief at freedom from war, a natural desire to make the most of happiness. The French Revolution had occurred only twenty-six years earlier. A social revolution was changing Europe. The middle classes were not now merely the stable element of the population. For the first time in French history, they were enjoying power. They enjoyed it largely through their money.

For money was not now the privilege of the upper classes; it was there to be made by anyone with financial sense and determination. Political upheaval had produced its speculators; the industrial revolution opened a thousand projects to the perceptive. The social revolution meant that new strata of society must be considered. New markets and new inventions beckoned the enterprising bourgeois. There were the needs of commerce (a new clientèle took increasing interest in sophisticated food and fashion). There was the establishment of the popular Press, the existence of a new audience for theatres and concerts. 'The consumption of plays is so great today,' wrote Gautier in 1843, 'that the dramatists cannot keep up with it ... One of the conditions of our time is to impose continuous work, without break or pause, on artists and writers. There is always a voice behind you which says, as it did to Ahasuerus, the Wandering Jew, "Go on!"' An immense new readership was opened for popular novels, travel books, and books of a more edifying nature. By the middle of the century, the network of railways, spreading over France, would largely have changed conceptions of travel, and presented more magnificent opportunities. It was small wonder that money became the leitmotif of existence. By the 1860s, Gautier could write that 'the religion of money is today the only one which has no unbelievers'.

In such an atmosphere, it was not surprising that women should determine

Opposite. Edouard Manet, *Nana.*

to seek their fortunes: that they should explore the unbridled love of pleasure, the gold mines that were there for the taking. 'If golden louis were meant to roll, and diamonds to glitter,' Cora Pearl would write in her *Mémoires*, 'no one can accuse me of diverting these noble things from their true channel.' The calculations of Cora Pearl (more in love with louis and diamonds than with men) brought her a spectacular success; though even her triumph paled beside that of the hideous la Païva, who rose from the Moscow ghetto to the Champs-Élysées, from destitution to almost indecent wealth, and, had she lived a few years longer, would have seen herself a princess.

The nineteenth century was an age for dazzling careerists; and some of its most spectacular careers were those of the great courtesans. Some of them died in sad neglect, some of them died respectable, some of them died in quite astounding grandeur; but most of them, at some time or other, enjoyed their own *hôtel*, perhaps their own château, their impeccable horses and carriages, their magnificent clothes and jewels, their influence over eminent men of the day. They made their mark in the Bois de Boulogne, in their boxes at the theatre, at Longchamp, Vichy, Baden, sometimes further afield. They constituted a class apart, an extraordinary sorority. They created, in fact, what Dumas *fils* was to recognise in fiction: they were the makers of the demi-monde.

Some of them simply entertained the Parisian of the nineteenth century, but they are still worth recalling as social phenomena which could not have existed before their time, or since. Others have earned (and the word is deliberate) immortality. Marie Duplessis earned it by her death, and her inspiration of *La Dame aux camélias* and *La Traviata*. Madame Sabatier, who compels our affection and admiration, earned it in her lifetime, from Baudelaire.

In this book I have tried to present some of the most distinguished courtesans of nineteenth-century France. Some of them were not French by birth, but all were French in spirit, and all of them were, at some time, established in Paris. Most of them were born during the Bourbon Restoration (1814–30), and their careers were part of French social history in the days of Louis-Philippe and the Second Empire. There have, of course, been *grandes cocottes* since 1870, but the fall of the Second Empire ended the empire of the courtesan. She was a brilliant, exotic bird that flourished in the days of a permissive Imperial Court, of widespread social licence and political irresponsibility. There could be no such careless *joie de vivre* after 1870. The courtesan could not thrive so well in the new Republican world. The First World War made her survival almost impossible.

Since the courtesan is a professional woman, I have had to exclude many celebrated women who were courtesans only for pleasure. Among them are Mme de Staël, who was the mistress to an age, and Mme Sand, who was mistress to another; Rachel, who led a turbulent life on and off the stage, and Sarah Bernhardt, who declared: 'I have been among the great lovers of my time.' Hortense Schneider remains, above all, the interpreter of Offenbach, however famous her private life may have been; and La Castiglione, who was sent by Cavour to seduce Napoleon III, was a fine political agent, a superbly beautiful ornament of the Second Empire, but she cannot be called a *fille de joie*.

Yet such women as these, if they cannot enter the ranks of the great courtesans, helped to create the climate in which the courtesans could flourish. They helped to define the demi-monde on the social map; they reflected it, sometimes, in their books, their songs, their stage performances, their own way of life. And, like their professional sisters, they invite the question: is it mere coincidence that the age of the courtesan should also have been a magnificent age for the arts?

Some of the twelve women I have chosen have been richly documented; others have eluded biographers and, somehow, escaped the memoirs and periodicals of the time. Some of my 'sitters' have therefore been given full-length portraits, and others have been rather briefly sketched. The most significant courtesan is undoubtedly Madame Sabatier. She is a radiant figure in literary history. I have always wanted to pay tribute to *la Présidente*, at 4, rue Frochot.

I should like to thank Mr Robert Speaight for his help with this book, and I am most grateful to Mr Graham Greene for lending me *The Pretty Women of Paris*.

J.R.

Hampstead,
January, 1966.

1
Blanche d'Antigny

Marie-Ernestine Antigny (1840–74)

Marie-Ernestine Antigny, better known as Blanche d'Antigny, was born on 9 May 1840, the eldest of the three children of Jules Antigny, a carpenter in Martizay, a little town near Bourges, in the Indre.[1] Her father was not only skilled at his work, he was practised in the art of seduction, and when Marie-Ernestine was seven, he finally left his wife, and went off with a local girl to Paris. The following year his wife set off in search of him, and entrusted her children to their aunt at Mézières-sur-Brenne.

Adélaïde was already delicate, but Marie-Ernestine was radiantly healthy, with dark green eyes, champagne-coloured hair, and a milk-white complexion. She thrived on the outdoor life, riding horses and wandering in the fields. When in 1850 her mother summoned her to Paris, she hid herself in the attic at Mézières in despair; she could not bear the thought of leaving the countryside – which in fact she would not see again.

Her little brother, Zacharie, had died at the age of seven; in Paris, her sister Adélaïde died, and Mme Antigny concentrated all her affection on her surviving daughter. Mme Antigny did sewing and housework for some distinguished families, and the Marquise de Gallifet, so it is said, helped to send Marie-Ernestine to the Couvent des Oiseaux, a convent school where most of her fellow-pupils had excellent backgrounds, and she learnt poise and good manners as well as the subjects on the curriculum. The only subjects she enjoyed were geography, which appealed to her sense of adventure, and Holy Scripture. It may be that the Bible satisfied her emotional nature, her love of drama; certainly she exulted in the organ music in the chapel, and sang and prayed with intense devotion. Had it not been for the death of the Marquise de Gallifet, she might have become a nun.

However, the Marquise died, and she was taken away from the convent at fourteen; her mother soon found her a job as a saleswoman in a draper's in the rue du Bac. The girls at the convent had called her Blanche because of her fine complexion, and she proudly kept the name. She was already well aware of her powers of attraction, and she already longed to wear fine clothes. She wanted fame and luxury and admiration – and she found a path which led to them, one evening, when a young shop assistant took her to the Closerie des Lilas. There, in the gaslit pleasure-gardens, excited by the wine, the rich, conflicting smells of scent and cigars, she threw herself into dancing a can-can; her escort vanished, and left her to drink champagne with some chance admirers. One of them, a Wallachian, seduced her; a few weeks later he took her to Bucharest.

There, on the banks of the Dambovnic, they stayed at a disreputable inn. Their fellow-guests seemed dubious, sinister characters. Blanche soon longed to escape from her lover. She joined some gipsy minstrels, and danced to their violins and mandolines, but the gipsies ill-treated her, and again she fled. One night she was found in the ruins of the convent of Kotorceny, ragged and distraught, and thinking once again she would take her vows. But the world of gallantry still remained more attractive than the cloister, and she could not abandon her career. She made countless conquests; and among them, so people said, was an Armenian archbishop, whom she nearly married. Since her life often resembled one of Perrault's fairy-tales, she also met a prince, who fell in love with her and introduced her into the highest Wallachian society. At last, exhausted by her life of pleasure, she became gravely ill; and then nostalgia took possession. Early in 1856, when she had recovered, she returned, like a homing pigeon, to Paris.

She needed her independence too much to go back to her mother. She went to live with a wardrobe-dealer, a Savoyarde by the name of Ambroisine, who encouraged her extravagant tastes, and hoped to exploit them. Blanche had herself engaged as a rider at the Cirque d'hiver; she allowed herself to be admired cantering in the Bois de Boulogne. She had recognised the possibilities of the Closerie des Lilas; now it was time to explore the more select delights of the Bal Mabille. In August 1858, for the first time, she entered the illuminated gates in the avenue Montaigne. And there, by chance, she met a journalist in search of a love-affair; and, with his encourage-ment, she began to dance. Her final *galop* was a triumph. A few days later, on the recommendation of Gustave Lafargue, the dramatic critic, she offered herself to the Théâtre de la Porte-Saint-Martin. She signed her first engage-ment for d'Ennery's *Faust*, and in this, on 27 September, she made her début as the living statue of la Belle Hélène. She had nothing to say; but 'the

6

whole audience, including Jules Janin, admired the plastic beauty of her harmonious form'.[2] Paul Baudry, the artist, took Blanche as his model for his picture of *The Repentant Magdalen*.[3]

★

At the age of eighteen, Blanche Antigny was already a celebrity; and she already understood how to exploit her fame. After ten days at the Porte-Saint-Martin, she renounced the stage; but her first public triumph had launched her finally into the demi-monde. Some of her lovers were artists and journalists who were far from rich; and Arsène Houssaye, the man of letters who chronicled the *vie galante* of his age, recorded that

she is so little made to be a courtesan that, according to one of her friends, she does not know how to get paid when her lover goes. This is because she sleeps like a log, and the chance admirer takes advantage of her leaden slumber, and beats a quick retreat. However, she has found a way to outwit the man who pulls a fast one: she sews his nightshirt to her own before she goes to sleep.[4]

Fortunately, some of Blanche Antigny's lovers were wealthy; and her income rose to four thousand francs a month. She moved from student lodgings into a furnished suite of three rooms; and there, in a four-poster bed which was hung with embroidered, lace-edged curtains, she dispensed her favours. On rosewood tables, round the room, artificial flowers blossomed for all eternity under glass bells. The suggestive scent of ambergris filled the air. Ambroisine received the clients and kept the accounts.

At eleven in the morning, Blanche would install herself on the terrace of the Café de Madrid, where, perhaps, her first lover would meet her, and take her to lunch at Bignon's or Tortoni's.[5] After lunch she would go home to dress for the regulation five-o'clock drive in the Bois de Boulogne. Since she needed to attract attention, she hired a handsome coupé in winter, an elegant *américaine* in the summer from the Crédit Voiturier. When it was time for absinthe, she went to the Café des Variétés, or the Café de Bade, where she met financiers and writers, or actors and actresses who encouraged her taste for the theatre. She often went to the Délassements-Comiques or the Italiens; and here, it seems, enthroned in her box, she caught the attention of a Russian prince, who swept her off in his *daumont* to supper at that renowned restaurant, the Maison d'Or.[6] It was, perhaps, in the Prince's honour that Blanche Antigny suddenly became ennobled as Blanche d'Antigny.[7]

The prince determined to set her up in a palace in St Petersburg – no doubt to remove her from his rivals; for Blanche still encouraged the French nobility, among them the Vicomte de Turenne. But she was naturally loath to leave Paris: her box at the Italiens, her suppers in the Grand Seize at the

Café Anglais; and she had not forgotten her unfortunate adventures in Wallachia. During the spring of 1863 she constantly refused the Prince's offer.

When summer came, however, and brought the great annual exodus from Paris, she allowed him to take her to Wiesbaden. Like Homburg and Baden, Ems and Spa, it was one of the watering-places in fashion. At Wiesbaden she created a sensation. She gambled wildly, patronised fêtes which were given in her honour, and received the dedication of a waltz. The prince was relieved, when the season ended, to take her to St Petersburg at last.

She settled at the Hôtel de France, while her protector had a handsome house nearby furnished in her honour. At the Restaurant Vert he introduced her, superbly, to the gilded youth of the city; and at dawn, when the exhausted guests were still asleep in a stupor of champagne, she calmly left the restaurant on his arm. She could hardly have felt much further from the reedy ponds of her native Indre.

A few weeks later she moved into her residence in the Grande Morskoï. In her warm rooms, hermetically sealed against the Russian winter, with their carpets, tapestries and gleaming icons, and royally attended by her moujiks, her porters and coachmen, her chef and her maître-d'hôtel, Blanche received the prince's friends and made herself a legend. The élite of St Petersburg would assemble round her samovar at eleven o'clock at night; and at five next morning, continued gossip, the silent moujiks would pick up the guests who were snoring in corners, besotted with French wines and kümmel, and take them home. Blanche could hardly remain content with a single lover; she captivated Mezentseff, the chief of the secret police, and General Levachoff, the Governor of St Petersburg. Levachoff wanted her to join the French theatre in the city; she did so, and appeared triumphantly on the stage.

After four years and more in Russia, the constant applause and adulation finally went to her head. In wild defiance of protocol, she decided to attend the traditional gala performance which ended the winter season at the Opera. She also determined to wear a dress in which she might outshine both play and audience. At the couturier's she found exactly what she wanted. The dress was naturally superb: it had in fact been ordered by the Empress. But the couturier made his protests and explanations in vain. Blanche thrust a bundle of notes in his hand, and hurried out with the dress. That evening, she wore it in view of the Empress's box.

Next day Mezentseff was commanded to expel her from Russia.

★

In the spring of 1868 Blanche d'Antigny returned to Paris, and established herself in a small apartment at 36, rue des Écuries-d'Artois.

One morning, at Dinochau's, the bohemian restaurant on the corner of the place Bréda,[8] Carjat the photographer and his friends saw Godfrin, an actor from the Gymnase, make his appearance with a handsome woman. She was wearing a fur toque, and she was wrapped in a blue fox-fur pelisse. She sat down smilingly at the table, sipped a glass of wine, 'and lit up the room with the sparkling gaiety of her blue eyes'.[9] When they reached dessert, she went to Carjat's to be photographed. She took the arm of a journalist whom she addressed by the familiar 'tu', though she had only known him for ten minutes. It was typical of Blanche d'Antigny.

Before she went to Russia in 1863, Blanche had already been a celebrity in the demi-monde. Now, nearly five years later, in the spring of 1868, she was more seductive and prosperous than ever. 'She was simply smothered in diamonds that her Russian admirers had given her,' remembered William Osgood Field, in *Things I Shouldn't Tell*, 'and she used to put them on all together and look like a jeweller's shop window.' One day, as Field was passing the door of her entresol apartment with a friend, a Miss Reed, 'this little door opened, and Blanche appeared – one mass of diamonds! She saw us, winked at me and disappeared, closing the door. Miss Reed, who was just ahead of me on the stairs, turned and looked at me and said with a comical smile: "Who *would* be virtuous?" '[10]

Blanche d'Antigny seemed to embody the demi-monde of the Second Empire. Zola's *L'Assommoir* inspired Édouard Manet to paint *Nana*, and Manet's painting in turn inspired Zola to write the sequel to the novel, in which Nana played the principal part. But when Zola talked to a *bon viveur* of the Second Empire, when he took notes on the courtesans of the imperial age, Blanche d'Antigny and Nana became identified in his imagination. They became merged in a single creature, the prototype of the *cocotte*. Zola's Nana did not only have the build and colouring of Blanche d'Antigny, she closely followed her theatrical and amorous careers. Early in 1881, when *Nana* was dramatised, Pierre Desgenais, the journalist, remembered: 'There was a fine woman who would have been the complete incarnation of Nana, and who *was* Nana, but she is dead . . .' And, waiting for the play to open at the Théâtre de l'Ambigu, he recalled the life of Blanche d'Antigny. 'That is the real drama,' he insisted. 'The Ambigu gives us the fictional drama, the secondary drama. It is romanticised, in spite of Zola's systematic realism.'

'Blanche d'Antigny was, of course, the original of Nana,' confirmed William Osgood Field. 'Everyone knew that; and, in fact, Zola told me so himself; but he admitted he had never even seen her, and was much interested in what I told him about her. That was, of course, long after he had published his book. As a matter of fact, Blanche was in no wise like Nana, except, indeed, that they both died of smallpox.'[11]

Field was one of the very few people who did not admire the beauty of Blanche d'Antigny. 'Poor Blanche! She was ugly, and very *canaille*, but she was very kind-hearted and amusing.'[12] This comment on her appearance seems almost unique. 'Her mouth is made for laughter and songs,' declared a French admirer, 'her sensual lips are made to be kissed, and to empty glasses of champagne.'[13]

Once again, on her return from Russia, Blanche determined to seek her pleasure and notoriety on the stage; perhaps she was also inspired by the thought of revenge on her Russian friends. She took lessons in declamation; and Mme Marchal, the pianist of the École Lyrique, made her practise songs from opéra-bouffe. She visited dramatic critics and celebrated actors; and, armed with an introduction from her friend Joseph Cappelmans, the editor of the *Journal de Saint-Pétersbourg*, she presented herself to Henri de Pène, the editor of the *Gazette des Étrangers*. He welcomed her warmly, and began to rouse public interest. At the end of June 1868, the week before her début at the Palais-Royal, the *Gazette des Étrangers* published no fewer than eight provocative paragraphs on the future star. Paris grew impatient to admire her. De Pène continued, until October, to sing her praises loudly (though an anonymous writer explained that 'compliance always finds its reward').[14]

Henri de Pène was not Blanche d'Antigny's only supporter. Raphael Bischoffsheim, the banker,[15] who happened to be her official lover, helped to organise the Press for her débuts. In spite of her many liaisons, she kept 'Bisch', as she called him, for a long while. A banker was a heavensent ally. She also enjoyed the support of Nestor Roqueplan of the *Constitutionnel*, of the dramatic critic of the *Figaro*, and the gossip-writers of the *Gaulois*. But this concert of praise was broken by a few discordant notes; and among the adverse critics was Barbey d'Aurevilly. In *Le Nain Jaune*, on 8 August 1868, he denied her all aptitude, all knowledge and all beauty.

Mlle Blanche d'Antigny [he wrote] isn't an actress, she is an intrigue. Some makers of whipped-up publicity omelettes have whipped up this one, too. Mlle Blanche d'Antigny isn't pretty, she doesn't act well, and she sings badly. But she has *people* . . . who create her celebrity for her and work at her notoriety . . . One curious fact, moreover, which the moralist must take into account, is the part played by this lady's diamonds. They certainly perform better than she does . . . Diamonds are the women's decoration. They aren't always the Legion of Honour, it is true, but I can see quite well that women like to have them and display them . . . But that people who wield the critic's pen should allow themselves to be spellbound by this luxury, as if they were kept women or keepable women, that they

Blanche d'Antigny

'The original of Nana . . . Zola told me so himself': Blanche d'Antigny, whose appearance and career suggested those cf the heroine of *Nana*.

Opposite. The Closerie des Lilas, after a lithograph by Rivière. It was in these pleasure-gardens that Blanche d'Antigny started her career. *Below*. A grove at the Closerie des Lilas in 1853: two ladies of the town and their admirers. One of the *biches* is bold enough to smoke a cigar.

Above. La vie parisienne. Dancing in the
open air during the Second Empire.
Left. 'The head of a Bacchante':
Blanche d'Antigny, from *les Jolies Femmes
de Paris* (1870).

Above. Even winter could not chill the *joie de vivre* of the era, as this fur-wrapped *parisienne* suggests.

Right. The Théâtre de la Porte-Saint-Martin. It was here, in 1858, that Blanche d'Antigny made her stage début as the living statue of la Belle Hélène.

Opposite. Wiesbaden, the Prussian spa, was much in fashion during the Second Empire. It was here that Blanche d'Antigny stayed with her Russian prince.

Right. 'The religion of money,' said Théophile Gautier in the 1860s, 'is the only one which has no unbelievers.' The Paris Bourse drew many worshippers, among them Raphael Bischoffsheim, Blanche d'Antigny's *amant en titre*.

Above. Théodore de Banville (1823–91), poet, man of letters, and admirer of Blanche d'Antigny.
Opposite. A new quadrille arranged from the music of Offenbach's *la Belle Hélène*.

Above. 'I can still see her under the helmet with the floating plumes . . . ,' wrote Théodore de Banville after Blanche d'Antigny died. This was no doubt the vision he had in mind.
Right. Florimond Rongé, known as Hervé (1825–92). The composer is seen in the title-rôle of his operetta *Chilpéric*, in which Blanche d'Antigny played Frédégonde.

A J. OFFENBACH.

QUADRILLE NOUVEAU
sur les Motifs de

LA BELLE HÉLÈNE

4=MAINS

OPÉRA-BOUFFE

PAR

LE MARQUIS DE THUISY.

a 2 mains, 4f50
à 4 mains, 4f50

le même a 4 mains et avec
Petit Orchestre 6f.

Ancienne Maison Meissonnier, autrefois rue Dauphine,
Paris, E. GÉRARD et Cie Rue de la Chaussée d'Antin 1, au coin du boulevard des Capucines.

Right. Henri Meilhac (1831–97) and Ludovic Halévy (1834–1908), and Jacques Offenbach (1819–80). Their operettas, in which Blanche d'Antigny and Cora Pearl appeared, captivated Paris.

Below. Hortense Schneider (1838–1920), the greatest interpreter of Offenbach. Her private life also earned her the title *le passage des princes.*

A smoking party in the 1860s: Blanche d'Antigny enthroned among some contemporaries. On the left are Arsène Houssaye, Judith Gautier and her father and Jean-François Millet.

Above. 'The Venus who characterized an age': Blanche d'Antigny at the height of her career.
Above left. Emile Zola (1840–1902) in his study in the rue de Bruxelles.
Left. Nestor Roqueplan (1804–70), a well-known *boulevardier* of the Second Empire. A celebrated journalist, he fostered Blanche d'Antigny's stage career in *le Constitutionnel*.

should comment on the diamonds, and do so with their eyes popping out of their heads—isn't this a pity?

Blanche d'Antigny did not think it a pity. She revelled in her diamonds. She bought her clothes regardless of cost. Most of them were created by Mme Laferrière, in the rue Taitbout, and Blanche never missed a chance of advertising her *couture* on the stage. In the summer of 1868, at the Palais-Royal, she played the part of the Vicomtesse de la Farandole in *Le Château à Toto*, an opéra-bouffe by Meilhac and Halévy, with music by Offenbach. In the second act she wore a dress worth 16,000 francs; in the third act she wore a largely transparent peignoir, trimmed with Bruges lace, worth 6,000 francs. She also sang a song which seemed to epitomise her career:

> Autrefois j'étais villageoise,
>   On peut s'en souvenir,
> Un peu sauvage, un peu sournoise,
>   Pensant à l'avenir!
> Parfois on me trouvait songeuse
>   Et l'on s'en étonnait,
> C'est qu'une voix mystérieuse
>   Tout bas me répétait:
>   Va-t-en, la Falotte,
> A Paris va-t-en, marche, va ton train,
>   Petit pied qui trotte,
> A Paris souvent fait un grand chemin.
>
> Pour te conter mes aventures
>   Il me faudra peu de mots.
> J'ai maintenant quatre voitures
>   Au lieu de deux sabots.
> Autrefois je gardais vingt têtes
>   De bétail dans les champs,
> Je n'ai fait que changer de bêtes . . .
>   Notaire, tu me comprends . . .
>   Va donc, la Falotte,
> Paris est à toi, marche, va ton train,
>   Petit pied qui trotte,
> A Paris souvent fait un grand chemin. [16]

On 29 July, when most people in Paris were away for the summer, Blanche took the part of Mimi (created by Hortense Schneider) in *Les Mémoires de Mimi Bamboche.*

The Théâtre du Palais-Royal is an oasis for the few Parisians who are still here in these depressing dog-days [said *La Vie parisienne* on 8 August]. There is hardly anyone in the audience, but on the stage there is the most charming blonde you could wish to see, Mlle Blanche d'Antigny, with some dresses! And a figure! Six feet tall at least! What does she say? What does she sing? How does she act? Oh, well! that will come . . . Anyway, there's no time to listen, one's completely absorbed in gazing at her long trailing dresses overladen with jet and lace, her open transparent peignoirs, her jewels and aigrettes . . .

It was now that she made the acquaintance of Hervé, the composer; he was looking for an actress to play Frédégonde in his opéra-bouffe, *Chilpéric*. Contracts were made to be disregarded. Blanche paid amends to the Palais-Royal, and went to the Folies-Dramatiques. Here, on 24 October, she made her first triumphant appearance as Frédégonde. As Desgenais remembered:

She appeared, half-naked, in an operetta by Hervé, under the white sheepskin of Frédégonde, singing (though she had no voice), gaily throwing in Chilpéric's face the diamonds and jewelled belts he had given her, lighting up the whole theatre with a sort of jovial ardour, being familiar with the audience as she was with everyone . . .

Yes, as the Marquis de Villemer wrote, this Rubens was the Venus who characterised an age. Mlle Schneider was exciting, modern, ironic, the froth of the champagne. Blanche d'Antigny, with her 'dimples of gross lascivious love', was a sort of Clodion made flesh. Under the electric lights and the trained opera-glasses, she represented the apotheosis of Matter.[17]

On 23 April 1869, she created the part of Marguerite in *Le Petit Faust*, an opéra-bouffe by Hervé, Hector Crémieux, and Jaime *fils*. These last two parts, Frédégonde and Marguerite, established her as a star on the Paris stage.

After a visit to Homburg that summer, she returned to the Palais-Royal, and created the part of Georgina in the one-act vaudeville *On demande des ingénues*. Théodore de Banville, the poet, succinctly described the play in the *National* as 'a comedy by Mme X— (*couturière*), Mlle Blanche d'Antigny, MM. Eugène Grangé and Victor Bernard.'

The dress [he continued, in lyric vein], is a marvel! Green, the colour of the waves, . . . it does not seem to have been cut and stitched, as dresses usually are, but trimmed and tossed into shape by the delicate hands of a fairy. It is like the draperies which tremble and billow out in the amorous fantasy of Clodion, and in every little corolla of green crêpe . . . a diamond shines and glitters and sparkles in sidereal whiteness, and the light audaciously comes and kisses it. As for diamonds, they are everywhere, at the ears, on the neck, in the tousled hair, they are even swarming on the small hat on the streaming golden hair, and I think there are some on the little slippers! People have said that Blanche d'Antigny is a woman by Rubens, and it is indeed in this style that the Master of Antwerp formed his great Nymphs out of roses and lilies, and shaped his big-breasted Nereids to whom he entrusted the task of guiding the ship of Marie de Médicis. Like these superb and terrible goddesses, Hervé's Marguerite pays in ready money, and shows all that could be desired for the pleasure of the eyes . . ., all the living marble needed to make a beautiful Galatea. But, unlike the Nereids and the Nymphs, she has these lights, these white flames, these captive stars, these decanter-stoppers at ten thousand francs apiece, a big enough pile of diamonds to build a barricade.

So what do we owe MM. Grangé and Victor Bernard, who are mentioned on the Palais-Royal poster? Is it the diamonds they've cut and polished, or is it perhaps the green dress that they have run up and put together? For as far as I can see, this green dress, the little hat and the diamonds are all the comedy that the Palais-Royal has given us . . . [18]

*

Such a diamond-covered deity needed to have her décor; and in September 1868, Blanche d'Antigny rented a charming *hôtel*, 11, avenue de Friedland.

In the hall, which was hung with tapestries, and decorated with exotic plants, two liveried footmen received the visitors and led them to the salons. Chandeliers shone from the ceilings, tapestries lent mystery to the walls, and the heavy blue velvet hangings on the doors were redolent of patchouli and vetiver. In the drawing-room, a bust of Dante gazed into space; and, on the clock on the mantelpiece, a figure of Peter the Great recalled the scintillating past at St Petersburg. Here, among the palms and hydrangeas, the fancy-dress balls were held. The drawing-room led into the oriental smoking-room, furnished with low, red-lacquered tables encrusted with silver and mother-of-pearl; and on the tables were cigarette-holders (Blanche enjoyed cigarettes) and golden boxes filled with exotic tobaccos. Then came the lovers' room: the little *salon des amoureux*, where the curtains softened the light, and a large portrait of Blanche smiled down on the deeply cushioned divans.

The dining-room, next to the smoking-room, looked over the avenue de Friedland; and here, on tables illuminated by candelabra each with fifteen candles, and decorated with large baskets of out-of-season flowers, the glasses glittered, the crystal glowed with a thousand fires. Bischoffsheim presided over these banquets, where the demi-monde, the half-world, entertained the world of literature: where Caroline Letessier and Léonide Leblanc inspired the admiration of Houssaye and Banville. The apéritifs were served with blinis and caviar. Saint-Émilion and Volnay accompanied the *terrine de foie gras*, Chablis and Château-Yquem escorted the lobster and the peacock in galantine. Then came Château-Lafite, *les asperges sauce aurore*, and *poulardes à la gelée*. Then, enhanced by marsala, malmsey and sherry, came *fraises au kirsch, bavarois aux fruits, napolitains* and *mille-feuilles Pompadour*. Champagne sparkled in silver-gilt goblets, each of them in the shape of an animal's head:

21

stag, fox, or wolf, or boar. If, for a moment, it ceased to flow, a butler would be summoned by a silver bell: a reproduction of the famous bell in Moscow; and champagne would flow again, like the Neva.

The *hôtel* in the avenue de Friedland was not only devoted to Comus; it was, above all, a temple to Venus. In the bedroom, hung with turquoise satin, the four-poster bed, under its enormous baldaquin with blue silk, lace-trimmed curtains, looked like a throne half-hidden under clouds. A broad white bearskin served as carpet. On a console table stood an ivory statuette of the flagellated Christ. In Blanche d'Antigny's bathroom, the bath was made of the finest Carrara marble. (The *Figaro* reported that she had had two hundred bottles of Montebello poured into it: a mineral-water bath which she found reviving.) From time to time, no doubt, Blanche d'Antigny would slip into her boudoir, which was hung with blue silk; she would take her jewels out of a little Boule writing-desk, and admire them. And yet she remained, at heart, as simple as a peasant girl from her native Indre, and she was never without her little gold crucifix. She was both religious and super-stitious. And, unlike some of her fellow courtesans, she did not know the value of money; she merely revelled in life, and wanted to please her numerous admirers.

★

They were certainly numerous. Maharajah, khedive and shah frequented her on their visits to Paris. Aristocrats and bankers and clubmen made their way to the *salon des amoureux*. The two careers of Blanche d'Antigny remained intertwined: the courtesan lent glamour and power to the actress, and the actress played the rewarding part of the courtesan. Vavasseur, who was acting with Blanche in *Chilpéric*, explained that he was too poor to buy her favours. She handed him an encouraging document:

List of my poor lovers

PILOTELL	– because of his hair
HERVÉ	– because of his talent
MILHER	– because he is a bachelor
JAIME	– because of his candour
LUCE	– because of his distinction
HAMBURGER	– because of his chic.

X., Y., Z., etc., etc., because they asked me to![19]

Vavasseur added his name to the list.

The total of Blanche d'Antigny's lovers defies calculation. If she had no engagement with a theatre, she might go to Berlin to meet a Russian prince, even for an idyll of a few hours. In the summer she would visit a fashionable spa. She set out in style: on 10 September 1868 the *Gazette des Étrangers* recorded: 'The evening before she was due to leave Paris, the rue des Écuries-d'Artois was blocked by the arrival in procession of her toilettes, each of them with a carriage to itself. Thirty-seven toilettes, thirty-seven carriages in a row.'[20] When she returned to Paris, she would announce her arrival by driving out in the *drojky* she had brought back from St Petersburg. The driver, in scarlet silk blouse and white breeches, would whip up the Ukrainian horses; and along the avenue de l'Impératrice they would canter, to the Bois de Boulogne. Like some terrestrial Queen Mab, Blanche d'Antigny would rejoin the evening promenade of *le tout-Paris*.

She was terrestrial indeed. In 1870, in that sensual anthology, *Les Jolies Femmes de Paris*, Charles Diguet drew her portrait:

Blanche has the bosom of Antiope and the head of a Bacchante. The famous head is proudly attached to plump, milk-white shoulders, moulded like those of Rubens' goddesses. The brow keeps a quasi-serenity, a relic of the chastity which sits upon the brow of every young girl. The cheeks have cast the lilies to the winds and kept only the roses, those flowers of passion. The eyes, almost childlike, have the fixity of sparkling minerals . . . They are two marcassites with gleaming facets . . . The sensual mouth is made to sing or to drain a glass of champagne, the wine of love.

Blanche d'Antigny might be called the muse of easy delights.[21]

On 26 February 1870, Victor Koning, the dramatic critic, recorded the interview he had had with her at Offenbach's reception at the Grand Hotel.

Mlle d'Antigny arrived, and cries of joy were heard. Here she came, the beautiful blonde, she was wearing the same light, blue-and-white costume that she wore in the first act of *Le Petit Faust*. I made my deepest bow; and with all the emotion which one must feel at such a moment, as this, I enquired in a trembling voice:

'Is it true, Mademoiselle, that you are reviving *L'Œil Crevé* at the Folies-Dramatiques?'

'Yes, it's true, you can tell them so. Just imagine that Moreau-Sainte [the director of the Folies-Dramatiques] only wanted to give me three louis an evening.'

'Three louis for you?' I cried in amazement. 'But he should have given you three hundred!'[22]

However, on 25 March Blanche duly made her appearance in the revival of Hervé's *L'Œil Crevé*.

Nothing is changed [wrote Banville] . . .; there's only another Frenchwoman, Blanche d'Antigny, who plays Fleur de Noblesse! Fleur de Noblesse she is indeed!

... She is a flower like those great Indian flowers which receive the tears of heaven in their calyx, and let the whole race of gods come and quench their thirst.[23]

★

On 18 June, she left with the company on a provincial tour. She was in Toulouse a month later, on the eve of the Franco-Prussian War. She came back to Paris for the siege, and turned part of her *hôtel* into a hospital, where forty Breton soldiers were cared for at her expense. She looked after them herself; and, two years after the war, a journalist recorded that 'these soldiers have not forgotten their good little Sister of Charity, as they called her, and from time to time they send her chickens, pigeons, even potatoes ... Often the presents arrive with charmingly naïve messages, like this: "We pray to the Virgin for you every day. Good-bye, dear lady! Our greetings to all your husbands." '[24] On the eve of the Battle of Champigny, five hundred people, all that remained of *le tout-Paris*, assembled at Arsène Houssaye's to support a charity performance in aid of the hospitals. Blanche d'Antigny, in a white apron, helped to serve champagne and liqueurs, and sold her kisses at five louis each.

She also gave fêtes at her own *hôtel* in aid of the wounded. The laughter and music and brilliant lights offended public feeling, and she was so attacked in the Press that she could not appear on the boulevards without being hissed and threatened. The fall of the Second Empire had unleashed violent emotions, and there were many people who blamed the national débâcle, the tragic inadequacy of the old régime, on the courtesans, who had drained men of their willpower and moral sense. When the bombardment of Paris began, Blanche d'Antigny felt obliged to ask the new Prefect of Police, Ernest Cresson, for protection. Her request was greeted with quite extraordinary vehemence.

It was in the first hours of the bombardment [Cresson would recall] that a demi-mondaine begged for the protection of the law and the prefecture of police.

Blanche d'Antigny was celebrated in the little theatres and among the people who take notice of the publicity given to courtesans. During the siege, certain newspapers had found time to bother about this woman. Several of them had denounced her luxurious mode of living, recorded the festivities and rowdy entertainments that had come to the notice of the poor; some papers had provoked threats. Blanche d'Antigny decided to ask for an interview with the prefect of police, in order to complain; she claimed to have an important communication to make. When I learnt of her insistence [here Cresson relapses into the first person], I received the visitor. I made her sit down, and asked her gravely to explain herself...

Blanche d'Antigny described the threats and insults which assailed her. She had reason for anxiety; her emotion seemed to be genuine. Her life was in danger, she ended, and the prefecture of police could not refuse her its protection.

At this point, Cresson's narrative becomes worthy of M. Prudhomme, that personification of bourgeois pompousness:

'You gave a noisy dinner-party last night,' replied the prefect, with a gesture which imposed silence upon her. 'And then there was dancing at your house; your windows were open, the brilliance of the lights lit up the street. Now listen to me: these festivities are an insult to the grief and suffering of the people. One day they are going to hang you . . . I shall come to your rescue too late, when they have finished.'

Blanche d'Antigny's face was drained of colour. She attempted to speak. 'It is no use,' said the prefect, 'you understand me. You have two horses: why haven't they been given up for requisition? You will take them yourself, tomorrow, to the authority concerned. You may go.'

The visitor gave no more parties during the siege; she did not ask for help again, she had no further need of it. The impudence of vice justifies the severity of the lessons which it dares to bring upon itself.[25]

When the Siege and the Commune were over, Blanche d'Antigny turned back to the theatre. In 1871–3, she created five parts on the Parisian stage, and performed the whole repertoire of the opéra-bouffe abroad. The month of June 1872 found her in London, where she was engaged at the Globe Theatre and wore a set of jewels worth £3,000. Her success displeased Hortense Schneider, who was playing at the St James's Theatre.

It was about now that Blanche fell in love for the first and only time in her life. Luce, the tenor, had begun his career by singing in the dives on the Left Bank; he was now at the Folies-Dramatiques. He had performed with her in *Le Petit Faust*. He was 'a tiny little tenor as round as a ball'.[26] But she loved him exclusively and truly, and she had found a lover who adored her in return.

Early in 1873 Luce died of consumption. It is said that Blanche asked for an advance of a thousand francs from the director of the Folies-Dramatiques. 'Yes, I have money,' she explained, 'but this is for Luce's funeral, and I don't want him to be buried with the money I've earned in bed.'[27]

She mourned him for the few months that remained to her. The idyll gave her the deepest happiness that she was to know; it was also her first step towards financial ruin, for she had dismissed Bischoffsheim, her official lover, and he had not forgiven her. She had lost her banker and her credit. Her creditors drove her from the avenue de Friedland, confiscated her horses, carriages and jewels; she went to a furnished house in the rue d'Antin, and sold furniture and *objets d'art* to repay the most urgent creditors, but she could not satisfy them all, and they descended on her, all at once, from London, from Brussels . . . She felt obliged to go to Egypt, and 'take her revenge on the Pashas'.[28]

Taillefer, the director of the Alexandria theatre, had signed a contract with her for the winter season; he was paying her almost three times her salary at the Folies-Dramatiques, where her contract expired in June. She embarked at Marseilles on 15 October, accompanied by her lady's maids, Henriette, Ambroisine and her daughter, and even by her coachman, Justin, who was having pleasure at her expense. On 1 November she made her appearance at the Zizinia Theatre, in Alexandria; but a cabal had been organised against her, and she was greeted by such commotion that she took fright, and the curtain was hastily lowered. Next day she broke her engagement with Taillefer, and left for Cairo. She was splendidly received by the Khedive, who appreciated her charms and her talent. She telegraphed every day to Paris to announce her triumphs, and the *Figaro* recounted them. She ended the season with the viceregal company in Cairo, and returned to her company at Alexandria. Taillefer suggested that she should take part in a benefit performance for them.

On the eve of the performance, Louise France, a journalist, interviewed her:

She was desperately worried, although a number of seats had been booked in advance.

'That's all to the good,' she said to me, 'but I shall subscribe like the others, though I'm poor.'

'Poor?'

'Yes,' answered Blanche. 'The Khedive behaved royally to me; but I have so many debts and such devoted servants.'[29]

She played a part which had been among her triumphs in Paris: Marguerite, in Hervé's *Le Petit Faust*. Once again there was a cabal against her. She had good reason to be anxious. Some of her creditors had even followed her to Egypt, and she was so afraid of arrest that she entrusted all her remaining jewels to her servants – except for a turquoise, which Luce had given her. On 28 May 1874, she reached Paris, to hear of the death of her mother, whom she had greatly loved. She was deeply unhappy, pursued by her creditors, and without a roof over her head. She found a room at the Grand Hôtel du Louvre; on 9 June she was suffering from a fever.

There are several conflicting accounts of what happened next. William Osgood Field, who knew her, recorded that she had smallpox, and that she was turned out of the hotel.[30] Her biographer, Vauzat, says that on

Opposite. A journalist admired Blanche d'Antigny as 'this Eve escaped from Paradise Lost'. Paul Baudry took her as his model for *The Repentant Magdalen*.

15 June her illness was diagnosed as typhoid, and the doctor said that she must be moved before she became too ill. Auriant, in *Les Lionnes du Second Empire*, maintains that she had caught consumption from Luce.[31] Whatever her illness, it was mortal. Henriette approached Caroline Letessier, the courtesan, who rented an entresol at 93, boulevard Haussmann, and sent a superb *dorsay* to fetch Blanche d'Antigny. She died there on 28 June, and was buried at Père-Lachaise. She was thirty-four.[32]

She left her love-letters to Henri Meilhac, one of the authors of *La Vie parisienne*. 'All the great names were there, and so was that of Luce, the tenor.'[33] She remains in the repentant Magdalen of Baudry's painting, in Zola's Nana, and, above all, in the criticism of Théodore de Banville. Banville had loved her as a poet who appreciated her beauty; he had loved her more than most of the men who had possessed her. And perhaps the most touching tribute to Blanche d'Antigny was the tribute which he paid her in his first article after her death:

I am not one of those who say 'It's nothing!' By dying so young, in all the brilliance of her swift, frivolous life, Blanche d'Antigny has taken with her one of the smiles of Paris, a city which does not have too many smiles . . . As an actress, she had nothing, in fact, except those robust arms, those crimson lips and white teeth, and the beauty of a Rubens nymph who wore fiery diamonds and rich clothes like the natural accessories of her triumph. She had nothing except the white shoulders and the radiant face of a young Gallic woman of the *Heptameron* or the *Cent Nouvelles Nouvelles*; but isn't that enough for us to cast at least a humble little flower on the tomb where she lies asleep, now that she has so cruelly expiated the triumphs of Mimi Bamboche and the brief intoxications of her carefree hours? How charming she was! I can still see her under the helmet with the floating plumes, under the damascened cuirass of a Pallas of fantasy . . . She had at least the happiness of not feeling her brow torn by the nail of old age, and of passing, like a brilliant apparition, quickly fled, through this city which forgets its idols and its toys.[34]

La Barucci

Giulia Beneni (1837[?]–70/1)

Giulia Beneni, who would earn fame as La Barucci, was born, it seems, in about 1837.[1] As a young girl, she came from Rome to Paris to seek her fortune; and her black eyes, her luxuriant ebony hair, her golden Italian skin, her queenly figure and bearing, her air of languor, won her an immediate place (some said the highest place) in the world of Parisian gallantry.

It seems to have been a Monsieur de Danne who first discovered her. He dressed her superbly and took her to dine in a restaurant well known to the demi-monde; from time to time (recorded a friend of M. de Danne's, who was invited to come and admire his conquest), La Barucci would rush to the mirror which decorated the *salon particulier*, and exclaim, in all naiveté: 'Grande Dio! que je suis belle!' She was beautiful, indeed; and within a few weeks the Prince d'Hénin had persuaded her to leave Monsieur de Danne, 'poor Anatole'.

Some months later, Anatole's friend from the *salon particulier*, the unknown man who had witnessed her début, was walking slowly up the Champs-Élysées. As he turned the corner of one of the streets which came out on the *rond-point*, he heard someone call his name. La Barucci was leaning out of an entresol window, and inviting him to come up and see her.

He congratulated her on the splendour of her surroundings. She took him into her bedroom, and showed him her jewel chest. It stood as high as the mantelpiece, and each of its drawers, lined with quilted silk, was filled with a single kind of precious stone. There was a compartment for diamonds, a compartment for emeralds, another for pearls, and another one for rubies; and, finally, there was a compartment for rings and earrings and bracelets of pure gold. The diamonds flashed in the sunshine. La Barucci was as pleased as a child with her treasures, which were said to be worth a million francs. But as for showing gratitude or affection for the donors, it did not occur to her.[2]

It was said that she never refused herself to a member of a fashionable club, and that all the Jockey Club, in turn, had entered her alcove – and, somehow, had continued to be her friends. But she was especially drawn to soldiers. 'From the glittering fuglemen of the guard, who opened the procession, to the magnificent Cent Gardes who closed it, by way of the elegant lancers, every notable officer, every officer in fashion, passed through her boudoir.' She would pursue her favourite lover with Italian fury. 'She would follow him step by step like a tigress,' wrote Zed, in *Le Demi-Monde sous le Second Empire*, 'watching the way he spent his time, and not leaving him a moment of freedom. She would abandon everything to go and see him at Melun or Compiègne, and spend several days with him in his bachelor quarters. She went as far as to slip into the duty-room of the captain commanding the escort at the Tuileries; and, one fine evening, she stayed there till dawn, and the authorities had to be asked to enforce her departure. The story of her adventure even reached the Emperor, who was, incidentally, much amused.'[3] On another occasion she suddenly arrived at the camp at Châlons with her younger sister, who followed the same profession. They brought two personal maids with them, not to mention endless luggage, and the Mayor of Mormelon gallantly gave them rooms in his own house, while the military authorities played music for them, and let them inspect the camp.

All fashionable Paris knew La Barucci's apartment at 124, avenue des Champs-Élysées. It was said that she sometimes lent it to society women who needed a clandestine rendez-vous. She herself did not only use it for receiving lovers; Zed, the Comte de Maugny, maintained that 'in her spare moments she privately received people of great distinction, and they told her secrets which she kept with scrupulous discretion. Sometimes she did them very important services, and they were not afraid to address themselves to her when a situation was delicate.'[4] The Goncourts, in their *Journal*, confirmed the astonishing number of eminent visitors. In November 1863, La Barucci's latest lover, the wit and journalist Aurélien Scholl, took them to dine with her at the Champs-Élysées. After dinner he thumbed through the mountain of visiting-cards which she kept in a china bowl by the fireplace; he read out nearly every name in high society. There were cards from the Imperial Family, cards from the Court, crested cards from the Faubourg Saint-Germain, and cards – so it seemed – from the entire *corps diplomatique* of Europe. The Goncourts had never been more aware of the ramifications of power, the secret apotheosis of the courtesan.

The décor of La Barucci's apartment richly confirmed her triumph. The splendour began at the porter's lodge, and continued up the grand white carpeted staircase, with its velvet-covered banisters. The door was opened by a footman in elaborate livery, who led the visitor into the great white salon; a silver-gilt goblet – the Goncourts deplored it – gleamed under a glass bell, on a velvet-covered stand which bore the initial N and the imperial crown. No doubt it represented one of the Emperor's nights of love. The dinner itself was sumptuous – the Goncourts called it insolent. As they unfolded their napkins, they caught their fingers in the thick embroidery; as they ate, they criticised the over-spiced, ostentatious food beloved of all courtesans. After dinner, La Barucci showed them her bedroom, and they deplored the 'horrible copy of the horrible *Vierge à la Chaise* by Raphael,' which she had chosen to hang over her bed.[5]

Marie Colombier, a courtesan herself, wrote more kindly of La Barucci and her hospitality:

No-one understood better than she did the grandeur and the beauty of her mission of love: she was proud to call herself *la Grande Puttana del Mondo* . . . All the princes passed through her alcove; with her slow movements, her noble attitudes, she was the idol of the universe.

Everything in her apartment had wonderful style. She had a personal maid, Sidonie, who anticipated all her wishes: there was no need to give her orders; she foresaw everything. It might happen that as La Barucci left the Opéra, or a première, she would ask the friends who had been in her box to come back for an impromptu supper. The Prince d'Hénin, the Duc de Fernan-Nunez, the Duc d'Aremberg . . . would follow her in their carriages. 'Sidonie,' she said, when she arrived, 'there are eight for supper.' And while they exchanged their impressions of the evening's entertainment, and drank a glass of madeira, Sidonie would take a cab to the Maison d'Or, and bring back some cold fish, some fillet of beef, some partridges *à la gelée* and a basket of fruit, not forgetting some flowers from Isabelle, who sold her wares alternately outside the Café Anglais and the Maison d'Or. Within the hour, the supper was ready; Sidonie opened the door: 'Madame is served.' . . . It astonished even the people accustomed to princely houses. [6]

As an Englishman in Paris observed, La Barucci's parties were 'anything but small tea';[7] and sometimes a great deal of gambling was done. On 4 February 1863 the Garcia and Calzado affair burst on Paris. Garcia was an impenitent gambler; he and his friend Calzado, the director of the Théâtre des Italiens, played the Comte de Miranda at *rouge et noir*, and then Garcia played Miranda at baccarat. The Duc de Grammont-Caderousse, a celebrated man-about-town, accused Garcia of cheating. La Barucci gave the order to shut the doors, and Garcia was told to return his winnings, and to let himself be searched. He protested, but he gave back about forty thousand francs; some of the rest of the money was discovered behind the chairs and curtains, but about thirty thousand francs were still missing. Miranda took the case to law; Garcia fled to Monaco, but Calzado was arrested. On 20 March the case was heard at the Palais de Justice. It was proved that the packs of cards had been incomplete, that there were five or six packs of each colour, and that there were only low cards, which were the most useful for winning at baccarat. Garcia was sentenced by default to five years' imprisonment, and Calzado was given eighteen months. 'There were evil tongues who whispered that the mistress of the house was in the swindle,' wrote Bingham, in his *Recollections of Paris*. 'However that may be, she soon afterwards disappeared from the scene, and people no longer beheld her, magnificently attired, driving round the lake in the Bois de Boulogne reclining in a splendid phaeton, horses and liveries all to match.'[8]

If La Barucci had vanished from Paris, she had probably gone on some errand of love; she was probably possessed by one of the passions which, every six months or so, seemed to overcome her. There was something disarming about these sudden infatuations: about her overwhelming love for the student in the Quartier Latin who was so in awe of her fifteen strings of pearls, the two hundred thousand francs' worth of jewels round her neck, that he failed to respond to *la Grande Puttana del Mondo*.[9]

There was indeed an almost endearing naiveté about the courtesan who cried, triumphantly, in her Italian French: 'Je souis la Vénous de Milo! Je souis la première p— de Paris!' When she was invited to meet the Prince of Wales, at the Maison d'Or, she was carefully instructed to behave with decorum, and, above all, to be punctual. She arrived some forty-five minutes late; the Duc de Grammont-Caderousse presented her to the future Edward VII. 'Your Royal Highness, may I present the most unpunctual woman in France?' At that moment, without warning, La Barucci dropped her diaphanous dress to the floor. 'Did you not tell me to behave properly to His Royal Highness?' she enquired, when the Duc upbraided her. 'I showed him the best I have, and it was free.'[10]

She remained in many ways a simple Italian. Her casual lovers did not give her money; if they wanted to please her, they gave her a length of silk or brocade for her Italian madonnas: she always sent her cast-off clothes to dress the statuette of the Blessed Virgin in some Italian church. And regularly, once a week, she kept a day free for her brother and younger sister. They would divide between themselves the best of the spoils which had ceased to please her – and the rest would be packed up, then and there, and despatched to the Holy Virgins of Tuscany.[11]

La Barucci seems to have been in Baden for the season of 1868; but some observed that she had 'a look of one marked for death'.[12] Marie Colombier remembered:

Despite her triumphant appearance, she bore the seeds of mortal disease within her. On those intoxicated evenings at Baden, while people were laughing and roistering around her, she used to say 'she was anxious to have her pleasure, because she hadn't long to live, consumption was waiting for her'. And then people laughed at her and said she was acting *la Dame aux camélias*.[13]

Paul Demidoff, in Paris, well aware that she had consumption, brutally paid her to sit between open windows in the Grand Seize, the famous Room Sixteen at the Café Anglais; roaring with laughter, he drenched her with Seltzer water.[14]

Perhaps La Barucci needed the money, for she had moved from the Champs-Élysées to a *hôtel* in the rue de la Baume. It was here that she summoned Marie Colombier in the early days of the Siege of Paris.

She had not left her bed for weeks . . . The moment Marie entered, she felt the chill of death, she had the impression that she was in a sepulchre. It was indeed a sepulchre, in which a dying beauty lay in agony. Her face had assumed the livid hue of candles which had been shut up too long in the ciborium, and only her mouth glowed brightly against this feverish pallor: a scarlet wound whence life would escape . . .

'Do you think I've changed?' asked Giulia.

'Of course not, my dear.'

'You know I have. You think I don't notice. You laughed at me at Baden, you and Letessier, when I was coughing, and when I said I should die because of my lungs. You said I was acting *la Dame aux camélias*. Well, you see, my lungs are killing me all the same.'

Marie kept back the tears that were rising into her eyes, and asked her why, if she felt ill, she had not left Paris this terrible year, why she had stayed there during the Siege. 'Oh, I know I should have gone,' answered Giulia . . . , 'but I didn't see what would happen. And then he wanted to stay, my *princhipe* (she pronounced the word with an Italian accent and the gentleness of a child). He is French, and I should have been too anxious if I had known that he was shut up in Paris.' She saw her friend's astonishment: Marie was aware of all her infidelities. And then she looked at her steadfastly: 'Yes, you see, in spite of everything, it's my only affection, my one true love. He is so handsome that one forgets he is so rich.'[15]

She died a week later.[16] Like la Dame aux camélias, she died of consumption, and she had one true love.

3

Cora Pearl

Eliza Emma Crouch (c. 1835–86)

None of the great courtesans of the nineteenth century knew the heights and depths of her profession more clearly than Cora Pearl. She was born Eliza Emma Crouch in about 1835; she was the daughter of a Plymouth music teacher, Frederick William Nicholls Crouch, who earned fame as the author of the popular song *Kathleen Mavourneen*. It is said that he sold the copyright for less than £20 to a publisher who made £15,000 from the work; certainly his financial sense did not equal his taste for music, and he found it hard to maintain 'the musical box', as neighbours used to call his house in Caroline Place, East Stonehouse. It seems that the family did not survive the financial stresses. They gradually drifted apart, and in 1847 Mr Crouch left his wife. Two years later he escaped his creditors, and emigrated to America, and Mrs Crouch, to salve her pride, explained to the children that he had died. She took a lover, a 'stepfather' whom her daughter Eliza detested; and, finding it hard to manage four young children, she then despatched Eliza to a convent school at Boulogne.[1]

The girl remained there for eight years; and though she did not learn to speak perfect French, she made a number of friends. When her mother finally sent for her, in 1854 or 1855, she was loath to leave a country of which she had grown very fond.[2]

There was no question of returning to live with her mother. She was sent to stay with her grandmother, Mrs Watts, in London; and she led a sober, godly, steadfast life which hardly suited her. Night after night she read travel books to her aged relative; Sunday after Sunday, when she had paid a visit to her mother, she was escorted to matins by a maid, who would wait outside the church to escort her home.

33

One Sunday (so she would write in her *Mémoires*), the maid was not waiting for her; and she set out, alone, for her grandmother's house. She was, whatever she claimed, herself, some twenty years of age; she was spirited, and well aware of her excellent figure and glossy red hair. She was soon aware that she was followed; and it is hard to think that she was displeased by the attention. She maintained that the man who followed her, a middle-aged diamond merchant, took her to a drinking den (it was probably near Covent Garden). She maintained that, in her innocence, she accepted the drink he offered; when she recovered consciousness, she found herself beside him in bed.

Eliza Crouch can hardly have been as innocent as she pretended; but one may well believe her when she says that she hated all men for the rest of her life. Henceforward she held them spellbound, used them, fleeced them, hurt them, and, almost invariably, left them. She never felt tenderness, she could never feel love.

I can say [she would write in her *Mémoires*] that I have never had a favourite lover. That is explained by my own feelings, which have always inspired me with an instinctive horror of men. It is not that I am less sensitive than other women, or that thoughtfulness, kind attentions, and handsome behaviour leave me indifferent. I have often sacrificed my own interest for the sake of gratitude or friendship. But as for what people are pleased to call blind passions, or fatal infatuations, no! I have not known them, luckily for my peace and happiness. I have always considered the favourite lover as an empty form of speech, a hollow phrase.[3]

After her ugly initiation, sex had no mystery, no significance for her; but she was aware that she possessed a power over men. It did not occur to her to return to her family. She washed the thought of her mother and her grandmother from her mind, and installed herself in a room near Covent Garden. She became, it seems, the mistress of Robert Bignell, the proprietor of the Argyll Rooms, a notorious pleasure-haunt; and, to her delight, he announced one day that they were going to Paris, travelling as husband and wife.

They climbed to the top of the Arc de Triomphe, descended into the famous Paris sewers, visited the Panthéon, the Tuileries, the theatres; they went riding at Meudon, and fishing at Charenton. Eliza later declared she had never enjoyed herself so much, even in Baden, where she spent two hundred thousand francs. But it was already clear that she preferred French life to life with Bignell. When it was time to go back to England, she sent him home, alone. She had by now adopted the euphonious name of Cora Pearl. She decided to make her future in France.

La Barucci & Cora Pearl

A subaltern in the Imperial Guard, *officier de la légion d'Honneur* and winner of the Victoria Cross in the Crimea. La Barucci made many conquests among the Imperial Guard.

Above. Aurélien Scholl (1833–1902), a well-
known wit and journalist, and the lover of La
Barucci and other *grandes horizontales.*
Top left. Albert Edward, Prince of Wales.
La Barucci caused a stir when she was
presented to him at the Maison d'Or.
Left. Ludovic, Duc de Grammont-Caderousse
(1835–65), an habitué of the Café Anglais, and
one of the most fashionable men-about-Paris.
Below. Isabelle la Bouquetière, a
familiar figure in *la vie du boulevard.*

'Grande Dio! que je suis belle!' Giulia Beneni, known as La Barucci, proudly called herself the First Courtesan of Paris.

Bottom. A courtesan bound for a *souper intime*.

Opposite. An inviting
destination for an
expedition: the Restaurant
de Paris at Asnières.

Above. 'Won't you come and
take the waters with me
at Baden? – we'll break
the bank!'
'No, Monsieur le Baron,
the only waters I know
are in the Seine, and
I'm off to Asnières to
pop corks.'
Top right. 'Courses,
concerts, théâtre,
on trouve tout à Bade,'
wrote a versifier in
1863. This photograph
gives a glimpse of
Baden-Baden, which was
the summer capital of
Europe.
Right. Boating on the
Seine in the days of the
Second Empire. An idyllic
scene at a landing-place.

'More than half seas over': two ladies of the
town take leave of a disabled admirer.

A *souper fin*, about 1860.
From a contemporary tableau.

Opposite
Far left. En route for Monaco. Some travellers wore their hearts
on their luggage.
Left. A *fille de joie* scorns the offer of a cheap dinner.

Above. 'One of the brightest stars in the firmament of the Second Empire' : Cora Pearl.
Opposite. The rue de la Paix, which furnished the jewels for the *haute bicherie parisienne*.
From a photograph taken in the latter years of the Second Empire.

MŒURS PARISIENNES. — LA SORTIE DE L'OPÉRA.

Above. A cab is summoned, a rendezvous arranged, a piece of gossip exchanged. Leaving the Opéra in the days of the Second Empire.

Right. 'This enchantress has the art of drawing all men to her': Cora Pearl at the height of her power.

Right. The most distinguished of Cora Pearl's lovers: Charles-Auguste-Louis-Joseph, Duc de Morny (1811–65). The natural son of Queen Hortense and the Comte de Flahaut, he was a brilliant political figure in Second Empire Paris. Photograph by Nadar.
Top left. 'Prince Citron': the Prince of Orange, a noted man-about-town in the Second Empire. He was one of the lovers of Cora Pearl.
Centre left. Prince Napoleon (1822–91), from a photograph taken at about the time he first met Cora Pearl. Their liaison lasted nine years and was one of the longest in her career.

Above. *The Bath* by Alfred Stevens (1828–1906). Stevens was born in Brussels, but he spent much of his life in France, recording the *parisiennes* of the Second Empire. In *The Bath*, one of them dreams, as no doubt Cora Pearl used to dream in her rose marble bathroom. *Opposite*. Part of the Imperial décor: a corner of Prince Napoleon's *Palais pompéien* in the Champs-Elysées.

Below. A scene at the races in the 1860s; an impression by Guys. A fine horse was
a status symbol in the Second Empire: races were important events in the social calendar,
and every self-respecting courtesan demanded handsome horses and carriages.
Bottom. *Gladiateur* winning the Grand Prix de Paris at Longchamps in 1865.

Top left. Riding in the Champs-
Elysées. From a caricature by
Gustave Doré.
Top right. A horse and its English
groom pose in front of a backdrop.
Bottom left. A winning horse with
jockey and owner in 1862.
(The same backdrop has been used
again.)
Bottom right. An Amazon of the
Second Empire. Cora Pearl, who
was a fine horsewoman, was said to
be kinder to her horses than she
was to her lovers.

Overleaf
Désespérée, by Alfred Stevens. The
expression on the face, and the opened
note on the table, suggest unrequited love.

She was, at first, obliged to live in a humble quarter of Paris, and to entertain undistinguished lovers. But Cora always had 'plenty of system'; and since it has always been evident that success creates success, she determined to have the outward signs of wealth: dresses by Worth and Laferrière and jewels from the rue de la Paix. It was Victor Masséna (the grandson of Napoleon's great marshal), third Duc de Rivoli and later fifth Prince of Essling, who obligingly bought them for her. Masséna, her first important lover, not only bought her clothes and jewels, but maintained her servants. He paid her chef, Salé, who sometimes spent thirty thousand francs on food in a fortnight. He gave her money to lose at the Baden casino and racecourse (on their last visit to Baden, in 1869, she spent, apart from gambling losses, over fifty-nine thousand francs).

Heir to a great name of the First Empire [Cora would write in her *Mémoires*], correct in every way, he was also the most attentive of men, the most anxious to please, the most adorable—and, I must add, the man who was paid least in return. It's terrible, but that can't be bought. He was horribly jealous of Adrien Marut, who . . . burned for me with all the ardour of his seventeen years.[4]

It was, naturally, impossible for Cora to content herself with one lover; and Masséna found, to his anger, that his wildly expensive mistress was also giving her favours to Prince Achille Murat: a youth eleven years his junior. Murat (Marut in the memoirs) was not rich, but he was incapable of refusing Cora's slightest whim. She persuaded him to take her out hunting, and he gave her her first horse. (Arsène Houssaye maintained that Cora, who rode like an Amazon, was kinder to her horses than her lovers.) She took a house at 61, rue de Ponthieu, where the stables were her pride and joy. She had not only a calèche upholstered in sky-blue, but at least a dozen horses: indeed, between 1863 and 1868 she bought more than sixty fine saddle and carriage horses, and in three years she spent ninety thousand francs with one horse-dealer alone. The height of fashion, she also employed English grooms, whose impassive faces earned them the name of 'the men who never smile'. She decked them out in bright yellow liveries, just like Princess de Metternich's. The *grand monde*, to their anger, saw themselves outclassed, and even Marie Colombier, one of the most spiteful of Cora's rivals, could only write that 'Cora Pearl personified what one might call the English type of courtesan. She was essentially a sportswoman, who rode like a jockey and liked to swank by cracking her whip . . . She had a perfect bust, it was worthy of being sculpted by some old master.'[5]

The British Phryne was one of the brightest stars in the firmament of the Second Empire [wrote Philibert Audebrand, in *Petits Mémoires d'une Stalle d'Orchestre*]. By unanimous consent she became, for twenty-five years, the prototype of the modern courtesan.

From 1852, Cora Pearl set the tone for that world of gallantry whose eccentricities always ended by leaving their mark on the real world. People who went to the Bois were determined to have a carriage modelled on hers, with little café-au-lait coloured horses, as like as possible to the ones that she drove herself. It went without saying that the women of Paris, beginning with those at Court, copied her clothes, her hair, her habits, and soon her fantastic behaviour. 'Since this enchantress has the art of drawing all men to her, of course,' said Mme de P***, 'we must do every mortal thing to be like her.'[6]

There were, of course, people who maintained that Cora Pearl was ugly. 'Cora Pearl,' noted Alphonse Daudet, the author of *Lettres de mon moulin*. 'A clown's head, a sewer of a mouth, a comic English accent. "Don't call me Cora! It's the name all the cabbies know . . . Call me Pearl . . . More chic . . . less dowdy . . ." A hideous head, a lithe young body.'[7]

Yet, despite the strictures of Daudet, it is not a plain but a piquant face which gazes out of the photographs. Cora Pearl proved, if anyone proved, that conventional beauty was not the only means of attraction. Perhaps her piquancy, her exotic accent, her toughness, her independence, even her outrageous behaviour, proved as seductive as her perfect figure. She found it easy to seduce the husbands and lovers of the most beautiful women in Paris. 'In those days she was as fresh as a moss rose,' recalled Gustave Claudin, the *boulevardier*, in the 1880s. 'Prince Gortschakoff used to say that she was the last word in luxury, and that he would have tried to steal the sun to satisfy one of her whims.'[8]

Cora Pearl had begun what she called her golden chain of lovers with a duke and a prince; she had soon added the Prince of Orange, the heir to the throne of the Netherlands. Indeed, some said that her golden chain was more than a metaphor. One journalist declared that she had a necklace which was a handsome record of achievement. 'From a massive gold chain depend twelve lockets of most exquisite workmanship, emblazoned with the devices of the best and oldest families of France. A central locket bears the arms of the lady herself, with this appropriate motto, *Honi soit qui mal y pense*. Within the lockets are twelve portraits of . . .'[9] Perhaps one represented the Duc de Morny; for one December day, as Cora was muffled up in furs, and skating on the lake in the Bois de Boulogne, she was noticed by the half-brother of the Emperor. She recalled the meeting in her *Mémoires*:

'Cora on ice?' he said to me. 'What an antithesis!'
'Well,' I replied, 'since the ice is broken, give me a drink.'
'I could ask no more.'[10]

Of all Cora's lovers, Morny was the most intelligent, the most gifted and distinguished. In appearance, he was a taller, handsomer edition of the Emperor. He also shared the Emperor's insatiable sexual appetites. But where the Emperor dreamed of politics, Morny would take action: it was he who had engineered the *coup-d'état* of 1851 which had made Louis-Napoleon Prince-President. While the Emperor showed small appreciation of literature, Morny dashed off a one-act operetta-bouffe, *Monsieur Choufleury restera chez lui*, between a diplomatic reception and an official speech. (He wrote it, under the pseudonym de Saint Rémy, in collaboration with Offenbach, and it achieved a notable success at the Théâtre des Bouffes-Parisiens.) Morny paid compliments with a natural grace, he was devoted to the arts (he had a deep admiration for Alfred de Musset), he played the piano to Cora for hours, charming in his violet velvet smoking jacket. He not only gave her a white Arab horse, he admired her riding. 'It seems,' wrote Cora, complacently, 'that I was not too ungraceful, for the donor, who worthily took his place at the Jockey Club, paid me compliments and asked who had taught me. "No one," I answered.' Morny had the qualities which Cora Pearl respected: toughness, intelligence, uncommon wealth and extravagance, and rank. He also showed her endearing loyalty: once, when she was turned away from the casino at Baden, he offered her his arm – and, escorted by the son of Queen Hortense, Cora entered the casino in triumph.

By the mid 1860s, she was among the most celebrated courtesans in Paris. In 1864, as the mistress of the Emperor's brother, she felt herself entitled to a château; and she rented the little Château de Beauséjour, on the banks of the Loiret, four miles from Orléans, where delighted guests played Chinese bézique in a boudoir with stained-glass windows, and admired the large bronze bath, cast specially by Chevalier of Paris, and engraved with Cora's monogram, three C's intertwined. The monogram was repeated on a marble slab on the terrace, with the proud Latin motto *Parcere subjectis et debellare superbos*. Since Cora was intensely house-proud, only the best English Wilton carpets were used; the parquet floors were scrubbed with soap and water every week, and when they were dry the carpets were laid over them. In front of every door was a mat, inscribed with the admonition WIPE YOUR FEET. The brasswork, from fenders to stair-rods, was brilliant, but it was never brilliant enough to please Cora. She was both house-proud and extravagant. She spent a small fortune on entertaining: there were rarely fewer than fifteen people to dinner, and her chef insisted that he could not buy less than a side of beef at a time. Cora was not content with such gastronomic extravagance: one day she wagered her guests that she would give them some meat which none of them would dare to cut. She had herself served up on a huge silver salver, borne by four men. She was naked, with a sprinkling of parsley.[11]

The Duc de Morny died, prematurely, in March 1865. (It was said that, as he lay dying, his friend the Marquis de Montguyon put all his love-letters down the lavatory: a scene which Alphonse Daudet, the Duc's former secretary, described with strict exactitude in his novel *Le Nabab*.) It was probably after Morny's death that Cora had her liaison with that impenitent *noceur* Ludovic, Duc de Grammont-Caderousse.[12] It could only have been a casual, brief affair, for the Duc was too enamoured of Hortense Schneider to become involved; and, besides, he died in September. Cora was not too disconsolate to take another imperial lover: in fact, she may already have embarked upon her affair with Prince Napoleon.

In his *Souvenirs d'un demi-siècle*, Maxime du Camp explained how the Prince was talking to Des Varannes, a naval lieutenant in the Emperor's household. 'Do you care much for Cora Pearl? I know she's your mistress. You don't, do you? Will you arrange for me to meet her? You'd be doing me a service.' Des Varannes replied: 'But, Monseigneur, it will be arranged this evening, if Your Imperial Highness so desires.' And so (continues du Camp) Prince Napoleon became 'the much too official lover of Cora Pearl, a knock-kneed tart with dyed yellow hair, whose real name was Emma Cruche [*sic*].'[13]

Maxime du Camp, like Arsène Houssaye, was not above confusing fact and fiction, especially if this improved his narrative. It was probably in 1868, after she had been hunting at Meudon with Prince Achille Murat, that Cora Pearl had met the Emperor's cousin. Prince Napoleon was then forty-two; he had been married for nine years to the dull, devout Princess Clothilde, daughter of Victor-Emmanuel of Italy. And while Princess Clothilde slept *seule et délaissée, dans ses complets de flanelle*, Prince Napoleon continued to earn renown for his many highly publicised liaisons. Yet for all his promiscuity, his political irresponsibility, his reputation as the *enfant terrible* of the Second Empire, this *César déclassé* had endearing qualities. The touching loyalty he had shown Rachel[14] he showed, now, to his latest mistress. Their liaison must have been one of the longest in Cora's career: it continued, at intervals, for nine years, and when it ended, it was the Prince, not she herself, who broke it. 'My first impression has not changed,' she would write at the end of her life. 'This man is an angel to those who please him, . . . profligate, unmanageable, insolent, and a devil to everyone else.'[15]

Prince Napoleon gave Cora a key to the Palais-Royal, where he lived. Indeed, she sometimes slept in the room next to that of the lady-in-waiting, and dined in the dining-room that was used by Princess Clothilde. But even

Cora was embarrassed to hear the Princess talking and the children playing next door. She was hardly the woman to be content with such a situation, especially as the Prince received a million francs a year from the civil list. Prince Napoleon was generous. He established her at 101, rue de Chaillot: a veritable palace of her own, which came to be known as *les Petites Tuileries*. He gave her twelve thousand francs a month, on the strength of which she regularly spent more than double;[16] and *la Lune rousse*, as she was called on account of her red hair,[17] bathed superbly in a rose marble bathroom, with her initials inlaid, in gold, at the bottom of the bath. As she did so, she could gaze complacently at her portrait; it smiled down from the bathroom wall, over a gratifying inscription:

> Et la riche Angleterre
> Plus d'une fois dans l'eau jeta ses filets
> Avant d'y retrouver une Perle aussi chère.

Dissatisfied with a single house, Cora allowed Prince Napoleon to buy her a second *hôtel* in Paris: 6, rue des Bassins.

In the last five years of the Second Empire, from 1865 to 1870, Cora reached her dazzling zenith. She was so rich that her jewels alone were worth a million francs, she had two or three houses furnished quite regardless of expense, and she showed the lavishness of all the *grandes cocottes*, choosing some of her clothes at Worth's, giving stupendous entertainments, grand dinners, masked balls and impromptu suppers (at which the peaches and grapes did not rest on the usual vine leaves, but on fifteen hundred francs' worth of Parma violets).[18] She threw herself into the febrile life of the Second Empire. Early in 1866 she appeared as Eve at a fancy-dress ball at the Restaurant des Trois Frères Provençaux. She looked very well, reported an English journalist, 'and her form and figure were not concealed by any more garments than were worn by the original apple-eater'.[19] On 26 January 1867, she appeared at the Théâtre des Bouffes-Parisiens, as Cupid, in Offenbach's comic opera *Orphée aux Enfers*.

Cora Pearl [snapped Philibert Audebrand] made her appearance half-naked on the stage, singing with quite a marked little Anglo-Saxon accent the couplets which begin *I know Love*. That evening the Jockey Club, in its entirety, graced the theatre. All the names which are blazoned in the Golden Book of the French nobility were there, complete with white gloves and ivory lorgnettes . . . It was success of a kind.

'There, now, I'm a French actress,' said Miss Emma Cruch [*sic*]. 'People can always be what they mean to be.'

Apparently [continued Audebrand] the beautiful Cora Pearl had already munched up a *brochette* of five or six great historic fortunes with her pretty white teeth. And why not? Just before he died, . . . the young Duc de Grammont-Caderousse summed it up in a phrase:

'If the Frères Provençaux served diamond omelettes, Cora would go and dine there every evening.'[20]

It was said that when she appeared at the Bouffes, she dropped two diamonds on stage, and left them for the dresser to retrieve: they were worth four thousand francs, which was twice the dresser's annual wages. (If the tale was true, Cora Pearl could spare the jewels: one critic remarked that she looked like a jeweller's window, with daylight lighting.) Her performance at the Bouffes was witnessed by many *grandes cocottes*; it created a sensation, and a count offered fifty thousand francs for the boots which Cora wore on stage. The astounding offer was made for some astounding footwear. 'I remember little of the performance,' wrote an Englishman then in Paris, 'except that Cupid played with great self-possession, that she was not much encumbered with garments, and that the buttons of her boots were large diamonds of the purest water.'[21] Not only the buttons. 'In one last extravagant gambol,' recalled William Osgood Field, 'she threw herself flat on her back and flung her legs up in the air to show the soles of her shoes that were one mass of diamonds.'[22]

A French spectator took the occasion much more seriously. Paul Foucher saw it as the official recognition of vice. 'The *moral* history of the modern theatre was,' he wrote,

completed by a celebrated evening at which I was present, and perhaps it would not be wrong to perpetuate the memory, because it alone would characterise an epoch. It is usual and, so to speak, traditional, to see venal love in distress turn to the theatre for self-advertisement. When you stop finding *protectors* in the Bois, at the Champs-Elysées concert, in the gallery of the theatre, you seek them out by cultivating the dramatic art; you make the stage into a boarded pavement. But until that particular evening we had not often seen the theatre exploit the scandals of common alcoves and cosmopolitan suppers. We had not seen it engage . . . a woman whose whole celebrity had so far consisted in the money she spent – I won't exactly say without earning it, but at least without hiding the nature and the multiplicity of her collaborators . . . At the reception at the Bouffes, vice was *presented*.[23]

Cora could afford to ignore such criticism of her stage performance. Few women led so resplendent a career as a courtesan. She visited the Universal Exhibition, where Prince Napoleon awaited her in his private room, which was furnished in Turkish style. She sat, enthroned, in her box at the theatre; she went to Monte Carlo, where she lost seventy thousand francs in eight months; she visited Vichy, where her presence was 'an era of benediction' for local tradesmen; she arrived, with a cart-load of luggage, six horses, and numerous retainers – 'an enormous staff,' she said – to gamble at Baden (though in 1868 she was compelled to raise money on promissory notes, and then to rush back to Paris, where her carriages and furniture had been seized by a bailiff). [24] 'Cora delighted – positively revelled – in the most wild and reckless extravagance,' wrote William Osgood Field, who knew her well, 'and no doubt she was quite right, for in her special profession it is more than half the battle to keep in the limelight, and have all the drums incessantly beating.'[25] Once, when he lunched with her in the rue des Bassins, 'she put her hand into a dish of cutlets or something and put a large dripping piece of whatever it was on the head of Ferdinand Bischoffsheim. He took it very meekly and smiled a weak smile through the veil of thick sauce that covered his face.'[26] When Prince Paul Demidoff, a Russian of untold wealth, insisted on wearing his hat at the Maison d'Or, just to vex her, Cora smashed his cane over his head—an incident which she regretted, because, she said, the cane was very fine.[27] When Demidoff claimed that her pearls were not real, she threw her necklace on the floor, where it broke, and the pearls rolled away in all directions. 'Pick up the pearls, my dear,' she said, 'I'll prove that they are real – I will leave you one for your cravat.' Demidoff sat transfixed. The nobility who were dining at the Maison d'Or went on their hands and knees to look for pearls. In 1863, it is said, Cora fought a duel in the Bois with another courtesan, Marthe de Vère, over the person of a handsome Serbian or Armenian prince. Both women used their riding-whips freely, and did considerable damage to each other's faces in the *rencontre*. They did not reappear in public for a week, during which time their Adonis vanished.[28]

Extravagant herself, Cora Pearl inspired outrageous extravagance in others. One of her lovers presented her with a box of marrons glacés, each marron separately wrapped in a thousand-franc note;[29] another admirer sent her a massive silver horse, which was carried by two porters, and proved to be full of jewels and gold.[30] Prince Napoleon offered her 'a large vanload' of the most expensive orchids. She gave a supper party, strewed the orchids over the floor and, dressed as a sailor, danced the hornpipe, followed by the cancan, over them.[31] Albert Wolff, the journalist, remembered a similar occasion when a prince had sent her a basket of flowers, and she threw them on the carpet and trampled on them, saying how tired she was of princely admirers. No doubt, he reflected, she was tired of being taken twice a week to grand restaurants, and given *une indigestion d'homard à l'américaine*.[32]

57

Every New Year's Day brought a queue of worshippers, bearing costly offerings to the goddess. At one moment, so it seems, Cora was conducting simultaneous affairs with Prince Napoleon, Demidoff, and Demidoff's compatriot Narischkin. She played her lovers against each other with fruitful calculation. Prince Napoleon would be told that Demidoff had given her a necklace worth £5,000; he would immediately buy her, say, a rivière of diamonds worth twice as much. Narischkin, not to be outdone, would hasten to the jeweller's; and so *ad infinitum*.[33] As the Comte de Maugny said, Cora had plenty of system.

In his book on the demi-monde of the Second Empire, written under the pseudonym of Zed, the Comte recorded that he had found an astounding register at Cora's. It was divided into three columns: in one were the names of her clients (most of them famous, and friends of his own), in the second were the dates of their visits, and in the third were 'the sums given by the pilgrims for the hospitality received'. There was also, said the Comte, a column of observations, which was 'not nice about everyone'.

It may be asked how the Comte de Maugny came across the register, and if, perhaps, he found some astringent comments on himself. In his book he wrote acidly about 'the inexplicable Cora Pearl. I humbly admit that that is one success I have never understood . . . For me she is a blot on the brilliant, refined, and, on the whole, aristocratic group of the *femmes galantes* of her age.'[34]

One suspects that the Comte de Maugny had been dissatisfied. Among the satisfied admirers (it is hard to specify the dates) were Khalil Bey, the majestic and blue-spectacled old Turk, whose Parisian *hôtel* was filled with the wonders of the East. The Queen of Sheba, said Cora herself, 'would have found her bed and board in his house, which was no less sumptuous than that of the divine Solomon.'[35] James Whelpley, an Irish lover, gave Cora Pearl his fortune, £80,000. She spent it in eight weeks.[36] Another admirer, the Comte Alonso of Cora's *Mémoires* (who has been identified as Aguado), met her in an unexpected way: he was anxious to find a mate for his Havana bitch, and his valet discovered that 'Madame Cornapile', of 101, rue de Chaillot, had a suitable Havana dog called Loulou. The Comte arranged both a canine and a human liaison.[37]

Cora's dog was no doubt the dog that died in Rome in 1873. Cora had dyed it blue to match a dress. For she was apt to set strange fashions. In 1867 she inspired a craze for a drink which the Parisians called 'Tears of Cora Pearl'. As Gustave Claudin would recall, in *Mes Souvenirs*, she introduced modern make-up into France.[38] Her bottles of toilet water and wonderful powders were sent from London. 'And then, oh glory without peer!' wrote Théodore

Opposite. 'There, now, I'm a French actress.' Cora Pearl as Cupid in *Orphée aux Enfers*, 1867. From a contemporary lithograph.

de Banville in his *Camées Parisiens*, 'Cora Pearl presented the world with that dye, thanks to which a brunette can have the pleasure of hearing a poet compare her hair, now red or pink, to a Bengal rose or a purple veil. Were it only for the love of red, oh Cora Pearl, I salute you!'[39] Cora did not restrict herself to red: Jean-Philippe Worth, the couturier's son, who found her make-up 'shockingly overdone', said that 'her lemon-coloured hair was so exactly the shade of the yellow satin in her carriage that it could scarcely be distinguished from it'.[40] Cora not only dyed her hair, she painted her eyelashes, brightened her eyes, and used face-powders tinted with silver and pearl. 'She tanned her skin,' remembered Claudin, in astonishment, 'and in spite of that many women copied her.'[41]

They could hardly have copied her clothes. In 1866 a journalist on *La Vie parisienne* met her at the house of a friend:

She was fit to put with the curiosities of the Barnum Museum. A pink satin dress, with a kind of mauve gauze flounce on the hem of the skirt, over which was some blond-lace sprinkled with white bugles. A gathered, décolleté bodice, with two little mauve flounces all round it. A loose belt, with four mauve gauze streamers, sewn with pearls . . .

She was going to the Théâtre-Lyrique. I am sure that people looked much more at her than they did at Mlle Nilsson, though Mlle Nilsson is very pretty.[42]

In July 1870 came the brief Franco-Prussian War; in September the Emperor surrendered with his troops at Sedan, the Second Empire fell, and the Bonapartes were scattered into exile: the Emperor imprisoned in Germany, the Empress and her son seeking traditional safety in England, Princess Mathilde in Belgium, Prince Napoleon in Italy. The Siege of Paris began. Cora's chief concern was her stables, and on the day when the gates of Paris were closed against the enemy, she contrived to smuggle out eight horses, 'for exercise'. She turned 101, rue de Chaillot into a small hospital, and (like other *grandes cocottes*) she ministered to the medical needs of the soldiers. Her fine linen sheets were used for shrouds, and she herself paid all expenses.

Prince Napoleon, in exile, remained touchingly constant; his letters showed solicitude and affection. When, at last, the Siege was over, they planned to meet in London. Cora boldly reserved a first-floor suite at the Grosvenor Hotel, and paid for a month in advance. She had planned without regard for Victorian principles. Soon after her arrival, the manager, suddenly aware of her profession, announced that she must leave the hotel. He refused, so Cora said, to return her money. However, the Prince arrived, incognito, and rented a furnished house for five weeks, and he and Cora toured the West Country, where squires' wives assumed that she was Princess Clothilde, and received her with due deference. They visited Dublin, where the Lord Mayor again mistook her identity, and asked to call and pay his respects. Cora had come a long way since the days of the diamond merchant at Covent Garden.

*

It was not the Franco-Prussian War, or even the fall of the Second Empire, which ended her career. It was a squalid melodrama, the *affaire Duval*. At the age of about thirty-seven, Cora captivated a rich young man, ten years her junior: he was Alexandre Duval, whose father had founded the chain of popular restaurants, known as the *Bouillons Duval*, in Paris. Alexandre Duval was invited to wear Prince Napoleon's nightshirt. 'With that crown on my stomach,' he said, later, 'I felt I had arrived.' Duval was young, besotted, and rich enough to give Cora the sort of presents she understood. Among them was a finely bound book; each of its hundred pages was a thousand-franc note.

There is no doubt that she preferred the banknotes to the donor; and when, having given her some horses from the ex-Emperor's stables, not to mention jewels, bric-à-brac, and the money to keep up the rue de Chaillot and the château near Orleans, Duval reached the end of his resources, Cora dismissed him. At three o'clock on the afternoon of Thursday, 19 December 1872, he returned to the rue de Chaillot with a revolver. It is said that he meant to shoot Cora; but the revolver went off, wounding him so gravely that he was in danger of death. The *affaire Duval* caused such a stir that Cora was banished from France. 'A singular thing,' observed *Le Figaro*, on 26 December. 'Since we have been a republic only two people have been banished from France, Prince Napoleon and Mademoiselle Cora Pearl.' 'I was paying dearly,' wrote Cora herself, 'for someone else's unexpected moment of aberration.'[43]

She went to Monte Carlo, and on to Nice, where she stayed with another *grande cocotte*, Caroline Letessier, who was then kept by the Prince of Monaco's son. Then she travelled to Milan, where, by some happy chance, she found Prince Napoleon, 'still the same, very liberal, very much above gossip, judging everything by his reason alone. He did not seem displeased to see me.'[44]

Alexandre Duval recovered from his injuries, and prospered; on his death in 1922 he was described by *The Times* as 'the last real boulevardier'. But the *affaire Duval* ruined Cora Pearl. In February 1873 she sold 101, rue de Chaillot to a fellow-courtesan. 'The establishment will be carried on as before,' wrote a journalist, 'but without the pistol.' In May 1877 the contents of the rue de Chaillot were auctioned.[45]

In 1874, no longer able to solve the problems of separation and financial strain, Prince Napoleon had broken his liaison.

Faced with my duty [he wrote to Cora], I can have no choice. I have decided against you, against myself, in favour of what must be done. I have a life of work before me, it must not degenerate through dissipation, or allow itself to be dominated by pleasure. You have always been charming, you give me great happiness, but you will understand that today I cannot act otherwise. I am sending you a last present, which may be useful to you. I shall not see you for some time, but one day I shall clasp your hand and kiss you with great joy, my dear Cora.[46]

Cora Pearl was thirty-nine; and already she seemed old. After about 1880 she began to feel financial strain; and, a pathetic, over-painted figure, sometimes wearing a broad-brimmed hat to create an illusion of youth, she haunted – for she was back in Paris – the scenes of her former grandeur. Arsène Houssaye records that he advised her to return to England, 'but she had dreamed of having a pyramid in France for a tomb, just like Semiramis.'[47]

I had known Miss Cora Pearl in her ascendancy [Houssaye continued]. I wanted to see her again, in her decline . . . She was living then near the hôtel Païva, two doors further down, in an entresol full of odds and ends, over a carriage shop. One day I went and knocked on her door. 'Good afternoon, Cora!' She threw her arms round my neck, she was so glad to meet a friend from her good days again. 'Yes, Cora,' she said, 'but Cora without the pearls.' 'You're still pretty!' I answered, without conviction. 'No, I'm not. Look, my cheeks are furrowed with tears. Don't say that in the papers. Paris doesn't like women who weep.'[48]

She still had her clients, as Houssaye knew, at 23, avenue des Champs-Élysées, over the premises of Georges Pilon, the coachbuilder; and it was not until July 1885 that she was compelled to sell her château and estate at Olivet. But when, in 1881, she paid another visit to Monte Carlo, she was reduced to playing roulette with five-franc pieces.

In his memoirs, *Giants in Dressing Gowns*, Julian Arnold remembered her as she was then:

Her days became as dolorous as the gentle rain which was falling as I descended the steps of the Casino at Monte Carlo one evening in the eighties. Across the wet pavements the street lamps cast pathways of gold scarcely less tangible than those of the roulette tables which I had just quitted. Beyond the gardens I found a woman seated on the kerbstone and weeping pitifully. She appeared to be about fifty years of age, handsome, fair-haired and well-complexioned but much bedraggled. Her sobbings were so persistent that I might not avoid stopping to enquire the cause of her tears, and, answering my questions she told me in mingled

French and English that she had been turned out of her apartment, that her port-manteau containing her few belongings had been retained against arrears of rent, that she had neither lodgment nor money, and that she was wet and hungry and miserable.

'But the weather does not invite your camping out like this, Madame; what do you propose to do?"

'Nothing.'

'Have you no friends?'

'None.'

'Your English accent is so good, Madame, that I would venture to ask your name?'

'I am Cora Pearl.'

Arnold took her back to his villa, where two bachelor friends were staying with him. Over dinner, Cora Pearl recalled her career. Late that night, while he was reading alone in the library, she entered in a borrowed dressing-gown, and suddenly let it fall to her feet. 'A woman's vanity,' she said, 'should be sufficient excuse. I found it difficult to rest until I had shown you that, if Cora Pearl has lost all things else, she still retains that which made her famous – a form of loveliness.'[49]

In 1883 (her address was given as 6, rue Christophe Colomb), she was listed in *The Pretty Women of Paris*; but she figured there as a relic of the past.

One of the most celebrated whores of her time [noted the compiler]. She has charmed a generation of votaries to Venus, and still goes on undaunted . . . Now she is poor, almost friendless, and up to her neck in debt, but she has not lost her merry disposition. No woman was ever so really good-hearted and generous when she had money, and none of her old lovers ever speaks of her except in terms of praise. Her features are not pleasing; her hair is dyed fair, but her teeth are mag-nificent and healthy; and her skin is of dazzling milky whiteness . . . She has never omitted using cold water, and is continually drenching her frame with an enor-mous sponge. To these ablutions and healthy exercise on horseback, we may ascribe the marvellous preservation of her bodily beauty. Every man of any note for the last fifteen years has passed a few hours with Cora, . . . who after sleeping in black satin sheets, embroidered with the arms of the Empire, now sheds tears of joy when an amateur slips a bank-note in her hand.[50]

Cora Pearl, who had once charged as much as ten thousand francs a night, had fallen to the ranks of the women who accepted five louis or even less.[51]

She had enough spirit to take up the study of Volapük, an artificial language which had recently been invented; indeed, she had some idea that she herself might propagate the study of Volapük at the Paris Exhibition of 1889 (but she would not live long enough to see it). She said – for she was still determined to project her image – that since her childhood she had dreamed of a universal language; it might well be called Corapük.

In 1884, in more practical mood, she sold her *Mémoires* to the publisher Jules Lévy. The book mingled fact and fiction, it was an autobiography *à clef*, in which the names of her lovers were thinly disguised, and their letters recalled her extraordinary spell. It was in her *Mémoires* that she set down her philosophy:

I can say [she wrote] that I have never had a favourite lover ... A handsome, young and charming man, who has loyally offered me his arm, his love, his money, has every right to think that he is really 'my favourite lover', my lover for an hour, my escort for a month, my friend for ever. That is how I understand the matter.[52]

Mémoires de Cora Pearl was published in March 1886, and it had a kind reception. The news of it even reached Cora's emigrant and ageing father in Baltimore; Mr Crouch was interviewed, and admitted that the author was his daughter.

In his *Mémoires d'un Parisien*, Albert Wolff dismissed the book as worthless, as the last cry of a vanished Parisian gallantry. 'In our new way of life,' he wrote, 'if I may be bold enough to say so, it has lost the importance it once possessed. The courtesan of our day has gone democratic like everything else. Under the Empire, she belonged to a few; today, she belongs to everyone.'[53]

On 8 July 1886, four months after her *Mémoires* had appeared, Cora Pearl died at 8, rue de Bassano, of cancer of the intestines. She was about fifty-one. She was buried in the cemetery at Batignolles.

If I had to live my life again [she had ended her *Mémoires*], perhaps I should be less wild, and more highly considered, not because I should have been worthier of esteem, but because I should have proved myself less clumsy. Should I regret my actual situation? Yes, if I think of my poverty. No, if I understand what my peace of mind would have cost me ... Honour and justice are satisfied. I have never deceived anyone, for I have never belonged to anyone. My independence was all my wealth: I have known no other happiness.[54]

4

Esther Guimond

Le Lion, la Paysanne (d. 1879)

Esther Guimond, who would be an influence on the Press and politics of her time, began life in complete obscurity. Her family, her date and place of birth remain unknown; it is only certain that her origins were humble, that she was born at about the turn of the century, and that her education was minimal (Frédéric Loliée, that chronicler of the Second Empire, said that Esther Guimond could hardly write).[1] She herself left a single clue to her early career. When she was reading her unpublished memoirs to Maurice Talmeyr,[2] the novelist, she suddenly exclaimed: 'Ah, here are my beginnings, when I was in a dressmaker's workroom . . . Ah! dressmaking . . . No, dressmaking didn't suit me!' And, warming to her subject, she added: 'Just try to guess who launched me . . . Come on, come on, guess . . . Do you know who it was? . . . Guizot! The great Guizot! . . . Yes, my dear . . . I was twenty, and I was in my dressmaker's workroom at the time.' Talmeyr was speechless. François Guizot had taught history at the Sorbonne, he had written massive works on the history of civilisation, he had been Foreign Minister and Prime Minister under Louis-Philippe; and he had been renowned for his austerity. But then, as Esther would observe, 'we courtesans are really the only ones who are worthy to talk to philosophers'.[3]

When she died in 1879, *L'Événement* gave a different, but romantic account of her début in the world of Parisian gallantry:

One evening, Esther Guimond ventured to the ball at the Opéra; she was dressed as a pierrot, but with all the coquetry of a little hoyden who wants to throw dust into people's eyes. She was a pierrot in white taffeta trimmed with white roses, she had white satin slippers, and perfect white teeth. She still had all her teeth when she died. It was a gay evening, but of all the men who came with Esther Guimond, none deserved to be taken seriously.

Next morning, one of her friends, who lived at the end of the rue du Bac, took her off to breakfast with some other women she knew. They breakfasted and chatted and dozed; it was noon, but she had to go home. It was pouring with rain, she hadn't got the money for a cab, in fact not even for an umbrella: she had spent her last sou on the taffeta pierrot's dress and the satin slippers. You can imagine the girl of twenty going from the rue du Bac to the rue Saint-Lazare, with nothing to protect her from the jibes of the passers-by but a black pelisse which only half covered her. It couldn't be helped, a carnival was a carnival. And then, on the Pont-Royal, one of the notable figures of the time, a peer of France and mayor of one of the first three cities in the country, passed by in his carriage drawn by three horses. He smilingly observed the pretty feet, shod in white satin, and all spattered with mud. 'What's that?' he said. He couldn't believe his eyes: the girl was pretty, devilish pretty; she was gaily braving wind and rain; she was slanging the passers-by with diabolical wit. The peer of France, a bored man if ever there was one, got out of his carriage and went up to Esther Guimond:

'Why the devil are you walking on a day like this, and in white satin slippers?' Esther Guimond, who had all her wits about her, answered then and there: 'Because I knew perfectly well you'd tell me to get into your carriage.'

And so he did. The peer of France took the young lady home – not to her home, but his own. He had money, and gave it to her; he had no wit, and she gave it to him. So it was that Esther Guimond made her first appearance on the stage of *la haute galanterie*.[4]

According to all other accounts, Esther was far from beautiful. The Goncourts decided that she looked like a repulsive concierge;[5] and people who did not call her le Lion (a nickname of which she was proud), called her la Paysanne. She was, explained one virulent critic, 'depraved and in fashion, and she saved everything by her wit, even her face.'[6] She had a great deal of natural wit, a great deal of audacity. Marie Colombier, the actress and courtesan, recorded that Esther's cynicism was applauded and her witticisms were repeated. When her passport was examined at Naples, she was asked her profession. 'A woman of independent means.' The official looked bewildered. 'Courtesan,' she cried, impatiently. 'And take care you remember it, and go and tell that Englishman over there.'[7]

★

Once she had found a distinguished lover, Esther Guimond established herself as a power. During the reign of Louis-Philippe, her salon was frequented by the most distinguished writers and politicians of the age. Despite her liaison with Guizot, her proudest conquest was no doubt Émile de

Girardin: the formidable publicist who founded *La Presse* which, in 1836, initiated the cheap Press in France.

When Girardin decided to sell *La Presse* at half the price of the other national papers, 'he caused a revolution in journalism, a pacific revolution which has brought benefit to us all'.[8] Girardin may not have realised his political ambitions, but he was the most powerful, most significant French journalist of the century. Gautier, Dumas, and Eugène Sue were among his contributors; Prince Napoleon would be among his friends, Dickens would be dazzled by his hospitality, Rachel would be among his mistresses, and Delphine Gay, the Tenth Muse, so loved by the men of letters of her time, would marry him. Girardin was determined to forget his illegitimacy in his own success; he has been aptly described as 'more American than French'.[9] He was ruthless, vigorous, self-made, difficult with subordinates, and delightful to his equals. He was hated and admired. 'But when he drives past in the Bois,' observed a journalist when he was over sixty, 'he is still the same: stiff and erect, a satirical expression on his face; he laughs, he lives, and he wants to prove that he is still there, alert. And so it is that death will one day find him.'[10]

The observation was made in 1868; death was not to find him for thirteen years. When it did, he would be buried in the brown frock of a Capuchin monk: the frock in which (like Balzac, who had been another of his contributors), he had worked throughout his life.

Esther Guimond conquered Girardin, so she said, by making him laugh. One day, when he had seen her home, he left two hundred francs on the mantelpiece. She returned them with a note: 'No cheap Press for me!' Girardin built her a small *hôtel* on the corner of the rue de Chateaubriand; he gave her a mere thousand francs a month, so she maintained, and he passed her on his discarded coupés.[11] He also sent her some of his newspaper articles, so that she could slip in an occasional observation, or a sharp and useful witticism; her anecdotes, and, indeed, her slander, helped to fill his gossip columns, and she readily suggested articles to him.

Since he had (wrongly) suspected his wife of infidelity, Girardin had been 'the husband of every wife in Paris except his own'.[12] One of his biographers has suggested that his long liaison with Esther Guimond owed something to his cool concern with publicity. In his Life of Girardin, Maurice Reclus makes light of the affair: 'We should not mention Esther Guimond if this fashionable prostitute had not once or twice played a small part in Girardin's political life.'[13] But the part she played was not perhaps so small.

'She had been young about 1831,' wrote Gustave Claudin acidly, in his

Esther Guimond & La Païva

The north side of the boulevard des Italiens in the 1850s, showing Tortoni's, and the other cafés and restaurants which were focal points of boulevard life.

BOULEVARD DES ITALIENS (côté nord).

Café de Paris.   Rue Taitbout.   Tortoni.   Maison-Dorée.   Rue Laffitte.   Café Riche.   Rue Lepelletier.

'Everyone who counted in Paris,' wrote the journalist Henri de Villemessant, 'used to pass Tortoni's every day, at about five o'clock.' Many of Esther Guimond's friends were among its habitués.

The Opera Ball in Paris in the days of Louis-Philippe.

Above and left. Two friends of Esther Guimond: General Cavaignac (1802–57); and Emile de Girardin (1806–81), the greatest French journalist of the century.

Arsène Houssaye (on the extreme right), lifelong friend of Esther Guimond and La Païva, talks to some of his guests at one of his famous *redoutes* in the avenue de Friedland.

Left. François Guizot (1787–1874), historian and statesman, reputedly Esther's first lover. *Right.* Louis-Philippe and Marie-Amélie, King and Queen of the French. Their refusal to receive La Païva probably explained her profound and lifelong aversion to France.

Above. Henri Herz, the Viennese pianist, who introduced the future La Païva to artistic society in Paris.
Left. La Païva. This is the only known engraving said to represent the most outrageous *grande horizontale*.

Opposite. The Hôtel Païva in the Champs-Elysées was intended to be the most splendid private *hôtel* in Paris. This photograph shows the hall and the famous onyx staircase.
Left. Ems, the Prussian spa where Mme Villoing met the eligible Henri Herz.

Above left. Three of La Païva's guests: Richard Wagner (top), one of the first to come to her *salon* in Paris; Emile de Girardin (centre), seen here in middle age; and Paul de Saint-Victor (bottom), the critic.

Top right. The ceiling in the *salon* showed 'Day chasing Night away'; some critics said it was worth all the other treasures in the *hôtel*.

Centre. One of La Païva's beds, a marine carriage drawn by four swans and attended by a mermaid. It was made of three separate pieces of mahogany, richly carved, and weighed a ton and a half.

Left. Portrait of Cydalise: Gautier's sketch of his first mistress, drawn from memory at the Hôtel Païva.

Above left. Arsène Houssaye, a close
friend of Girardin, who continued to
visit La Païva after the disgrace of 1870.
Top right. The Marquis de Païva, the
husband who 'ennobled' Madame Villoing.
Centre. Alexandre Dumas *fils* in about 1868.
His play *la Femme de Claude* (1873) was
written as an attack on La Païva.
Left. Edmond and Jules de Goncourt, from a
sketch by Gavarni. Occasional guests at the
Hôtel Païva, the brothers made devastating
comments on it in their *Journal.*

Above. Guido Henckel von Donnersmarck, the Prussian who became La Païva's third husband. He insisted that France should pay 5,000,000,000 francs as war indemnities in 1871. From a caricature by Sem.
Left. Emile de Girardin in old age. As the editor of *la France*, he campaigned for close links between France and Germany after the war of 1870.

Below. The end of the Franco-Prussian War: Prussian troops in the Place de la Concorde, 1 March 1871.

Souvenirs, 'in the golden days when the *garde nationale* were mounted. She claimed that one evening M. Guizot had come to tea with her to meet Émile de Girardin. This was apparently true . . .'[14] No doubt it was. In 1846 Girardin had begun a Press campaign against the minister who had disappointed his political hopes. But the two men, who had officially quarrelled, still had their private contacts through Esther Guimond, who was then more in fashion than ever, and remained on excellent terms with her first lover.

Claudin maintained that Esther lacked the wit with which she was accredited. She was, he said, a *poseuse* who would interrupt a frivolous supper to talk about Saint-Simon, whom she had not read. But Claudin did not enquire why men of distinction troubled to come and see her: why she entertained Nestor Roqueplan, sometime director of the Opéra, and contributor to *Le Constitutionnel*; why she entertained Sainte-Beuve himself. She was also a friend of General Cavaignac, who was the chief of the executive power in 1848, and suppressed the revolution that June: indeed, she claimed that when Girardin was imprisoned that month, she probably saved his life. She forced her way into Cavaignac's presence and demanded to know why he had arrested Girardin. 'Because he's conspiring!' 'Conspiring?' she cried. 'What nonsense! He can't conspire, no one ever shares his opinions!' Cavaignac laughed, so Esther would recall, and Girardin was freed. Maurice Reclus says that Esther Guimond and Mme de Girardin both pleaded with Cavaignac for his freedom.[15]

In 1853, when Roger de Beauvoir was involved in a lawsuit with his wife, he could not make any plans for his children without permission from President de Belleyme, of the Tribunal de Première Instance de la Seine. He wanted access to his children at Easter. He dined with Esther Guimond. She sat there, squalid and middle-aged, in the midst of her luxury; on one side of her sat Prince Napoleon, on the other side sat Girardin. It was, apparently, through Girardin – and through Esther's good offices – that Roger de Beauvoir obtained the permission he needed.[16]

Her political powers were considerable. The former mistress of Guizot was a close friend of Prince Napoleon, cousin of Napoleon III. 'Gifted with such intelligence and cunning,' wrote Loliée, 'what resources she could have used had she put them at the service of a lasting ambition! Had she not been intimately concerned in a thousand intrigues, in every kind of clandestine adventure and secret machination?'[17]

*

Arsène Houssaye, in his *Confessions*, suggested that Esther Guimond had asserted the rank of the courtesan in society. At a fashionable race-meeting, attended by the Jockey Club, high society had been enraged to see *ces demoiselles* enter the grandstand escorted by the men-about-town. The *grandes dames*, said Houssaye, despatched their master of ceremonies to tell the courtesans that they were intruding. Esther replied that she was there by the will of these gentlemen, and that only bayonets would move her. On the return from the races, she gave her coachman a louis to drive neck-and-neck with the coachman of the Comtesse de Courval. It was not, as Houssaye mildly explained, so that she could toss the Countess flowers. As Esther's little victoria drove alongside the Countess's landau, she improvised a song in thirty-six couplets (it lasted all the way home): a song which was 'a masterpiece of impertinence'. She sang it to the tune of *La Rifla*; all Paris sang it next day, and everyone added 'their grain of salt and pepper, Gallic salt and Cayenne pepper'. 'And that,' Esther Guimond used to say, 'is how I made my entry into society.'[18]

As the incident occurred in the reign of Louis-Philippe, a virtuous and family-minded sovereign, Paris was delighted to take Esther Guimond under its wing; and 'this woman,' wrote Houssaye, 'who was not pretty, who had neither charm nor grace, became the darling of the *jeunesse dorée*, just simply because she was foul-mouthed . . . One even met her at diplomatic suppers; she made fair weather and foul behind the political scenes, because she used to see all the statesmen.'[19] And just as Louis XIV, before he embarked on an enterprise, used to ask: 'Qu'en pense Ninon?', Guizot more than once asked Esther what she thought of things, and especially what she thought of men in power and aspirants for power. 'Often she only needed a line to paint a face. If her *Mémoires* are ever published, people will find . . . some pages of the intimate history of the nineteenth century.'[20] In his *Men and Manners of the Third Republic*, Albert Vandam went further:

I do not positively assert that Esther Guimont, a kind of second-rate Aspasia of the Citizen Monarchy, had a direct and clearly defined mission of espionage, but several of her letters to Guizot prove beyond a doubt that at least on one occasion she was engaged in very delicate negotiations on behalf of the Government with certain journalists of the Opposition; while her salon – save the mark! – in the middle of the forties was looked upon in the light of a political centre.[21]

When Arsène Houssaye wrote his *Confessions*, he was particularly anxious that Esther Guimond's letters should be published. 'But where are they to be found? When she died, all the interesting letters that she had received were stolen from her.'[22]

This theft – if theft it was – seems dramatic justice. Esther was the least scrupulous of women, and some said that she had made a fortune through blackmail.

Alphonse Karr in his *Log-book* [recorded D. Bingham, in his *Recollections of Paris*] says that the first exploit of this *coquine*, who afterwards became famous, was to captivate a greenhorn who had a liaison with a lady of quality, and, feigning jealousy, to persuade him to hand over the letters of her rival. With these letters in her possession she proceeded to levy blackmail, and their writer had to sell her jewels in order to procure money enough to save her honour. This was the commencement of Esther Guimond's fortune.[23]

Some people added that she had been indirectly responsible for the sudden, mysterious death of the first Mme Bazaine. She had threatened to disclose a secret passion of the Marshal's wife; and Maria Bazaine, distraught, had sought refuge in poison.[24]

Whatever the truth of this story, it is certain that Esther delighted in causing trouble. She advised Comte Edmond de Lagrené to write about another courtesan, Antonia Sari, who was selling her effects in the rue Scribe. Lagrené wrote a lively column, Girardin published it in *La Presse*, and society women hurried off in their carriages to the rue Scribe to enjoy a preview before the sale. The day after the auction was said to be held, Antonia Sari, with a male escort, burst into Edmond de Lagrené's office. 'It's Esther who told you that, isn't it? Pure feminine jealousy. She hasn't forgiven me for stealing her Girardin.' The angry repercussions continued. Girardin rebuked his contributor, and the furious Lagrené asked the printers to publish a note which they assumed to be Girardin's work: 'We must acknowledge our mistakes. We were wrong to say that Mlle Antonia Sari had been sold by magistrate's order. Faithful to the principles which she has always followed, *she sold herself*.'[25]

★

One day in the 1870s, when Maurice Talmeyr was writing an article on Girardin for the *Revue bleue*, he was sitting at Tortoni's: the café which had known its golden days in the distant age of Louis-Philippe. Tortoni's would not have been Tortoni's if there had not been some friends of Esther Guimond's among its veteran habitués; and one of them took Talmeyr to see her.

Old and forgotten as she then was, she still held a place of importance in Girardin's life. She still lived in the rue de Chateaubriand: in a sullen, one-eyed little *hôtel* across a dark little courtyard. The door was opened by Blanche, her old cook, who led Talmeyr into a salon so dim that at first he could not see how it was furnished; as he adjusted himself to the twilight, he saw that the room seemed large and red – not like a woman's room, but the room of a magistrate or a lawyer. And then, into the crepuscular salon, there came a little old squat, grey woman, hunched, with a neckerchief round her head, and her hands in her apron pockets. She said good morning, gruffly; and, at last, the formalities over, she began to talk about Girardin. 'There's Girardin and Girardin . . . There's the serious Girardin, and the Girardin who is less serious, or, maybe, not serious at all . . . And there's the political Girardin, too . . . Ah! the political Girardin!' Talmeyr was fascinated by the wrinkled, cynical face, the violent, scarlet mouth, the broken, retroussé nose 'which was a phenomenon of insolence. Her whole person had an air of concentration, of lying in wait, which was unique. Add to that a manner of speaking which ranged from buffoonery to tragedy, and little clenched, soft, tormented, meddlesome hands, frogs' legs which she plunged feverishly into her apron pockets and raised again in melodramatic gestures. She also had an infernal wit, an amusing cynicism, a gay vitriol with which she inundated everyone, Girardin first and foremost.'[26]

She gave Talmeyr a mischievous picture of Girardin in slippers, diminished, ridiculed, greedy, full of fads, enjoying his sensual pleasures; and then the gossip gave place to the serious critic: 'Ah, the political Girardin! Ah, that was the whole of an epoch.'

Talmeyr's article was published in the *Revue bleue*; next day arrived two letters. The first, in the microscopic writing of Girardin, asked Talmeyr to come and see him at eight one morning. The second, in a wild, baroque scrawl, 'like that of a frenzied cook', was from Esther Guimond, who was delighted once again to be in the public eye. Her letter was largely illegible, but Talmeyr could discern that he had earned her approval. 'Je te tutoie,' she scrawled in a postscript, 'je te fais Grand d'Espagne!'

Girardin's morning habits, like those of Thiers, were legendary. It was said that he was up, unfailingly, at four, and he had written his article by six. (In the portrait of Girardin, which hung in a place of honour at Esther's, his pen was prominently displayed – and, it seems, the legend *Inde fortuna*: 'Hence my fortune.') Girardin lived in the same *quartier* as Esther, in a princely *hôtel* which gave on to the rue la Pérouse on one side, and on to the avenue Kléber on the other. To Talmeyr it was like a ministry. At the top of the steps, an usher opened the tall, glazed double doors which led into a vast ante-room. The room was enhanced by a marble copy of Clésinger's most celebrated statue, *la Femme piquée par un serpent*; and round the figure of the young Madame Sabatier, the best beloved courtesan of her time, waited Girardin's clients: journalists, actors, actresses, artists, financiers, priests and politicians. Talmeyr's name was written down, and taken to Girardin; and, a few moments later, he was led up the imposing staircase to a large, square room. 'And there stood a well-built, elderly man with a staring gaze, in the frock of a Capuchin monk. With his piercing, squinting eyes, his clean-shaven face, marked by a lock of hair in the middle of his forehead, he looked like a squinting Napoleon disguised as a monk, and at first I didn't recognise him as the visitor in white tie and evening dress whom I sometimes saw at Victor Hugo's.'[27]

The interview lasted for five minutes; Girardin commissioned Talmeyr to write a series of portraits for his newspaper, *La France*. Soon afterwards, Talmeyr called again on Esther Guimond; he was high in favour, she discussed the famous men in her life: Sainte-Beuve, Roqueplan, Dumas *fils*, Houssaye, Prince Napoleon, Guizot. The journalist's routine continued: Talmeyr went every week to take an article to Girardin, while Girardin's clientèle awaited their audience round the Clésinger statue. One day he was invited to dine at Esther's; *le grand Émile* was among his fellow-guests.

On Girardin's arrival, she rose dramatically to receive him. He was wearing evening dress, as he did at Hugo's, but he had a familiar, half-gay, and vaguely sly expression. 'He was neither the severe Girardin of Victor Hugo's, nor the busy, laconic Girardin who received you, in a monk's frock, in his *hôtel*, but a third Girardin who was almost totally unlike either, and proved that Esther had been right when she said knowingly that there was "Girardin and Girardin".'

Esther's dining-room, like her salon, was strikingly unfeminine. You could still imagine yourself at a lawyer's or a doctor's. The guests were widely spaced out, 'and, in the middle of them, opposite Girardin, old Esther sat enthroned, hunch-backed, myopic, with her mouth like a penknife gash, and her broken nose'.[28] On one side of her, on the table, were two slip-on sleeves, and on the other, like a surgeon's case, was a whole set of carving instruments, because she always carved for herself, as if she were taking part in a rite. The servant slipped the sleeves on her arms, and she attacked the meat in an energetic but nervous way, as if she were committing a murder. When the deed was done, she meticulously detached a little piece of the victim and sent it to Girardin,

who tasted it and tasted it again, clicked his tongue and clicked his tongue again, paused for reflection, and finally pronounced the young wild boar or turkey to be good or mediocre, ordinary or succulent. At the last course, a pâté with truffles caused a sensation. It gave forth such an aroma that the whole table uttered a cry of delight, and *le Lion*, knife in hand, her loose sleeves round her upraised arms, with one of those grand gestures which Rachel had taught her, enthusiastically pronounced the name of a foie-gras merchant in Colmar.[29]

The evening ended gaily enough, and Girardin himself seemed to be almost in a good temper – but a good temper which still suggested the habit of giving orders. On the stroke of eleven, not a moment later, he left. 'Well,' said Esther to Talmeyr, 'what do you think of *le grand Émile*? . . . A little stuffy, sometimes, isn't he? . . . That's his way . . . And when are you coming to hear me read my memoirs?'

The memoirs were a journalist's dream. 'And now, here are my friends . . . There's Sainte-Beuve, there's Musset, there's Roqueplan, there's Jérôme . . . And there I've even got a note from Hugo. Listen to this, it isn't bad: "When is Paradise? . . . Would you like Monday? Would you like Tuesday? Would you like Wednesday? Are you afraid of Friday? I am only afraid of delay!" '

She softened suddenly as she came to Dumas *fils*, and spoke of his wretched childhood, of the little collégien who had later drawn himself in *L'Affaire Clemenceau*. He had been put *en pension*, and virtually abandoned, and she and two other women friends of his father's had gone to console him. Sometimes they had taken him out, and tried to raise his morale by gorging him with cakes. Years later, in the fifth act of *La Dame aux camélias*, the dying Marguerite Gautier was modelled on Esther Guimond. 'You see, I was ill,' she explained to Talmeyr, 'I had typhoid fever, and he was there once when I was unconscious . . . Oh, he wasn't ungrateful, he had a heart, and he remembered my cakes . . . He still remembers them, he was talking to me about them the other day . . . Well, he came to see me, he sat down by my bed, he didn't take his eyes off me, and do you know what he suddenly said as I came round? . . . He stood up and took my hands and cried: "Now I've got my fifth act!" '[30]

It was these memoirs which Esther Guimond asked Talmeyr to ghost. Quite unbelievably, he refused to do so. He withdrew from the interview, she wrote to him twice to ask if he would undertake the work. Then she understood, and there was silence. Girardin abruptly refused to publish any more of his articles. 'You have displeased . . . I warned you that you must not displease.' When Talmeyr met him again at Hugo's, Girardin was still mysterious; he would offer no explanation.

*

Esther Guimond seems to have wondered how to dispose of her papers. Early in 1879, Edmond de Goncourt recorded her surprise: she had eight hundred letters from Girardin, all of them compromising, and he had refused to buy them back from her.[31] But Girardin was too shrewd to be blackmailed. Esther had set the fashion for selling compromising correspondence; now she had met her match.

There were numerous letters she did not sell: Houssaye, a close friend of Girardin's, said that she had two pillows on her bed: one to sleep on and one to dream on. The pillow for dreams was full of letters from her friends. Some of the correspondence came, perhaps, from Dumas *fils*, who had written part of *La Dame aux camélias* in her *hôtel*, and, it was said, had used certain circumstances in her life when he was working on *Le Demi-Monde*. 'The Baronne d'Ange,' said a journalist, 'resembles la Guimond in many intimate details which had been taken from life, and had a great influence on the value and success of the play.'[32] It was claimed – somewhat wildly – that Byron had been among Esther's lovers; but certainly, as Marie Colombier said, she had been 'a great collector of celebrities.'[33]

Esther Guimond, who had spent much of her life among tragedies and scandals, came at last to suffer herself. Comte Edmond de Lagrené, who knew the harm she had done, saw her when she was dying of cancer. 'It's like a jackal devouring me,' she cried. 'Why must I suffer so? I have never done any harm to anyone.' As Lagrené left her, he could not resist saying, cynically, to the servants: 'Send for the doctor: she is delirious.'[34]

She died in her seventies, in the summer of 1879. Girardin wrote briefly to Houssaye: 'She died today. Take care of yourself – let us both take care of ourselves.'[35]

Girardin would take good care of himself and his reputation. He spent the whole of the following day shut up in her library.[36] He was probably the only person to know the fate of his eight hundred letters, and of the vanished memoirs of Esther Guimond. 'Oh, you know,' she had cried to Maurice Talmeyr, 'my memoirs aren't the memoirs you might think . . . They are the memoirs of a politician!' 'Ah! the political Girardin,' she had added. 'That was the whole of an epoch.'[37]

5

La Païva

Thérèse Lachmann, later Mme Villoing,
later Mme la Marquise de Païva,
later Countess Henckel von Donnersmarck (1819–84)

The nineteenth century was an age for fabulous careers, for unbelievable, well-nigh outrageous triumphs; and some of the courtesans who were humbly born lived to dazzle and infuriate honest women. The most successful courtesan, in material terms, was, without much question, la Païva. She was also the one *grande horizontale* who appears to have had no redeeming feature.

Thérèse Lachmann was born in the Moscow ghetto in 1819 (she was born, said someone who knew her, of a witch and a broomstick-handle). Her father was, in fact, a weaver; and on 11 August 1836, at the age of seventeen, she was married to Antoine Villoing, a consumptive young tailor. Marriage brought her a son, and it brought independence from her parents; but she could not tolerate the thought of spending the rest of her days as a tailor's wife. She determined to take her destiny in hand.

After a year or two, it seems, she left her husband and infant son, and worked her way to Paris – for there, as Rivarol, the eighteenth-century wit, had often said, Providence was greater than anywhere else; and in Paris she lived in the slums near the Église Saint-Paul. Her education was minimal. She was far from beautiful: her hair was blue-black, her eyes were slightly protruding, her nose was Mongolian, while her mouth and chin suggested energy rather than gentleness. But if she was unlikely to attract conventional lovers, she possessed a flamboyant exoticism which appealed to more original men. She had some rare, disturbing quality which commanded the attention. She also had extraordinary willpower: some inner dynamism drove her on when any weaker woman would have failed.

By 1841 Mme Villoing had acquired a large enough wardrobe to try

Opposite. An amazon riding in the forest at Pierrefonds in the 1850s.
From the painting by Alfred de Dreux.

her fortune; and, calculating, no doubt, that a spa was a likely décor in which to find a rich, *désœuvré* lover, she set out for Ems, in Prussia. In this watering-place, where the world of fashion took the cure and idled at the casino, Fate (which rewards the adventurous) presented her with an eligible client.

Henri Herz was Jewish, like herself; and it is always possible that some semitic sympathy drew them together. It is also true that Henri Herz was gifted, affable, charming in the Viennese manner, and kind. It is, however, certain that Madame Villoing soon recognised the advantage of attachment to a rich and famous pianist. Had she not heard of the Salle Herz, in Paris, the concerts which Herz himself gave to an eager and discriminating audience? Was she not aware that, in these days of Louis-Philippe, a Herz piano was a symbol of taste and sensibility? She listened, ardently, as Herz played to his Prussian audience; she asked if he would take her as a pupil. She exerted her charm to such effect that she was soon his mistress.

It is said that he married her in England. One may question the tradition. When Monsieur and 'Madame' Herz returned to Paris, he took her to a reception at the Tuileries, and they were turned back at the ante-room. It did not suit King Louis-Philippe or the pious Queen Marie-Amélie to accept this irregular alliance.

The rejection was understandable; but it probably explained the profound aversion to France which Thérèse would feel for the rest of her life. She could achieve much with her willpower, and still more with money; but she could not gain recognition in the highest French society. She would always want it, pretend to despise it, and try to make herself amends for her social failure.

However, if Herz did not give her the *entrée* to the Faubourg Saint-Germain, he brought her the company of musicians, journalists and men of letters; Richard Wagner came to her salon, Hans von Bülow, the pianist and son-in-law of Liszt, Théophile Gautier[1] and Émile de Girardin. Herz also brought her the possessions for which no doubt she had craved since her childhood: he indulged her fancies for brilliant clothes and jewels. It was not surprising that at last he needed to earn a fortune; and in 1848 he set off on a tour of America, leaving her to help supervise his interests in Paris. When he had gone, she merely became more extravagant than ever. At last the Herz family, enraged by her accumulated debts, turned the so-called Madame Herz out of the house.

Once again she found herself destitute; and it was at this moment, said the Goncourts, that she sent for Gautier. He found her at the hôtel Valin, near the Champs-Élysées. She was gravely ill. 'You see what I've come to,' she said to him. 'Perhaps I shan't get over it . . . And then that's that . . . But if I get out of this, I'm not the woman to earn my living running up dresses – and one day, a few yards from here, you mark my words, I mean to have the finest *hôtel* in Paris . . . Remember that.'[2]

Years later, when the *hôtel* was built, and the Goncourts were dining with her, she expounded her terrifying theory of willpower. She said that everything happened through willpower; circumstances did not exist, one created them when one wanted. And, talking of concentrated willpower, she quoted the example of a woman who was determined to achieve a certain purpose, and shut herself up, away from the world, hardly eating, for three years, utterly absorbed in her plans. Silence fell round the table. She added: 'I was that woman!'[3]

One suspects that the tale was exaggerated; but possibly Thérèse referred to the days of her destitution at the hôtel Valin. Destiny was kind to her, then. Her friend Esther Guimond took her to Camille,[4] the milliner; and Camille, foreseeing that Thérèse would be a valuable client, advised her to go to London, and to go like a conquering heroine. She provided her with an arsenal of clothes. The day before Thérèse embarked, Gautier saw her again, with all her flamboyant dresses spread out round the room, trying them on, as a soldier might try his weapons before a battle. 'Not badly equipped, am I?' she said. 'But you can never be sure . . . I might misfire . . . and then *finita la commedia*.' She asked for a flask of chloroform to take in case of failure. Gautier procured one.[5] She was not as confident as she later pretended.

The chloroform was not to be needed. In a profusion of hired silks and satins, Thérèse went to Covent Garden. Late, and alone, she entered her box. It was next to Lord Stanley's, and she ensnared him.

She returned in a confident mood to Paris, well aware of the benefits of a title; and since Antoine Villoing had tactfully died of tuberculosis in 1849, she was free to take a titled husband. Once again she set out for a spa. In Baden she discovered a presentable Portuguese marquis, Albino-Francesco de Païva-Araujo. On 5 June 1851 she married him.

★

The history of la Païva (as she would henceforth be called) fascinated Horace de Viel-Castel, the historian and man of letters; he duly recorded it in his memoirs of the Second Empire.

On top of the scum of Parisian society [he wrote in 1857], there is a certain Madame de Païva who is the queen of kept women, the sovereign of her race.

This woman, who is of Russian origin, was for a long while the mistress of Herz, the pianist, then the mistress of the Duc de Guiche (now the Duc de Grammont), and then the mistress of a number of more or less notable notabilities. However, as the years went by without bringing her either position or fortune, she firmly resolved that she would win them both.

To begin with she made a Portuguese fall madly in love with her: he was the Marquis de Païva, a cousin of the present Portuguese envoy, and she made him so loving and so mad that the wretched man offered to marry her and, as you can imagine, was accepted.

The morning after the marriage, when the new husband and wife awoke, Madame de Païva addressed her satisfied lover more or less as follows:

'You wanted to sleep with me, and you've done so, by making me your wife. You have given me your name, I acquitted myself last night. I have behaved like an honest woman, I wanted a position, and I've got it, but all you have is a prostitute for a wife. You can't take me anywhere, and you can't introduce me to anyone. We must therefore separate. You go back to Portugal. I shall stay here with your name, and remain a whore.'

Ashamed and confused, Païva took the advice of his wife. In the solitude of a Portuguese castle he buried the memory of his deplorable adventure.[6]

In his memoirs of the Second Empire, Viel-Castel sometimes preferred readability to truth; and the truth was that the Païva ménage lasted for some months before the Marquis vanished from the scene. He was to shoot himself in 1872,[7] but his suicide would disturb la Païva as little as the premature death of her son by Villoing and the early death of her illegitimate daughter by Henri Herz. She had acquired a title, and now she had to ensure that she was wealthy enough to be the envy of Paris. She discovered a Prussian count eleven years her junior. His name was Guido Henckel von Donnersmarck. He was one day to be a prince, and the friend of the Kaiser. He happened to be a man of glittering wealth.

Viel-Castel described la Païva's conquest of the Count:

The ex-Herz, now Païva [he wrote], could not live the life she had dreamed of for so long with the dowry that her husband had brought her. She set off in search of a rich and generous prince whom she could enmesh in her net.

She encountered this prince, or count, or duke, on her travels, and she followed on his trail to Constantinople, St Petersburg, Naples and Paris; the prince always found her in the lap of luxury, dazzling in her strange, voluptuous beauty, a beauty which was a little contrived, a little painted, and very artificial. La Païva did not seem to pay any attention whatever to the prince, but one fine day it was not she who followed the predestined mortal, but the predestined mortal who pursued her.

He was in love to such an extent, to such a degree, that he went to her, not to offer her his hand – la Païva would have had no use for it – but the accessories.

'I have three million a year,' he told her. 'If you'll live with me, we can share it.'

La Païva, who had spent three hundred thousand frances on the conquest of the prince, accepted to recover her expenses.

I don't know the name of the count, duke or prince, but today [1857] la Païva has the best and most elegant *hôtel* in Paris, her dinners are reputed to be exquisite, she entertains many artists and men of letters, and her conversation is said to be witty . . .

I have seen [continued Viel-Castel] the plans of a palace which Mauguin, the architect, is building her in the Champs-Élysées. The land and the building, without the furnishing, will cost a million and a half.

La Païva displays two million francs' worth of diamonds, pearls and precious stones on her person. She is the great debauchee of the century.[8]

One aspirant for her favours (so the story ran) made his request so often that eventually she came to terms. 'Bring me ten thousand francs in notes,' she said. 'We'll set light to them, and I will be yours as long as they are burning.' Next day Adolphe Gaiffe, the would-be lover, arrived with twelve thousand francs – a magnificent gesture, since he could ill afford them. La Païva set the first note alight. The young man took advantage of his good fortune, so Viel-Castel recorded, 'like a man who knows that time is money'. When the last of the banknotes had turned to ashes, la Païva's latest lover told her, triumphantly, that they had all been forged.[9]

La Païva, acidly portrayed by Viel-Castel, was more kindly described by Arsène Houssaye. Handsome, worldly, endowed with the art of writing engaging (if largely inaccurate) memoirs, this ex-director of the Théâtre Français had been presented to her when she gave her inaugural reception at her *hôtel* in the place Saint-Georges.

Her guests were chosen, he said, for their wit; but only one woman was asked, and she was asked because of her beauty. Houssaye, for once, showed little understanding of women's nature. La Païva, who had built her career on her powers of attraction, was hardly likely to select a beautiful woman, younger than herself, to delight her guests. However, if it is hard to explain why she welcomed Mme Roger de Beauvoir (once Mlle Doze, of the Comédie-Française), it is easy to see why no other women came to the place Saint-Georges. In a city where manners were hardly puritan, in an age when morals were lax and love was cheaply bought, la Païva could never divest herself of her ugly notoriety. In an age of *parvenues*, she remained the most immoral of *parvenues*; in an age of *nouveaux riches* she remained the most derided of the *nouveaux riches*. Years ago, in the days of Herz, Louis-Philippe had refused to acknowledge her; throughout his reign, and the reign that followed, the Faubourg Saint-Germain would consider her untouchable. No woman of good family would ever cross her threshold, let alone consent to receive her. La Païva used to remind her guests: 'When you want women from the Faubourg Saint-Germain, just let me know, I'm rich enough to buy duchesses.'[10] But she knew that duchesses could not be bought.

Arsène Houssaye glossed over the fact that no duchesses were invited. 'We did not,' he wrote, in *Les Confessions*,

condemn [the Marquise de Païva] to such an extremity. We were too happy as we were. Never were conversations more lively and original. I think that that sumptuous table . . . stimulated wit quite as much as the frugal table of Mme de Maintenon.

There was no need to banish politics from the conversation, though Émile de Girardin was among the guests. But art, literature, *l'éternel feminin*, sparkled round the table, with the topaz of champagne, the pearls of Rhenish wine, and the rubies of all the châteaux of the Bordelais. Never had artists and men of letters been more royally fêted.[11]

Théophile Gautier, whose conversation made one forget even sleep, and the passage of time, was glad to turn from his journalism, and his all too modest way of living, and to earn his superlative Friday dinner by verbal pyrotechnics. Across the table the dramatic critic of *La Presse* would face his editor, Émile de Girardin. Next to Girardin, the observer might find Sainte-Beuve of *Le Constitutionnel: l'oncle Beuve,* the doyen of critics, hiding his baldness under his skull-cap. Next to Sainte-Beuve might be Delacroix.

One evening, at Mme de Païva's [recalled Houssaye], when Eugène Delacroix had been acclaimed as the king of colour, the conversation turned to colourists. Suddenly Léon Gozlan broke his silence, and went off like a rocket.
'I may be a bit odd,' he said, 'but I've always associated colours and shades with different feelings – I don't quite know why. But, to me, piety is pale blue, resigna-tion pearl grey, joy is apple-green, satiety is coffee-coloured, pleasure is deep rose . . . Going to a first rendez-vous is the colour of weak tea, and going to a twentieth, strong tea; as for happiness, . . . it's a colour I don't know.'
Gozlan was acclaimed with a general salvo of compliments.
The Marquise wanted to know everybody's favourite colour . . .
The conversation [at Mme de Païva's] was always sparkling, original, rich in unheard-of ideas and expressions. As at Dr Véron's, the bores were not invited a second time . . . Anyway, none of us would have ventured to repeat a platitude. 'Be careful,' the mistress of the house would sometimes say, 'there is Théo picking up his pencil.' And in fact, when someone uttered a truism, like Monsieur Prudhomme, Théophile Gautier used to take his pencil and draw faces on the back of the menu. The Marquise used to keep them, and say: 'That will pay me for my

dinner.' One evening, she had pen and ink and paper brought to the table. 'My dear Théo, you draw so well, draw me your first mistress.' The poet set to work at once and drew the portrait of Cydalise . . . Mme de Païva gave it to me because I had known the original.[12]

Arsène Houssaye was a courtier. Delacroix himself recorded two evenings at la Païva's; and, with the honesty of a true artist, he expressed distaste for the philistine ostentation he found. 'I dislike this terrifying luxury,' he noted in his *Journal* on 7 February 1855. 'There's nothing to remember about an evening like this: you're just duller next day, that's all.'[13]

Édouard Houssaye, the brother of Arsène, found much to remember. On 25 February he paid tribute to la Païva in Arsène's magazine, *L'Artiste*. He also recorded the conversation of Delacroix himself – a conversation that seems to have pointed certain morals to his hostess.

Mme de Païva [wrote Édouard Houssaye] is a real Circassian in the heart of Paris, a woman who dares to be beautiful in the Circassian style. She has a salon whose style and colour prove her artistic nature. Every Wednesday she receives men of quality who are wits, and wits who are also men of quality . . . There's no gambling or singing, no dancing or smoking; instead of all that there's a dinner where the roast has not been forgotten (as it was at Mme de Maintenon's), and where Mme de Païva is as witty as if the roast was not there. And then people talk, and then they talk some more, and then they go on talking.

Last Wednesday, they were talking of that fatal moment in life when the pitiless clock of Time strikes the last hour of youth. Eugène Delacroix said wisely: 'Oh! if one heard it strike, how many fewer stupidities, how many more fine pages there would be in the lives of artists and poets! They, too, like women, believe in eternal youth, and exhaust themselves trying to hold it back by the wings when the feathers are left in their hands . . . There should be a stern voice to warn them in time, all these prodigal children who only adulterate their wine when they are past drinking altogether. Someone should warn them, as they warn people who linger in public gardens: 'It is closing time, gentlemen, closing time.'[14]

On 2 May 1855, Delacroix went again to la Païva's, but he found the atmosphere more distasteful than ever: 'This evening at the insipid Païva's . . . I was petrified by so much futility and insipidity . . . When I came out of this soporific pestilence at half-past eleven, and breathed the air in the street, I felt I was at a feast; I walked on for an hour, alone, still dissatisfied, morose . . . Conclusion: I must stay in solitude.'[15]

Delacroix shunned la Païva; Vivier, the famous horn-player, who was known for his hoaxes, is said to have played a practical joke on her.[16] Vivier bore an astonishing likeness to Napoleon III. One day he arrived after dinner, had himself announced as the Emperor, and promised decorations and sinecures to the speechless guests. At last, with extraordinary audacity, someone tore the false goatee off his face. He was not invited again.

However, there was no lack of celebrities at la Païva's. François Ponsard, the dramatist, came, and Emile Augier (who is said to have found some features for his play *Le Mariage d'Olympe*). Paul de Saint-Victor, the critic, came; and, among the artists, Paul Baudry and Jean-Léon Gérôme. The *hôtels* in the place Saint-Georges and, later, in the rue Rossini, seemed too humble to house la Païva's guests. Besides, they did not satisfy her love of ostentation. The tailor's wife from Moscow still needed to display her wealth; the pariah who had been rejected by the Faubourg Saint-Germain still needed to show some sort of domination over Paris. On 4 May 1856, *L'Artiste* announced:

> The Marquise de Païva's *hôtel*, which will stand in the avenue des Champs-Élysées after Mme Le Hon's *hôtel* and M. de Morny's *museum*, is beginning to rise from the earth. The masons have spent three months underground. It seems that the *hôtel* will be a meeting-place for men of letters and diplomats, and that it will contain the rarest treasures – not to mention the mistress of the house, that Circassian woman who is witty as if her beauty did not excuse her from being so.

★

The *hôtel* Païva was to be, as its châtelaine intended, the most luxurious private *hôtel* in Paris.

Its architect was Pierre Manguin; and for ten years he laboured at his creation. He organised what were virtually workshops in the Champs-Élysées, where all the work was done in his presence, after his designs. Even the marble and onyx he ordered were carved on the site, as cathedral-builders might have carved them in the Middle Ages. La Païva would often arrive, on her way back from the Bois, and inspect the building; once, it is said, she found a carpenter who had been happily settled in some obscure small room for five years. 'What!' she cried. 'You're still here! You must be God Everlasting.'[17]

As the year 1866 began, the *hôtel* was almost finished. 'The only thing left,' said Dumas *fils*, well aware of the châtelaine's morals, 'is to lay the pavement.'[18] 'Several people,' noted *La Petite Revue*, on 13 January, 'persist in announcing that M. Baudry has just finished the paintings at MONSIEUR de Païva's *hôtel*. It's *Madame* they should say. Oh, it isn't the same thing . . .'

The new *hôtel* stood in a Champs-Élysées which, at the end of the Second Empire, was still unspoilt by signs of plebeian commerce. There were no shops, but half-a-dozen nearby private *hôtels* dazzled the eye and imagination. There was Prince Napoleon's neo-Pompeian palace; there was Émile de Girardin's Roman palace, a scholarly reply to Plon-Plon's architectural paganism. There was the Gothic castle of the Comte de Quinsonas, the Tunisian château of Jules de Lesseps, the remarkable rose-coloured *hôtel* of the Duke of Brunswick. And, finally, among these grandiose pastiches, there was now the *hôtel* Païva (which alone remains, as The Travellers' Club, today). The *hôtel* Païva was mentioned in the guide to the sights of Paris. It stood out, like la Païva herself, as a symbol of the Second Empire; and whether or not one admired the intensity of its ornamentation, it represented, and that with splendour, the taste of the time.

The vast salon, lit by five tall windows, seemed a kind of temple dedicated to the worship of physical pleasure: it was hard to take ones eyes off the magnificent ceiling where Baudry had painted Day chasing Night away. The four quarters of the day were represented by mythological divinities: Apollo bending his bow, Hecate with her silver crescent preparing to wrap herself in her starry mantle, Aurora still asleep on her rosy cloud, Vesper melancholy and pensive. All the figures converged towards the centre of the oval vault, and they were connected by pairs of genii which symbolised the hours. Cabanel and Gérôme had also contributed paintings, famous sculptors had carved the mantelpieces in the smaller rooms; but some critics thought that Baudry's ceiling (which would prepare him to paint his great frescoes in the new Opéra) was alone worth all the other treasures in the *hôtel*. 'I want to have been the only person on earth to enjoy your delectable painting,' Mme de Païva had told Baudry. 'I think I have the right, since I paid you the price you asked for it. You must pray to God that I live!'[19]

Yet what other treasures there were! The salons were hung with crimson damask, specially woven at Lyons for eight hundred thousand francs. The staircase, lit by a massive lustre in sculpted bronze, was made – steps, baluster and wall – entirely of onyx. Mrs Moulton, the American banker's wife, seems to have heard some rumours of its splendour. She recorded that 'a lady, whose virtue is someone else's reward, has a magnificent and much-talked-of *hôtel* in the Champs-Élysées, where there is a staircase worth a million francs, made of real alabaster. Prosper Mérimée said: "C'est par là qu'on monte à la vertu." '[20] (It was reported that Augier, the dramatist, asked to compose some lines in honour of the staircase, replied with the devastating quotation: 'Ainsi que la vertu, le vice a ses degrés.') The first

floor, to which the staircase led, was reserved for la Païva: for her bathroom, bedroom and boudoir, and a room for Henckel von Donnersmarck.
The bathroom, said Gautier, was worthy of a Sultana in the Arabian Nights.
Its walls were onyx and marble, enhanced by Venetian ceramics, and by a
ceiling in the Moorish style. The bath was solid onyx, like the lavatory
under the window; it was lined with silvered bronze, with gilt, engraved
designs representing fleurs-de-lys. The three taps, sculpted and gilt, were
set with precious stones. The bedroom insolently proclaimed the triumph of
la volupté. The locks on the doors were said to be worth two thousand
francs apiece. The bed, encrusted with rare woods and ivory, delicately
wrought, stood like an altar in an alcove, under a ceiling on which Aurora,
Goddess of the Dawn, hovered in the empyrean. It had cost a hundred
thousand francs. 'Fifty thousand francs?' la Païva had cried, when she saw
the original estimate. 'Do you want me to have fleas? Put a hundred thousand
francs!'[21] The visitor felt himself in the presence of a single idea: the
defiant, obsessive idea of personal glorification.

This overwhelming proof of wealth was not the only proof which the
mistress of Henckel von Donnersmarck could display. Her devoted lover
had presented her with that other essential sign of opulence: a château.
He had bought her (some said for two million) the sixteenth-century château
de Pontchartrain, on the road from Paris to Rambouillet. The park, designed
by Le Nôtre himself, the château which had known the presence of Louise de
la Vallière and le Roi Soleil, were now the décor for the marquise of the
demi-monde. The hothouses provided her guests with grapes and cherries
and peaches in mid-winter. One day, so the legend goes, Girardin and
Houssaye were walking in the grounds, estimating their hostess's fortune.
Houssaye declared that it must be eight to ten million francs. 'You're mad!'
cried la Païva, bursting out of an arbour where she had overheard the
conversation. 'Ten million! That would hardly bring in five hundred
thousand livres a year. Do you think that would let me give you peaches
and grapes in January? Five hundred thousand francs, that's what my dinners
cost.'[22] Whatever the truth of the anecdote, her dinners cost a fortune:
her Clos-Lafite and Château-Larose were beyond all praise, and one visitor
long remembered how he had seen uncommonly large truffles, in porcelain
dishes, set beside each plate; these were meant to be nibbled between the
courses. 'All your great ladies want *display*,' said la Païva, once, 'and they
more or less ruin themselves to be sure of it. I couldn't ruin myself, if I
tried. Henckel and his mines are inexhaustible.'[23]

They were, indeed, and they created one of the legends of Paris; and
while Viel-Castel declared that la Païva was rouged and painted like an old

tightrope-dancer, Henri de Villemessant, the journalist, recorded the living legend with a keen financial sense and boyish wonder:

One morning [he wrote in his *Mémoires*] I found myself in a house which she had often visited during her second marriage; she counts by marriages, like the Kings of France count by dynasties. There arrived at the door a carriage drawn by horses which cost 10,000 francs apiece: they were the morning horses, it was 10 o'clock. Imagine what the others must have been like! The coupé, a masterpiece by Bender, bore a coat-of-arms – it was certainly that of the third dynasty. The interior was lined with white satin, in exquisite taste. I am told that the carpet, which was sable, cost at least a thousand écus.

She emerged from this vehicle, enveloped in a blue fox fur pelisse of inestimable price; beneath the pelisse she wore some flamboyant dress . . . No, I'm wrong, it wasn't flamboyant; on the contrary, it seemed a mere nothing. She just wore lace, cashmere, diamonds on every finger, earrings worth twenty thousand livres apiece; in short, she showed a luxury, simplicity and taste . . . as if she had been born in swaddling-clothes which were woven by the fairies. It was magical.

Since then, she has never stopped growing in Parisian legend. She follows a path which is hers alone, she has made herself a place which many envy her and none could hold so well . . .

Now she has an *hôtel* in Paris, every detail of which is a marvel. The taps are gold, the kitchen stoves are made of Dresden china and the paving-stones are made of jewels, as they are in the fairy-tales of Perrault. It seems as if a magic wand has conjured it all from the earth; the genie who has created these thousand and one nights has given Scheherezade eternal youth. I defy you to give her the fifty-two years which are in fact her due. It is all so extraordinary that one expects another wave of the wand to make all these splendours return into the earth just as they came out of it . . .[24]

Henckel's mines were indeed inexhaustible. La Païva, said Arsène Houssaye, had sent an emissary to India to find unfindable hangings for her salon. The seat beside her bed was solid silver, recorded Jean-Philippe Worth.

Her bath was lined with gold, and the faucets were of the same pure metal with enormous turquoises set in the tops. She herself told my father that on the very spot where she built this house of Oriental opulence she had once stood shaking with cold, and starving.

No jewel casket could approach hers in the magnificence of its contents. She was the first to wear what are now commonly called *bouchons de carafe* – glass stoppers for decanters – or enormous stones as big as nuts, bigger than any franc piece.[25]

La Païva saw her jewels in precisely that light: when one of the Goncourts admired her diamond earrings, she replied: 'Yes, they're good for a hundred francs a day.'[26]

She appeared, in opulent glory, at Longchamp, at first nights, at the Opéra; her box at the Théâtre des Italiens faced the Imperial box. One evening, when the glare of the footlights hurt the Empress's eyes, la Païva offered her the delicate Japanese screen which she was using; the Imperial aide-de-camp took it to the Empress, but she 'swept it contemptuously out of her way'.[27] La Païva remained untouchable.

Her one resource remained her wealth. She was conscious of every franc she possessed, and of every single centime that she spent. Émile Bergerat, the journalist, a son-in-law of Gautier, wrote the simple truth when he called her

the archetype of those courtesans who are only courtesans for money, and fall in love with money alone. La Païva was a coffer. She was never known to have a passing fancy . . . She had a horror of dogs and cats and birds and children, of everything that is an expense and brings in no reward, and may divert one from the hunt for the Golden Calf. But she would have given herself to a miner for a nugget. She was harder with her household than a Roman patrician, implacable about their slightest failings, magnificently hated . . .[28]

At Pontchartrain, so the legend went, there was a servant whose only task was to open and shut one hundred and fifty windows; he began his work at six in the morning and finished it at midnight, and he finally died of exhaustion. The park at Pontchartrain was Dante's Hell for the gardeners, who were said to be fined fifty centimes for every leaf found on the ground. Mme de Païva, in person, collected the fines at dawn.[29]

If her meanness was notorious, her financial sense was remarkable; she profited largely from the talk of visiting economists and bankers. She helped von Donnersmarck to manage the fortunes he enjoyed from his coal and iron and zinc and copper mines in Silesia, his vast estates, his industrial interests (when he died, he would be worth more than two hundred and twenty million marks; he would be the richest person in Germany, after Mme Berthe Krupp von Bohlen). La Païva showed a shrewdness and flair which would have won the respect of any speculator on the Bourse.

La Païva, who had established herself by her feminine attractions, also showed a masculine toughness. She had no time for fires in winter: the Goncourt brothers declared that she lived in icy air, like a monster in Scandinavian mythology. It is recorded that, one day, when she was thrown by a horse, she took a pistol from her belt and shot it.

Brutal, opulent and ageing, she entertained the Goncourts as the Second

Empire approached its end, and she was devastatingly drawn in their *Journal*:

I look at the mistress of the house, and study her [went the *Journal* in May 1867]. White skin, good arms, and fine shoulders bare down to the loins behind. The red hair in the arm-pits shows under the slipping shoulder-straps. Big round eyes; a pear-shaped nose with a flat Calmuck piece at the end . . . A mouth without inflexion, a straight line, the colour of paint, in a face all white with rice powder . . . Under the face of a courtesan still young enough for her trade, it is a face a hundred years old, and, at moments, it takes on some terrible likeness to a rouged corpse.[30]

The Goncourt *Journal* is rarely kind; but its savage comments on la Païva have an air of uncompromising truth. As aesthetes, the Goncourts were revolted by the painted woman whose hair – they maintained – was as false as her smile. They disliked her bourgeois concern with the price of her possessions, they despised the fact that she hoarded her jewels in safes on either side of her bed. They considered that – Baudry's ceiling apart – her *hôtel* was an upholsterer's job. They found that its atmosphere killed conversation. Round the splendid table, lit by blazing lustres, where the decanters were too heavy to hold, there fell the cold peculiar to the *hôtels* of prostitutes who played women of the world. It was an icy cold compounded of boredom and malaise, which froze the ease and wit of all the guests. No doubt the Goncourts knew that every window in the *hôtel* Païva had iron shutters.[31] The *hôtel* had then, as it has today, a sinister air.

It was also said to be more than a décor for grandiose prostitution, for lavish dinners every Friday and Sunday. It was rumoured to be a centre for Prussian espionage. Henckel von Donnersmarck was well known to Bismarck; and though his liaison with la Païva kept him in Paris, his sympathies remained with his own country. La Païva made no secret of her own political sympathies. Russian by birth, French by her first marriage, Portuguese by her second, she now shared her Prussian lover's views. She had used France in her career, but she had not forgotten that France despised her; and while she and Henckel may not have corresponded with Berlin, they had long been fostering Prussian interests. In the last years of the Second Empire, la Païva had often talked to Prussian diplomats about the political indiscretions and military weaknesses, the tendentious opinions, the signs of social decadence in France. She had reported the terrifying optimism of the liberal Empire. She had foreseen the coming conflict between France and Prussia; it seemed to her inevitable and not unwelcome. And when, in July 1870, it came, she had no regrets. She went, immediately, to live in Henckel's castle at Neudeck, near Tarnowitz, in the wilds of Silesia. He himself joined the Prussian forces which were invading France. On 23 August, before hostilities were over, Bismarck made him Prefect of Lorraine.

In his book on the origins of the Third Republic,[32] the Marquis de Roux declared outright that Henckel was Bismarck's man. On 23 February 1871, when the peace preliminaries were discussed, Henckel and Bleichroeder, on behalf of Bismarck, examined the financial clauses of the treaty with Thiers. Bleichroeder suggested that France should pay war indemnities of three thousand million francs. Henckel, well informed about French resources, made the Chancellor demand five thousand million.

With characteristic Prussian tact, Henckel had wagered Girardin twenty thousand francs that Prussian troops would be in the Champs-Élysées within a month of the declaration of war. He lost his wager; but the War was soon over, and in March 1871 the Prussians entered Paris. The statues of the cities of France in the Place de la Concorde were draped in black; every *hôtel* in the Champs-Élysées was locked and shuttered but for one. From the steps of the *hôtel* Païva, in full uniform, Henckel von Donnersmarck watched his compatriots march past.

The fall of the Empire brought the final triumph of la Païva. On 28 October, when her marriage to Païva had been annulled, she and Henckel were married at last at the Lutheran Church in Paris. She was fifty-two. Jean-Philippe Worth recorded that Henckel had given her, as his wedding present, the Empress Eugénie's necklace, which the ex-Empress had been forced to sell. The three rows of diamonds were faultless, and this example of the jeweller's art was considered the finest of its time.[33] It was the ex-Madame Villoing's revenge on the Faubourg Saint-Germain.

The von Donnersmarcks continued to hold their receptions, and to make appearances in Parisian life, though from time to time they were reminded of their unpopularity; one day, the Marquis de Roux records, Henckel was horsewhipped in the Champs-Élysées.[34] When his wife appeared at a performance of Offenbach's operetta, *La Périchole*, she was hissed by the audience (Thiers, then President of the Republic, glossed over the situation by inviting her to dinner).

It was in the theatre that she received the most public of all affronts: Dumas *fils*, who had invented the word demi-monde, had always kept his distance from the most outrageous demi-mondaine, and it was against her that he wrote his play, *La Femme de Claude*. Césarine, the wife of Claude, has many points of resemblance to the woman whom one can only call la Païva. She is original, exotic, attractive and sinister. She has a past that will not bear the light. She is ready to ruin men for money. And when she is asked if she is prepared to sell France itself, she simply answers: 'But I'm not French, am I?' Her husband finally shoots her in the act of betrayal, but he is not committing murder. As Dumas *fils* explains in his preface:

Claude is not killing his wife, the author is not killing a woman, they are both killing the Beast, the Beast which is foul, adulterous, prostituting, infanticidal, the Beast which undermines society, dissolves the family, profanes love, dismembers the country, and dishonours woman, whose face and form it takes: the Beast that kills all those who do not kill it.[35]

La Femme de Claude was a clear and devastating attack on an amoral woman who was prepared to betray her adopted country; and la Païva must have suspected a transparent reference to herself. The play was first performed at the Gymnase on 16 January 1873; it failed on account of a cabal which had been well organised by her supporters.

There are two likenesses of la Païva, in these post-imperial days. Jean-Philippe Worth remembered that 'her beauty, for which she was noted, was of rather a strange type, and she enhanced it by powdering her hair blond . . . The first time she appeared in the Bois with fair hair she started a storm of talk.' The first time he saw her, he continued, 'she was no longer young and her beauty was already on the wane. And I am afraid I did not appreciate it. Her eyelids were shockingly blackened, and this, combined with the prominence of her eyes, made her look fierce and hawk-like.'[36] Émile Bergerat was more outspoken; in his *Souvenirs d'un Enfant de Paris* he recalled her all too vividly:

It was [he wrote] at a Wagner concert, in the Nadar Rooms, two years after the war, that I saw her for the first and, thank God, the only time. She was coming forward between the chairs, like an automaton, as if she was worked by a spiral spring, without a gesture, without expression . . . Behind her, as a trainbearer, a magnificent human stallion shortened his giant strides to keep pace with this rolling puppet from a *danse macabre*. As he toyed with the trinket on his watch-chain, he looked as if he was ready to wind up the mechanism if it stopped. Now this man of thirty or forty, handsome, strong and proud, like a god from Valhalla itself, a multi-millionaire, a prince of our conqueror's imperial family, who, when he left the Nadar Rooms, was going to govern Alsace and Lorraine, was the third and ultimate husband – Clio, cast away your scrolls! – of the Hoffmanesque mummy. He had married her with his eyes open, out of love, and officially, if you please. Don't talk to me about your Ninon de Lenclos, the nineteenth century can offer you something better. At the age of sixty-five [*sic*], la Païva still 'made' a Hohenzollern!

I don't even dare to tell you all my thoughts on the subject. You either believe in vampires or you don't, I believed in them at that concert. If the terrible lemur who so patently held this Siegfried in bondage was not a known corpse, that is because there are some who return by the light of the moon to drink the blood of white cuirassiers. She had their purple on her lips, and all the rest was livid, glazed, and in dissolution.[37]

Émile de Girardin was less of a moralist than Dumas *fils*; he did not share Bergerat's feelings of repulsion. He had known la Païva since 1844; he and Houssaye, his inseparable companion, had been among her best friends. He was one of the first to return to the *hôtel* Païva after the war, and perhaps it was there that he first conceived the idea of campaigning for closer links between France and Germany. In December 1874, Bismarck showed his approval of the republican régime in France; there came the first public suggestion of a Franco-German rapprochement, and Girardin made himself its interpreter. He had recently resumed the editorship of a daily paper, *La France*. There was no one to whom the Donnersmarcks could more easily sell an idea: they only needed, it was said, to flatter the man who claimed to have an idea a day. It seems that Girardin helped to create a political mirage: the illusion that if France allowed Bismarck to make other territorial conquests, he would return Alsace and Lorraine. In January 1875, Prince Hohenlohe, the German Ambassador, congratulated Girardin on his campaign.[38]

As for Henckel von Donnersmarck himself, he fought to germanise Lorraine. In the general elections of 1874, when Alsace and Lorraine first sent deputies to the Reichstag, he had the audacity to stand against the Bishop of Metz, Monseigneur Dupont des Loges. 'The great bishop had 13,054 votes. The former spy managed to collect 2,346.'[39]

There were still friends in France who managed to forget such outrage. Houssaye often dined at the *hôtel* Païva with Prince Hohenlohe, drowning his conscience and his regrets in *bouillon de moules à la crème fouettée*, or in an 1859 Tokay like melted amber. If Houssaye is to be believed, Prince Hohenlohe once asked how he could please the author of the *Confessions*. 'Prince,' replied Houssaye, 'if you want to please me, it's perfectly simple, bring the keys of Metz to dinner one day, on a silver salver.' 'It's not as simple as that,' said the Prince, 'but it would not be impossible for destiny and diplomacy to contrive to make Metz a French city once again.' 'That,' answered Houssaye, 'would be good for Germany and for France. It would destroy the sterile hate between nation and nation.'[40]

When he committed the conversation to his *Confessions*, Houssaye could not help adding: 'It will soon be ten years since then. Where is the Marquise? Where is the silver salver? Madame de Païva has been buried, against her wish, in Silesia, and Prince Hohenlohe is governing Alsace and Lorraine.'[41]

★

As Houssaye implied, Fate had deprived la Païva of some of her dearest wishes. It had deprived her of the glory of being a power in politics. In the spring of 1878, she and Henckel had hoped to contrive a secret meeting between Bismarck and Gambetta, the virtual dictator of France, to negotiate about Lorraine; but Gambetta had finally refused an interview which would have brought no material gain to his country.[42] And, far from seeing the keys of Metz brought to her *hôtel*, la Païva had at last been compelled to abandon the monument she had created. The French Government had advised her, in terms which were virtually a command, that she and her husband should leave the country.

Would she destroy the Baudry ceiling, as she had implied? She left it intact. But the *hôtel* Païva and the château de Pontchartrain (spared by the Prussian invaders in the war) were abandoned, and the great debauchee of the century crossed the frontier to live in her husband's castle, Neudeck, in Silesia.

She was now a pathetic figure. She had had a stroke, and she had smashed the Venetian mirror in her room so as not to see her physical decline. Four personal maids had been unable to disguise the signs of her paralysis and degeneration. She would take a series of baths, in vain, to counteract the acidity of her blood: a milk bath, a lime-flower bath, a scented bath; and once, it was said, she tried to bath in champagne. But she had heart disease, and her body swelled unmercifully. She died at Neudeck on 21 January 1884. She was sixty-five.[43]

'All my wishes have come to heel, like tame dogs!'[44] she had cried, once, intoxicated by Fortune. She had embodied the triumph of willpower. She had known every pleasure that colossal wealth could buy. And perhaps, because of her wealth, because of her nature, she had never known real happiness.

'And when God took her back,' wrote Émile Bergerat, 'since He does take such creatures back, no one knew what became of the soul of this body, the body of this soul, for she had no tomb and she does not lie in consecrated ground.' Henckel von Donnersmarck's second wife, rich, well-born, beautiful and young, apparently found the answer to the enigma. She unlocked a room at Neudeck which was always carefully locked, and there, preserved in alcohol, the corpse of la Païva was dancing. Even in death, von Donnersmarck had not been able to leave her.[45]

98

Mademoiselle Maximum

Léonide Leblanc (1842–94)

Léonide Leblanc, who would earn the title of Mademoiselle Maximum, was born on 8 December 1842 in the hamlet of Burly, near Dampierre, in the department of the Loiret. She was the daughter of a local stonebreaker.[1] When she was five or six her father, weary of his lot, decided to take his wife and child to Paris; and since he could not afford transport, they set out, with their few belongings, on foot. One night, during their long walk, they were caught in a thunderstorm, and Léonide had to throw away her sodden, useless shoes and ragged stockings. She entered Paris barefoot. A historian later recorded the fact.[2]

Francisque Sarcey, the dramatic critic, maintained that the Leblancs wanted their child to be a governess, and sent her to school in Paris. Here, so he said, she displayed such precocious intelligence, such determination to work, that at twelve she constantly outstripped the girls of fourteen and fifteen. Sarcey, who appears to have been a friend of Léonide's, continued her tale with a certain naïveté: the child, he explained, worked so hard that she caught typhoid fever and almost died of it. During her long convalescence, when her parents humoured her every whim, she declared that she would not go back to school; and, despite their straitened means, the Leblancs were compelled to have her education finished at home, so that one day she might qualify as a teacher. But Léonide was already determined to become an actress. She had always taken the leading parts in the plays at school, and her closest friend there had been the cousin of a tenor, who supplied both children with theatre tickets. It became clear that Léonide would always do as she pleased, for one day she escaped from home with her friend, and spent the night at a hotel. At the age of fourteen, she went off again, this time to the Paris suburb of Belleville, in search of a theatrical career.

The director of the Belleville theatre, M. Fresnes, engaged her to play the parts of little girls; and – according to Sarcey – Léonide stayed at Belleville for four months.

One evening, Virginie Déjazet was acting there in *Les Premières Armes de Richelieu*. Léonide played the fiancée of the young Duc. At the end of the performance, on behalf of the cast, Léonide presented the famous actress with 'such a big bouquet she could hardly carry it. She herself was so pretty, so very pretty, that no one knew any more whether to admire the girl or the flowers.' When Léonide left the dressing-room, Déjazet observed: 'That child has all she needs to catch the coach to celebrity.' Déjazet made one mistake, so a critic would remark. 'Mlle Léonide went by train – and by sleeper, too!'[3]

The witticism probably contained the essential truth. Years later, in her preface to a *roman à clef*, a highly controversial novel called *Les Femmes du théâtre*, Léonide explained how an actress was forced to make her way, earning the good graces of the author and director, the actor and the critic. But however she established herself, she was helped by events. M. Cogniard, of the Théâtre des Variétés, paid a visit to Belleville. He was looking for a star to replace Judith Ferreyra. He was, went the chronicle, 'seduced by Léonide's beauty, and then by her talent, and he engaged her for three years'. According to Sarcey, she made her first appearance at the Variétés in 1859, in *La Fille terrible*; almost at once she became the darling of the theatre.

She stayed at the Variétés for eighteen months, until the director of the Vaudeville encouraged her hopes of becoming a great actress, and she eagerly signed a contract with him. She made her début at the Vaudeville in *Jobin et Nanette*, and took the part of Raphael in *Nos Intimes*, an early comedy by Victorien Sardou. 'And how pretty she was,' cried Sarcey, 'disguised as a man, and smoking a fat cigar which made her feel quite ill!'[4]

But Léonide had too little work at the Vaudeville, and she repeatedly asked Montigny of the Gymnase to engage her; she even promised that, if need be, she would learn a big part in twenty-four hours. One day Montigny accepted the challenge: he asked her to take a three-hundred line part that evening in *Le Mari à système*. She learnt the part that day and went on stage at eight o'clock. Montigny was so impressed that he signed her on for three years. It was an optimistic contract – and it was invalid, since Léonide had not yet come of age. She played a few parts, and then, without warning, disappeared to Italy.

Alphonse Lemonnier, her admirer, told the tale of her escapade.

And this [he wrote] is how she left Paris. One morning she went to the window and saw that the weather was glorious and there wasn't a cloud in the sky.

'Oh!' she said with a sigh to her maid, 'what a wonderful day! I wish the sky was always that colour.'

'In Italy,' answered the abigail, 'the sky is always blue.'

'So it is . . . Well, then, let's go to Italy.'

'But your part . . . ?'

'My part will survive, someone else will take it . . . *Quid mihi*, that's my motto.'

'What does that mean, madame, *Quid mihi*?'

'It's a Latin phrase you don't need to understand, but it roughly means: *To hell with it.*'

Two days later, Léonide had left France for the native land of macaroni.[5]

Sarcey looked on her escapade with his usual benevolence. 'Well, she was attracted by the Italian climate, and maybe by some handsome and famous Italian. And then, if you can't do something wild when you're seventeen, when can you do it?'[6] But, as Sarcey would recognise, the escapade was to have serious consequences. Paris came to believe that Léonide was not a serious actress; and gossip grew busy. Rumour said that she had entered the Grand Turk's harem at Constantinople.

People are talking a lot about Léonide Leblanc [reported *La Vie parisienne* on 2 December 1865]. The Turks have apparently stolen her from us for good and all. No one still knows exactly what she will do at Constantinople . . . There will be pilgrimages to see her, as there are at Mecca.

As for Loulou, she has departed [added the columnist, the following week]. Has she set off for Constantinople? Nobody knows, but someone has mentioned Milan.[7]

Alphonse Lemonnier confirmed that she had been there:

In two months, she visited Rome and Florence and Milan.

At last she cried:

'Really, this country's monotonous, the weather's always fine. I'm tired of sunshine and blue sky, I'm longing for snow and fog, I'd like to be able to skate. Suppose I went to London?' And behold our fine bird took wing and flew off to England. She stayed there three months, she went to all the races, she saw all the sights, she visited all the most interesting things in the capital.

She drank pale ale, she ate underdone meat and potatoes baked in their jackets. I think she even took boxing lessons.

But, one day, she said again to her maid:

'Have you noticed, Juliette, men and women are the same wherever you go?'

'Oh no, madame, in Africa they have black skins.'

'Do you mean it? Let's go to Africa . . .'

And so it was that Léonide travelled for eighteen months without stopping. At last, having seen almost everything that there was to see, she wanted the impossible, she would have liked a fantastic country to be created for her.[8]

It seems probable, as Sarcey says, that she longed for Paris, and came home. On 20 January 1866 *La Vie parisienne* recorded that she was no longer in Constantinople. She was writing a book: *Les Petites Comédies de la Scala, souvenirs de la Vie italienne.*[9]

★

Léonide Leblanc, who had earned applause in the theatre, and even braved the world of literature, had long ago won celebrity in a different fashion. As her jewels suggested, she had grown famous for her personal charms. She had begun, as some courtesans ended, by marriage: her husband was a German photographer working in Paris. But the marriage was brief, and the husband vanished, leaving Léonide to pursue her amorous career. Early in 1862, Aurélien Scholl, the journalist and *boulevardier*, informed the Goncourts that she was his mistress; he brought the 'little wonder of nature and prostitution' to see them. She filled the room with the frou-frou of silk and the radiance of diamonds. She had, said the Goncourts, the grace of a bird, and – they guessed – the brain of a bird.[10]

Scholl had hopefully given her a ring, inscribed: *Aurélien to Léonide: for ever*. But the ring was soon forgotten in a multitude of jewels: Léonide amassed a splendid collection of rings, including one famous one with a blue diamond; her pearl necklace became a legend, and she had more antique and modern bracelets than even she could wear. 'Léonide! What a long time ago it was!' Scholl would tell a friend. 'She was very beautiful. She still is. But you see, my dear fellow, if you put her on top of Mont Blanc, she would still be accessible.'[11]

Even among the men-about-town, she earned the name of Mademoiselle Maximum – perhaps for her fees, perhaps for her accomplishments, perhaps for her extravagance, but most probably for the number of her lovers. Prince Napoleon merely passed through her boudoir, as he did through many others; but her liaison with Henri d'Orléans, Duc d'Aumale, was the great event, the *lit de parade*, the state bed, in her professional life. When Léonide received an important client for the first time, she would show them round her *hôtel* in the rue d'Offémont, or her sumptuous apartment in the boulevard Haussmann, where many of her *bibelots* and *objets d'art*, and much of her valuable furniture, had been given her by the Grand Seigneur of Chantilly. And, it is said, at a certain moment, she would half-open a door: the door to His Royal Highness's study. The speechless visitor would catch a glimpse of the royal silhouette, 'in the attitude of a man absorbed in the effort of reflection'.[12] No doubt the wax model aroused much real jealousy, awe and esteem in the breasts of would-be suitors.

In the last few years of the Second Empire, Léonide was among *la garde*: the dozen most famous courtesans in Paris.

Speaking of Duleep Singh made me think of that very extraordinary woman, Léonide Leblanc [wrote William Osgood Field], for I introduced him to her, and on his rare visits to Paris he rarely failed to call on her . . . Léonide was a modern Ninon de l'Enclos; witty, very *intrigante*, very ambitious, very good-natured, and very amusing and *bonne fille*. She was not beautiful, indeed hardly pretty, but she had a clever and pleasing face. Like the famous Ninon, . . . she brought *la galanterie* up to the level of a fine art, and her admirers came from all sorts and conditions of men.[13]

'She was voluptuousness in flesh and blood,' wrote Zed, in *Le Demi-monde sous le Second Empire*, 'with the style of an eighteenth-century marquise.'[14]

When the theatres closed, and the lights were lit in le Grand Seize, the celebrated Room Sixteen at the Café Anglais, Léonide would be found there with the most notorious men-about-town, or *noceurs*, supping, and sometimes playing baccarat until nine o'clock the following morning. When Arsène Houssaye gave a *fête vénitienne* at the avenue de Friedland, Léonide would be asked to act there with Sarah Bernhardt, just as Adelina Patti would be invited to sing. And when, in the summer, before the hunting season began, the *noceurs* went to gamble at Homburg or Ems, Wiesbaden or Baden, Léonide and the rest of *la garde* made the pilgrimage with them.

In July 1863, at Baden, she was 'beautiful enough to write home about', and *La Vie parisienne* declared she did honour to the French flag. In 1864, at Homburg, recorded the same journal,

she appeared . . . with a federal Yankee, who was pretty well ballasted with dollars and gold dust from California . . .

Within a few days, Mlle Léonide Leblanc won two hundred and seventy thousand francs – that is the official figure.

Laden with this splendid booty, she came back to Paris, where she began to decorate and furnish a sumptuous apartment in the rue Laffite . . .

Not long ago Mlle Leblanc left again for Homburg. She started off by losing or rather re-losing thirty thousand francs at roulette. The bankers began to feel jubilant, and to hope for complete revenge. But next day she won sixty thousand francs, which brings her present credit at the Homburg bank to three hundred thousand francs. The management is kept daily informed of the phases of this great duel. If occasion arises, we shall recount its progress, and its probable result.[15]

The following week, the telegraph from Homburg announced that Léonide had brought her total winnings to half a million. 'You wait,' said *La Vie parisienne*, 'she will want the whole million.'[16]

It was, however, at Baden that Léonide twice broke the bank – a feat which earned her celebrity in Paris. And then, in possession of a fortune which she would spend in six months, 'she lit a Maryland cigarette with banknotes, laughing at the thalers and double thalers gone with the wind.' When he recorded the incident some forty years later, Jules Claretie added: 'Those who write the history of the manners of the Second Empire must not forget the legend of this corner of the world.'[17]

Baden in the 1860s was the summer capital of Europe.

The enchanted town, *par excellence* [confirmed Gustave Claudin], was Baden, which some people called the Pearl of the Black Forest . . .

There was nothing but hunts and races, banquets, galas and balls. The post offices were bursting with men who had ruined themselves, and were sending home for subsidies . . .

During the fortnight of the races, Baden was the land of Cocaigne. All the dandies and idlers from all the capitals assembled there . . .

Many Parisians had country houses at Baden. M. Émile de Girardin had a delightful châlet in which he received his colleagues in journalism; because, one might add, all the Press were there, as well . . . [18]

Among the French men of letters there in August 1868 was Maxime du Camp, the friend of Flaubert. 'Princes ought to live,' he wrote, 'according to certain formulas which distinguish them from other men and give them at least the appearance of some superiority . . . The Orléans princes are here at the moment . . . D'Aumale has become intimate with Léonide Leblanc, who is just a whore; Joinville is escorting Madeleine Brohan, of the Comédie-Française. On the terrace near the orchestra, people follow them, point them out to each other, and laugh at them. It would be so easy to shut one's door and respect the public, by respecting oneself.'[19]

★

It was not in Léonide's nature to shun publicity. She had always welcomed artists and poets, she had indulged in intellectual whims. In 1865 she had written the preface to *Les Femmes de Théâtre*, by Alphonse Lemonnier; the book was considered scandalous, and seized by the police. *Les Femmes de Théâtre* proved to be ephemeral; but the preface itself is still worth recalling, for Alice, the courtesan, giving advice to Lucie, the would-be courtesan, is probably expressing Léonide's own views on her profession. And coming, as it does, from one of *la garde* in the Second Empire, this advice cannot be dismissed as simple fiction. It is a kind of social document:

'To begin with, my dear,' said Alice to Lucie, 'have you a heart?'

'I think so,' answered Lucie, innocently.

'So much the worse for you,' Alice went on. 'If you have one, wrap it up in your handkerchief and put it in your pocket. The heart, you know, is an extra you must dispense with if you're going to be happy in this world . . .

But, above all, before you grant anything,

See that you're given:

(1) A nice apartment;

(2) A few expensive clothes;

(3) Some splendid jewels.

Then, when you're *chic*, when you have your lackeys, carriages, etc., don't gaily throw your money out of the window, lay by something for a rainy day.

Invest your capital!

Buy shares, speculate, speculate . . . Women are terribly lucky on the Bourse.

And when you are no longer twenty, you will at last be able to console yourself for your vanished charms with a handsome income, thanks to which you will marry Monsieur Someone-or-other . . . who will give you his name, and his youth, . . . and that's enough!

Modern writers always predict us a future as door-keepers or box-openers at the theatre. Prove them wrong.

When we have been easy women, we shall be honest women.

We shall end as we should have begun.

But alas! We aren't made of wood. You may fall in love. If you do, just remember this: if it's a poor young man, take care that you always put usefulness before pleasure.

The most delightful passions don't last any longer than the loveliest flowers . . .

Let me repeat, have a single aim: money, and more money, always money.

It's money which rules the universe, it's the real, the only king in the world.

I've said my say.'

And, at a draught, the bacchante drained her glass of champagne.[20]

Whatever the Goncourts may have said about her birdlike brain, Léonide Leblanc was known for her wit; and it is not surprising that soon after she had written this preface to *Les Femmes de Théâtre*, she wrote *Les Petites Comédies de l'amour*: a light-hearted series of tales about a would-be Don Juan. It went into three editions, at least, within the year.

I told you [wrote Alphonse Lemonnier, introducing the book], that Léonide did everything from caprice, and that is why this little novel, which is her first work, will doubtless be her last, for she doesn't pretend to rival George Sand.

She has gaily written *Les Petites Comédies de l'amour* to have a small printed volume of her own, since it is the fashion today.

What can I tell you about her book? . . .

It's the story of a butterfly in the wings of the theatre and of four women whom I'd like to name if I had the right to be indiscreet.

This book is not immoral. On the contrary, it proves something, it could certainly be a lesson to all the braggarts of vice, the cavaliers of love, the Don Juans of the century who treat women as toys and amuse themselves with the most serious thing in all the world: with *Love*![21]

★

Léonide was determined to be taken seriously. She knew how to talk. She had intellectual pretensions.[22] She liked to play Egeria. Towards the end of her life, she would say to a famous Parisian publicist: 'Telephone me about five o'clock every day, and we'll talk politics.'[23] While she was the mistress of Henri d'Orléans, she tried to make converts to Orleanism; but she was eclectic by nature. She not only smiled on the Duc d'Aumale, she appreciated Clemenceau. Indeed, William Osgood Field, in his *Uncensored Recollections*, records that

> for many a month she had Georges Clemenceau . . . and the Duc d'Aumale at her feet at the same time. Each of them knew about the other and they were not jealous – on the contrary, rather amused. One day the Prince would ask her, laughingly, 'Well, and what has your *communard sans culottes* friend got to say for himself?' And perhaps the day after Clemenceau would inquire with his cynical smile, 'Has your wicked old *Altesse Royale* been abusing me lately?'[24]

Léonide was not only eclectic in love, she was eclectic in friendship, and she broke with as few friends as she could. She remained friends – no small achievement – with most of the other *femmes à la mode*, and to one of them, Adèle Rémy, she showed particular kindness. But she was not a model of goodness and sincerity: her pet sin was lying, and, helped by her imagination, she lied to a quite remarkable degree. In *More Uncensored Recollections*, William Osgood Field disclosed one of the grandest lies she ever told.

> I am [he wrote] in a position to affirm with certainty that the famous blue diamond from the crown of Louis-Philippe which the Duc d'Aumale was supposed to have given to Léonide Leblanc, and which was the cause of so much trouble later, was never given to her by Henri d'Orléans. Léonide told me this herself. She used to pretend that the Prince had given it to her, but it seemed to me, knowing him as I did, that this was quite impossible. So one day I taxed Léonide with lying about it, and she not only admitted that the Prince had never given it to her, had never even heard of the gem, but that it had nothing whatever to do with Louis-Philippe

Caroline Letessier & Mademoiselle Maximum
Marguerite Bellanger

Young woman at her dressing-table. A Second Empire décor of the kind every courtesan must have known.

Above. One of the elaborate fairy tableaux which delighted spectators in the age of *féeries-revues*.

The courtesan who 'dealt in Grand Dukes': a photograph of Caroline Letessier.

Above. A typical mise-en-scène of the Second Empire.
Léonide Leblanc was one of the many courtesans who saw the
usefulness of a stage career.

Caroline Letessier in sailor's costume.

Opposite

Top left. 'If you put her on top of Mont Blanc, she would still be accessible': Léonide Leblanc, who earned the title of Mademoiselle Maximum.

Top right. Georges Clemenceau as a young man. For many months, it is said, Léonide Leblanc had both Clemenceau and the Duc d'Aumale at her feet.

Bottom left. Henri d'Orléans, Duc d'Aumale (1822–97). The fourth son of Louis-Philippe, the Duc was noted as a general and a historian. He was Léonide Leblanc's most distinguished lover.

Bottom right. 'She was voluptuousness in flesh and blood, with the style of an eighteenth-century marquise': Léonide Leblanc as the Comte de Maugny must have seen her.

Below. A dinner-party in the 1860s. From a contemporary photograph.

Opposite. A *bal costumé* at
the Tuileries.
La Castiglione as a
sorceress is on the arm of
Napoleon III, who is
wearing Venetian dress.
Left. The Emperor's
Cleopatra: one of the most
engaging photographs of the
young Marguerite Bellanger.

Top. Soldiers like these men from the
Cent Gardes were much favoured by
Marguerite Bellanger and La Barucci.
This imperial bodyguard, the élite of
the French army, was disbanded soon
after the fall of the Empire.
Bottom. To salute or not to salute?
The colonel's wife or the drum-major's
mistress?

The Théâtre de Vaudeville in 1866; it was here that Léonide Leblanc appeared in Sardou's *Nos intimes*.

Marguerite Bellanger's writing-paper
is said to have been embossed with a
marguerite, and the motto: 'All things
come to those who wait'. Here,
photographed in male dress, she still
wears a marguerite brooch.

Bottom right. Marguerite in male attire,
with her carriage and piebald horses.
Below. The Emperor's mistress.
Marguerite Bellanger, crowned with
marguerites. From a bust by Jean-Baptiste
Carpeaux (1827–75).

Marguerite Bellanger, again crowned with marguerites. From a contemporary photograph.

'Nothing,' wrote one of the courtesans, 'can give any idea of the first fortnight in September at Baden-Baden.' A view of the celebrated spa.

His Majesty Napoleon III, Emperor of the French. From a photograph taken on his fiftieth birthday.

Above. The Empress Eugénie,
who ordered Marguerite
Bellanger to give up
Napoleon III.
Right. Marguerite Bellanger
and her son, known as
Charles Leboeuf. His
paternity has been variously
attributed to Napoleon III,
to Olivier Métra, the
composer, and to one of the
Emperor's equerries.
Below. The Emperor's
châlet in the park at
Vichy. Marguerite
Bellanger sometimes came
here to visit her 'cher
seigneur'.

Top left. The courtesans
must have spent many hours
preparing for their conquests.
Here a lady's maid helps her
mistress at the dressing-table.
Top right. Trying on a
crinoline. A photograph that
suggests the exigencies of
Second Empire fashions.
Left. A bearded violinist,
Chinese lanterns, garlands of
flowers: at any moment the
quadrille will begin. A
glimpse of social life in the
Second Empire.
Below. 'Cocotte en délire'.

A family party and a *souper intime*. From a photograph taken in the latter years of the Second Empire.

'Vive la joie!'

A courtesan writing
her confessions.

Title-page to the so-called
Confessions of Marguerite
Bellanger. She is
manipulating a puppet
Emperor.

or any kind of crown! Yet at the death of Léonide, this stone was sold at auction with the Royal legend attached to it. It was set as a ring . . .[25]

Léonide was no doubt forgiven much by men, because of her beauty. At the age of twenty-eight, she seems to have reached rare physical perfection:

This is the dream made flesh [wrote Charles Diguet, in *Les Jolies Femmes de Paris*]. This is the celestial beauty which is not spoken of, but sung. This is the ideal which haunts the dreams of poets, enamoured of the impossible. This figure is a poem, all these curves are stanzas: stanzas written by God to astonish the children of men . . .[26]

Such was Léonide Leblanc at the end of the Second Empire. During the Franco-Prussian War, she was in London, giving performances in aid of French prisoners. The first year of the Third Republic saw her at the Odéon, and she was on the list of the *pensionnaires* of the Comédie-Française, though she never appeared on their stage. 'They held the frolics of her early youth against her,' Sarcey explained, 'and they affected to believe that, among these escapades, there were some which would, without any doubt, shake the very fabric of the House of Molière.'[27]

Léonide was obliged to stay at the Odéon, and she remained as audacious as ever. In 1873 she attended the trial of Marshal Bazaine, who had surrendered Metz during the war. The courtroom was full of spectators for this *cause célèbre*, and among them was a society woman who claimed that Léonide had taken the seat given to her by the Président du Conseil, the Duc d'Aumale. 'I am dining with Monseigneur this evening,' exclaimed the angry woman. 'I shall complain to him of this affront.' 'Ah! so you're dining with Monseigneur,' said Léonide, imperturbably. 'I am having supper and sleeping with him.'[28]

In 1883, when Léonide was forty-one, she was still catalogued in *The Pretty Women of Paris*, the directory of prostitutes; but she was listed as a fading beauty.

Here are the remains of true beauty and grace [wrote the compiler], but it is difficult to do justice to such a celebrated whore . . . She has charmed a generation, and in years to come will be almost as celebrated as a Dubarry, or a Nell Gwynne. Every notable rake has passed at least one night in her arms, for a modern Don Juan's catalogue would not be complete unless he could inscribe therein the honour of having 'had' Léonide Leblanc . . . Of all the old glories of Napoleon the Third's corrupt court, she is the best preserved relic, and our concluding advice to all real judges of female loveliness is – hasten to enjoy her at once, ere it be too late.[29]

Léonide had always wanted to love and to please. Once she had captivated men by her youth; now, in middle age, she attracted adolescents by her maturity. One morning, when she was over fifty, someone met her on foot in the Bois de Boulogne, hurrying to meet a young lover. It was, perhaps, the young coiffeur for whom she had lost 'the most extravagant and generous protection of the rich American Louis Tiffany'.[30] For though Léonide gave practical advice to aspiring courtesans, though she took a bulldog to guard her jewels when she was rehearsing at the Odéon,[31] she had no financial acumen. She had amassed a solid fortune, an Aladdin's cave of jewels; but just as she had failed to keep her lovers, she failed to keep her material possessions. She speculated unwisely, and was forced to leave her *hôtel*, and to live more modestly.

Today [wrote Sarcey, in 1884], she lives in retirement in a small *hôtel* where her friends come to chat to her . . . : for she is a well-informed woman, completely French in spirit, she likes books; she has some very fine ones, which is not unusual, but she reads them, which may be less common.

That does not mean that she has completely given up the theatre; one sees her in a stage-box at every first night . . . From time to time, the theatre offers her a chance to perform, and she seizes it . . . The public is fond of her, and never tires of applauding her: these are the last pranks of a child of success.[32]

It was said of Léonide that, unlike Napoleon's Old Guard, she always surrendered, and never died. But death came to her early. She developed cancer and vanished from the theatre, which had only been the springboard for her charms; she vanished from the world of the demi-mondaine. She died at 61, boulevard Haussmann in February 1894, at the age of fifty-two. The nun who was present at her death said that she had died better than she had lived, and that she was finally reconciled with God.[33]

Her death was recorded by an Irishman, W. P. Lonergan, who had long lived in Paris:

This Léonide Leblanc [he wrote], was one of the most fascinating women of her time. Her decline was darkened by the success of younger and more aggressive women, such as Madame Liane de Pougy, Armande Cassire (for whom foolish young Bixio shot himself, as young Duval had done for Cora Pearl), Cléo de Mérode, who riveted the momentary attention of a monarch, and four or five others who were, and are still, to a certain extent, the favourites of millionaires. All these, however beautiful, were eclipsed by the stately and statuesque actress who was the *amie* of the Duc d'Aumale. Intellectually she rose high above any of them, and she was similarly superior to Cora Pearl the horsey, and to another woman of the Second Empire, Marguerite Bellanger. And yet Léonide Leblanc was only a labourer's daughter. The vanity of earthly things came home to me as I saw her thinly attended funeral going slowly towards Père-Lachaise.[34]

Not everyone admired her like Lonergan. In a volume of memoirs which appeared the year after her death, Ernest Daudet, the brother of Alphonse, denied that she had been among the great courtesans of the Second Empire. Many distinguished men had known her, Daudet explained; but they all remembered her as a woman whose ambitions outstripped her powers. She could attract her worshippers, but she could not keep them. She was intrinsically vulgar, she had never been redeemed by genuine passion, and she had been a compromising gossip. Her liaisons, even those which demanded most discretion, had been known all over Paris, and they had been so embroidered in her telling that a casual pastime had reached the proportions of morganatic marriage. Léonide had longed to appear entrusted with state secrets, the inspiration of revolutions. She had always tried to throw dust in people's eyes, to simulate an influence which she did not possess, an influence in which (said Daudet) she would have trafficked had the need arisen.[35]

Her death inspired even jocularity. On 3 February 1894, apparently while she lay dying, Jules Claretie, Sardou, and Dumas *fils* had discussed her over dinner. 'She will have a national funeral,' Dumas *fils* had said, 'and the Duc d'Aumale will command the troops.'[36]

7

Marguerite Bellanger

Julie Leboeuf, later Mme Kulbach (1840–86)

I don't imagine I need to tell you the date of my birth. Posterity will hardly consider the fact worth recording; and I shall spare myself an admission which is painful for any woman who is no longer in the first bloom of youth . . . Shall I say where I was born? Again, why should I do so? Shall I say what I did when I was a girl, before I came to Paris? You're not interested, I'm sure . . .[1]

So Marguerite Bellanger – if she wrote her so-called *Confessions* – tried to cast posterity off her track, and left them free to make their speculations. One writer has suggested that she was a farm-girl from the French provinces, who was spellbound by the thought of Paris: that one day she stole her father's savings, and slipped away, at dawn, to catch the first train to the city of her dreams.[2] Another biographer says, precisely, that Marguerite was born at Boulogne in 1838, and became a lady's maid, a supernumerary at the Théâtre-Beaumarchais, a walker-on at the Opéra, and an ingénue at the Folies-Dramatiques.[3] A third writer has insisted that she was born at Villebernier, and worked as a sempstress at sixty centimes a day. A young merchant – so the chronicle continues – took her to Nantes, where she lived in furnished rooms in the *quartier* of the grisettes, behind the Théâtre-Graslin. An older prostitute, Adèle de Stainville, launched her on her *vie galante* among the swells of the Loire-Inférieure. She followed one of her lovers to Paris.[4]

The truth is that Julie Leboeuf – as she was really called – was born of humble stock at Villebernier, near Saumur, Maine-et-Loire, in 1840.[5] She made her way to Paris, adopted the less plebeian and more euphonious name of Marguerite Bellanger, and tried out her dramatic talent in *Mademoiselle de Belle-Isle*, by Dumas *père*, in a little theatre in the rue de la Tour d'Auvergne. Margot was gauche, and the audience were noisy and critical; she turned to face them, shouted: 'Zut!', picked up her skirts and abandoned her stage career. By about 1862 she was a *cocodette* of the second rank: 'the very type of the eight-day mistress for the man-about-town of the Second Empire.'[6] She was robust, attractive, gay, in her early twenties, radiating vitality and youth; but her ankles were decidedly thick, and her manner was rustic: she remained a woman from the fields. She was often found in the neighbourhood of the École Militaire, entertaining the officers of the Garde Impériale.[7] She lacked the class of a great courtesan, but she was still known. On 22 April 1862, the Goncourts observed her at the theatre with the Duc de Grammont-Caderousse.

In 1863 – at least according to the *Confessions* – Marguerite was installed in a little fifth-floor room in the boulevard des Capucines. This is a point at which the *Confessions* sound implausible: for the *cocodette* who claimed to live in one room also claims that she enjoyed certain luxuries, among them a lady's maid.

My maid had orders to wake me at two o'clock in the afternoon; not a moment sooner or later. I nibbled a few sweets in bed, drank a cup of chocolate; if I was tired, I drank a glass of malaga or madeira, and got up. I put on a peignoir lined with red satin, and stretched myself out, barefoot, on a sofa, to wait for that indispensable man, my hairdresser. At five o'clock I went out. My basket-carriage, one of those Lilliputian basket-carriages, the most elegant in Paris, was waiting for me at the door. I drove it myself, and I usually went to the Bois. There I was certain to meet the most famous mondaines of the time, and all the millionaires, . . . who were made more than generous by our charms and the hope of pleasure. Then the suppers were arranged. Should we go to Durand's? Should we go to Voisin's? Should we finish the night at the Café Anglais? When the last bottle of champagne was empty, which of these gentlemen would have the privilege of seeing us home?[8]

Among those who saw her home was, it seems, Daniel Wilson,[9] who, one distant day, would be the son-in-law of Jules Grévy, third President of the French Republic. Another lover was attached to the Emperor's household, and Marguerite followed him as the Court moved from Compiègne to the Tuileries, from Versailles to Saint-Cloud.[10]

*

There is a story, fit for Perrault, of the young Marguerite sheltering from the rain at Saint-Cloud: of the Emperor passing in his carriage, and throwing a tartan rug to the unprotected, handsome girl. Next day, so the legend goes, Marguerite determined to make the most of her adventure, and she requested an audience of His Majesty. She had, she said, an urgent personal message. The Emperor was fascinated by the request, and, perhaps, he suspected an intrigue. Marguerite that day became his mistress.[11]

The *Confessions de Marguerite Bellanger* give another account of the origins of her favour. One day, it appears, a member of the imperial household invited her to dine at the Café Anglais. She could not imagine which of the three men in the party was destined for her; but she took unashamed, unsophisticated delight in the dinner.

I still remember the menu: an hors-d'œuvre first, delicious prawns, strongly spiced, a Rhine carp *à la Chambord*, quails stuffed thick with truffles on buttered toast flavoured with basil, asparagus with *sauce à l'osmazone*, a pheasant . . . with Russian salad; Pontet-Canet with the first course, and chilled champagne from the second course to the coffee.[12]

None of Marguerite's escorts at this banquet was meant to be her lover. She was in fact being considered as a paramour for the Emperor; and soon afterwards, in a little hunting-lodge at Saint-Cloud, Napoleon III made her the last of his official mistresses. 'Of all the adventures of Marguerite,' wrote Hector Fleischmann, in *Napoléon III et les Femmes*, 'this is certainly the most wonderful and the most unexpected; it never ceases to astonish us.'[13]

Marguerite delighted the Emperor by her tomboyish ways, her refreshing, frank, plebeian manners; after the etiquette of the Court he enjoyed her spontaneity and naturalness. The liaison continued for nearly two years. Mocquard, his secretary, bought her a small *hôtel* in the rue des Vignes, at Passy, and the Emperor often visited her there. In his *Recollections of Paris*, the Hon. D. Bingham recorded:

I several times met the Emperor driving up the Champs-Élysées of an evening in his brougham to the Rue des Vignes, where Margot held a veritable court. 'The gravest and most frivolous persons flocked thither,' wrote a chronicler during the siege; 'ministers, senators, equerries, chamberlains, diplomatists, tenors, soldiers and buffoons, picking up crosses and places which the lady of the house obtained with the greatest facility from her *cher seigneur*.'[14]

It is said that Marguerite had her notepaper embossed with a silver-petalled, gold-centred marguerite, and the motto: 'All things come to those who wait.'[15] She followed her *cher seigneur* to Vichy, and once, in broad daylight, she arrived by carriage at his châlet, where he was presiding over a council of ministers. She went to Biarritz and to Plombières. When the Court moved to Saint-Cloud, she lived in a little house which adjoined the wall of the private park; there was a hidden door in the wall, for the Emperor's use.[16]

However, the Empress discovered that her husband's latest liaison was far from casual; and when, in the summer of 1864, she heard that he was taking his mistress to Vichy, she decided to spend a few weeks at Schwalbach, a watering-place in Hesse-Nassau. Indeed, she went there on her doctor's orders, for she was so perturbed by the thought of Marguerite Bellanger that she could not eat or sleep.[17]

It was said that Mocquard used Marguerite as a means of influencing the Emperor. He called every day at two o'clock to instruct her what to say; every day, at five, he came back to learn the result.[18] As for Marguerite herself – so Marie Colombier wrote in her *Mémoires* – her head was turned by the Emperor's constancy. She forgot that she was merely to minister to his physical pleasures. It was as if an actress who had played a servant in Molière, had chosen to act the heroine instead. Dorine could not play Célimène.[19]

Marguerite presumed too much of her influence. Her 'indiscreet barouche'[20] was seen too frequently in the Bois de Boulogne, in the Champs-Élysées, crossing the path of the imperial carriage. In October 1864, the Empress returned to Paris. Soon afterwards, the Emperor was brought home in a state of collapse from the rue des Vignes, and she decided that the liaison must end. France could no longer afford to have a ruler who endangered his health. She ordered Mocquard, the brother of the Emperor's secretary, to accompany her to Passy; and there, it seems, she told Marguerite that she was killing the Emperor and must give him up. By the beginning of 1865, Prosper Mérimée, who was the Empress's confidant, could write: 'Caesar thinks no more of Cleopatra.'[21]

★

Some say, however, that Cleopatra claimed to be pregnant by Caesar, so as to keep him; and here posterity comes across a tangle of facts which cannot be unravelled.

On 24 February 1864, at half-past ten in the evening, a child was born at Marguerite's house in Passy, 27, rue des Vignes. Two days later, four signatories registered the birth of a boy, Charles-Jules-Auguste-François-Marie, 'father and mother unknown'. Among the signatories to this quite extraordinary document was a friend of the Emperor's cousin, Princess Mathilde.[22]

It was later suggested that the child was the son of the Emperor and Mademoiselle Valentine Haussmann, the daughter of the celebrated Préfet de la Seine, and that Marguerite agreed to feign pregnancy and to own the child, to save the future of the society girl. This story is, however, discredited by Hector Fleischmann. He records that Valentine Haussmann's son by the Emperor was born a year later, on 26 January 1865, the month before she married the Vicomte Pernetty. Marguerite Bellanger was without doubt the mother of the child who was born in 1864. No one has yet ascertained the father.[23]

After the fall of the Empire, two undated letters from Marguerite were found among the imperial papers at the Tuileries; they were in an envelope, sealed with an N and a crown, and inscribed, in the Emperor's hand, *Lettres à garder*. They had, it seems, been written by request. M. Devienne, first President of the Cour d'appel de la Seine, recalled how, one day, 'he had arrived to get the letters signed, at the village of Villebernier, in Anjou, and, hastening to the farm where Margot was for the moment hiding her importance [her pregnancy?], he found her wearing a rough hood and clogs, and a short skirt. She was with her worthy parents, sitting round the cabbage soup, flanked by jugs of cider.' The result of the interview was two letters, presumably dictated by Devienne, and signed by Marguerite. The first was addressed to Devienne: 'You have asked me for an account of my relations with the Emperor. It is painful to admit that I have deceived him.' The other letter was addressed to the Emperor himself. 'I have been guilty,' Marguerite wrote, 'it is true . . .'[24] Perhaps the letters were written to soothe the fears of the Empress. The dynasty was none too solid, and a bastard son of the Emperor's might have harmed the Prince Imperial's future. Perhaps (as Henri Rochefort, the political journalist, suggested) the child was the son of the composer Olivier Métra;[25] perhaps he was the son of one of the Emperor's household, for 'it seems certain, according to one of her friends,' wrote Hector Fleischmann, 'that, even during her liaison with Napoleon III, Marguerite continued to have relations with her previous lover, one of the Emperor's equerries'.[26] The father of Charles Leboeuf, as she called him, may never now be known. Marguerite had him brought up by a jeweller in the rue des Moulins. But the Emperor gave him an estate in the Oise.[27]

★

The two Bellanger letters were published soon after the fall of the Empire; and on 23 September 1870, within three weeks of Sedan, an Englishman in Paris could write that the tide of scandal about Marguerite was 'now at the flood'. Mademoiselle Bellanger, he added,

Opposite. The Empress Eugénie's bedroom at Saint-Cloud.
A room like this was no doubt the ideal of most ambitious courtesans.

is the niece of the proprietor of 'Voisins'. Six years ago she was very handsome, now she is so fat that she has lost all expression. She used to dine frequently at 'Voisins', and blow up her respected uncle before the party, if the dinner was not good! I believe she is now a respectable married woman, and fled with all the rest of her former world (demi-monde) to London or Brussels. I hope we shall hear no more of her affairs.[28]

Marguerite had had an *hôtel* built for her in the avenue de Friedland; but after the Commune, when everyone with an imperial past felt uneasy about their future, she was afraid of sharing the fate of Mme Dubarry, and she sold the *hôtel* to another courtesan. However, she kept a handsome château at Villeneuve-sous-Dammartin, in the department of Seine-et-Marne. She owned land in Touraine and the Soissonnais; and she enjoyed a considerable income, which enabled her to finance several concerns, including a lacemaking firm. She led a somewhat retired life in a *hôtel* in the avenue de Wagram, though she had a number of liaisons: among them, perhaps, a liaison with Gambetta (who did not deny the suggestion when it was made to him). In 1872 she began a long affair with Colonel (later General) Lenfermé de Lignières; when he was commanding at Saint-Cyr, she lived in an apartment at Versailles, and when he moved to the garrison at Tours, she lived in a château in the neighbourhood. Lignières was a legitimist, but this did not prevent her from giving Bonapartist dinners in Paris; and when, in 1873, Napoleon III died in exile in England, it is said that Marguerite attended his funeral.[29]

Yet, like many courtesans, she longed for respectability. At Villeneuve-sous-Dammartin she was known for her charity work, her interest in social service; and after her liaison with Lignières was over, she married a Prussian by the name of Kulbach. It was not long before they quarrelled, and the marriage broke up; and Marguerite Kulbach ended her life as she had begun it: looking after her cows and sheep and hens.[30]

In the winter of 1886, walking round her estates, she caught a chill; it was followed by acute peritonitis, and Gambetta's friend, Dr Fieuzal, who was summoned, was unable to save her. Marguerite's death was worthy of Balzac: a jealous old servant turned away the village curé, who had come to administer the last rites, and slammed the door in the face of the family. Marguerite died alone, in her château, on 23 November 1886, in her forty-sixth year. Her husband and her son, Charles Leboeuf, issued the *faire-part* of her death, and announced that she would be buried at the Cimetière Montparnasse.[31]

8

Caroline Letessier

(dates unknown)

Caroline Letessier began her life, as she ended it, in obscurity. It is not known when she was born, or where; her parents remain in shadow, but probably she was an unwanted or illegitimate child, for Marie Colombier records that she had a foster-father: a butcher by the name of Graindorge.[1] Nothing seems to be known of her childhood; but Zed, the Comte de Maugny, in *Le Demi-Monde sous le Second Empire*, says that she began her career at the French theatre at Turin, under the protection of a diplomat. And though she did not then conform to the Rubens ideal of the Second Empire courtesan, though she was unfashionably thin, her wit and beauty earned her a triumph in the Piedmontese capital. 'I can still see her in fancy dress at the masked ball at the Théâtre Meynadier,' wrote the Comte de Maugny towards the end of the century. 'She was sitting on the balustrade of one of the boxes, shouting out at random to new arrivals, and enlivening the festivities, which were otherwise rather dull, with her unquenchable verve.'[2]

She was invited to *soupers intimes* by the Prince de Carignan, and much courted by the *corps diplomatique* and the aristocracy of Turin. She was already renowned for her elegance. A few years later she was in Paris, more Rubenesque, more beautiful, and among the foremost members of *la garde*. Some of the men most in demand found themselves at her feet; and Marie Colombier declared that, with Cora Pearl and Giulia Barucci, Caroline Letessier represented the *splendeurs galantes* of the Second Empire.[3]

While Cora Pearl (so people claimed) personified the English style of courtesan, Caroline Letessier was essentially Parisian. She had spontaneous grace, and a highly expressive face, lit up by a smile of remarkable charm;

her features were irregular, but she radiated intelligence. She was always gay, and full of verve; she was brilliantly satirical; and, above all, she was elegance itself.

She would be seen at every festivity, dressed in vivid satin, with multi-coloured, jewelled butterflies strewn about her black hair. She would always be recognised in her stage box, for she would always begin by setting out her accessories on the plush-covered ledge. She was never without her mirror, the golden apple in which she kept her rice-powder, and her lorg-nette, which scintillated and glowed with precious stones. Her elegance idealised everything about her, even her astounding luxury; and her luxury roused the admiration of her colleagues on the stage and in *la vie galante*. 'We very often talk about you,' Aimée Desclée, the actress, wrote from Naples, 'and I've told them that you had diamonds by the shovelful, property in Touraine, twelve servants, and horses which were worth twenty thousand francs apiece. In fact, I left them gasping.'[4]

Caroline Letessier earned and spent a fortune without counting; and her fortune did not come from the Théâtre du Palais-Royal, where she was an actress from 1855 until 1858.[5] She earned her wealth by more personal triumphs among the elect. Indeed, her elegance, her blithe disregard of money, seemed to destine her to be a prince's mistress. In 1859 she went to St Petersburg, where she was to stay for eight years, and there she played the princess at the Théâtre Michel and in society. She not only borrowed the title of Princess Dolgorouki from its unsuspecting holder, but in fact ensnared a Grand Duke.

At one magnificent ball, it appears, when her dress was nearly torn off in a waltz, His Imperial Highness repaired the damage by tying the pieces together with his Grand Cordon of the Order of St Andrew. 'It was said that Caroline Letessier dealt in Grand Dukes,' noted Marie Colombier in her *Mémoires*.[6] Caroline did not merely 'deal in Grand Dukes'; one of them (no doubt her waltzing partner) promised her marriage, and in 1867 the authorities thought it time to suggest her departure. Caroline ignored advice. Stricter warnings were given, and finally she took fright. She set off from Russia with her Grand Duke. They travelled as M. and Mme Letessier.

At Berlin, the chief of police came to demand their passports; Caroline reminded him that this was an unnecessary formality. 'Are you looking for me?' enquired His Imperial Highness. 'Yes, monseigneur.' 'What do you want of me?' 'We want Your Imperial Highness to go back to St Petersburg.' 'But I don't choose to return to Russia: madame is going to France, and I'm going with her.' 'I am sorry, monseigneur. Your uncle, the Emperor's, orders.' 'You wouldn't dare to arrest me?' 'No, monseigneur, but we shall detach the compartment from the train, and you won't go. As for madame, she can set off if she likes.'[7]

Apparently the problem was solved, and M. and Mme Letessier settled down in a sumptuous villa just off the Lichtenthal Strasse in Baden. Their arrival did not lower the temperature of gaiety in the season of 1868. When Caroline made her resplendent entry into the casino, the *jeunesse dorée* of Baden encircled her and gazed admiringly at her dress and jewels. Hortense Schneider, 'who was always "got up" like a bourgeoise from the Marais', observed: 'I have seen fatted calves in my time, but never such a pretty one as this.' The observation naturally hurt the foster-child of a butcher. 'And I've never seen such an ugly cow,' answered Caroline Letessier.

Uproar followed. The director of the casino came to investigate, but the Grand Duchess of Baden's son intervened in favour of Caroline, and the matter was dropped. Except by Caroline herself: every time she saw Hortense Schneider on the arm of Lord Carrington, she asked Carrington: 'How's your cook-housekeeper?'[8]

Apart from this incident, Baden enjoyed an uninterrupted kermesse; and even a tipsy, clumsy giant by the name of Bismarck danced the can-can.[9]

★

As for Caroline Letessier, she returned, it seems, to Paris, where she kept her reputation for elegance and extravagance. *The Pretty Women of Paris* declared that 'she always had money when all her dirty sisters in the trade were starving. During the siege of Paris, when a piece of white bread was a rarity, and the poor molls were dying off like rotten sheep, Letessier walked into the shop of a starving jeweller in the rue de la Paix, and nearly killed him with joy by buying with ready money a set of silver toilette utensils.'[10]

The story may be questioned, for, at some time during the Siege, Caroline Letessier found herself in England; she was accompanied by Caroline Hassé, the courtesan who was once unkindly said to resemble Louis-Philippe. The English visit of 'the two Caros', as they were called, occasioned one of the most entertaining episodes in the history of the *bataillon de Cythère*.

There was at Magdalen College, Oxford, an undergraduate who was looked upon with general favour: he had plenty of money, he kept four horses, he entertained a great deal, 'and yet with all was very clever and reading for honours'.[11] Since his parents happened to live in Paris, and since he was 'somewhat tempestuous', he had in vacations come to know a number of *la garde*; and hearing that his friends, the two Caros, had arrived in London, he invited them to Oxford and announced that two French cousins were coming to see him.

The two 'dainty girls' were duly installed at the Randolph Hotel, and since they were both very pretty, well mannered and well dressed, they created something of a sensation. They constantly went to lunch and tea at Magdalen, where one of the youngest dons, a callow divine, fell violently in love with Caroline Letessier. 'If he had seen her, as I did a few months before,' wrote William Osgood Field, 'throwing plates at the head of Lord Charles Hamilton in a *cabinet particulier* at the Café Anglais, he might have hesitated before offering her his hand and curacy.' However, only two members of the college suspected anything wrong: two sophisticated Fellows 'who could detect a Paphian perfume at a hundred yards'. They were Charles Reade, the novelist, and Reginald Bird. They acquainted the President of Magdalen with their suspicions, and Dr Bulley sent for the undergraduate, who expressed indignation and invited him to meet the ladies at a fête at the Botanical Gardens. The two Aspasias were warned, and – since it was their trade to fascinate, and to be all things to all men – they 'absolutely fascinated' the courtly and guileless old man. Dr Bulley told everyone, including the Dean of Christ Church, about these two charming and well-informed 'lady exiles from the now besieged French capital'.

The Dean of Christ Church, Dr Liddell, part-author of the Greek lexicon, Liddell and Scott, and the father of the original Alice in Wonderland, invited the two Caros to the Deanery to meet Ralph Waldo Emerson, who was captivated. The luncheon at Christ Church was followed by a garden party, but who should appear at the garden party but Sir William Vernon Harcourt, the historian, and it so happened 'that both these prettily bound duodecimos had claimed his attention by Seine-side'. The recognition was mutual and immediate; however, as Sir William had even more to lose by an indiscretion than the ladies, nothing was said. 'Few things to my mind could be more comic,' wrote William Osgood Field, 'than to see Caroline Letessier and dear fat blonde Caroline Hassé innocently playing croquet on the Deanery lawn with some callow undergraduates, while Emerson and Sir William Vernon Harcourt looked on.' The two Caros returned to London without any kind of scandal, but Reginald Bird later on discovered the truth, for he met them at the pleasure-gardens at Cremorne, and enjoyed the joke immensely. As for the undergraduate, whose name Field discreetly hides, he became 'one of the most respected members of society, and identified with clerical and religious matters'.

★

Caroline Letessier was later the mistress of the Prince of Monaco's son;[12] but her brilliance and extravagance were evidently misplaced in Republican days. The *grande cocotte* who had 'dealt in Grand Dukes' had saved nothing of her fortune, and she became a companion to one of the new generation of courtesans. She kept her little *hôtel* near the avenue de Villiers, and kept a few of her *objets d'art*; but the demi-mondaine who had lent a lover five hundred thousand francs now lived on a monthly allowance of fifteen louis which two of her colleagues, Adèle Courtois and Isabelle Ferrand, made her out of charity.[13]

In 1883 *The Pretty Women of Paris* gave a brutal portrait of Caroline in her old age:

She was one of the queens of prostitution some fifteen years ago, and when she passes in her carriage, a fearful wreck, we are forced to ask how it is that she could have accumulated the riches she possesses, for she is very ugly and has always been so. A pair of watery, moth-eaten, red-rimmed eyes; a big nose, with gaping nostrils . . . ; a bumpy forehead; her skin rough and pimply, cracked by the use of doubtful paint; her face shining with glycerine when at home, and covered an inch thick with red and white at night – such are the ruins of the whore of the Empire, the divine 'Caro' . . . Last year she sold off her collections of lace, pictures, jewels, and ancient furniture, and went to live at the [Avenue de Messine]. This auction, like every other action of her life, was a commercial speculation, as the best goods were not sold, but went to furnish her new abode. From all such cold, calculating, heartless syrens, half-women and half-leeches, good Lord deliver us.[14]

She had been completely forgotten, said Frédéric Loliée, when suddenly a newspaper reported that this star of the Second Empire demi-monde was extinguished. One sullen morning, hastily, with few flowers, in an almost empty church, Caro Letessier's funeral service was held.[15]

9

Alice Ozy

Julie-Justine Pilloy (1820–93)

It has been said that Parisians are French twice over; and Julie-Justine Pilloy, better known as Alice Ozy, would alone prove the axiom to be true. She was endowed with wit and elegance, quick emotions, coquetry, and a very keen financial sense. One of her grandfathers had been director of the Conservatoire, and chapel-master to the Emperor; it was therefore not surprising that she also had an artistic nature.

She was born in Paris on 6 August 1820, the daughter of M. Pilloy, a jeweller, and his wife, whose maiden name was Ozi.[1] Since Monsieur Pilloy took a mistress who bore him two children, and Mme Pilloy consoled herself with a lover, Julie-Justine was entrusted to a foster-mother. At the age of ten, since both her parents found her an encumbrance, she was forced to earn her living by embroidery; and in a Paris attic, with her foster-mother's daughter, she spent the long days of her childhood doing needlework. The woman who employed her soon became aware that the girl's potentialities were wasted: her classical beauty would draw customers to the shop. At the age of thirteen, Julie-Justine was installed behind the counter. She was soon made sadly aware of her powers of attraction, for she was seduced by the owner of the establishment. This seduction, for which she could hardly be blamed, lost her the chance of marriage to a kindly provincial doctor, and to a distant cousin, who had been enslaved by her beauty. Julie-Justine apparently decided, in her teens, that she was precluded from marriage. She had to find her happiness elsewhere.

She found it in the arms of Paul-Louis-Édouard Brindeau.[2] Six years older than herself, Brindeau had been a pupil at the Collège Bourbon; he had left it at sixteen to make his début, as tenor and actor, at the

Belleville theatre. In 1834 he had appeared at the Vaudeville, and, three years later, at the Variétés. He would in time become a *sociétaire* of the Comédie-Française, and, for some twelve years, he would be their most celebrated *jeune premier*. It was not surprising that Julie-Justine fell ardently in love with the young Brindeau, eloped with him, and turned towards the theatre. She could imagine no greater triumph than appearing with her lover on the stage. Early in 1840, she gave her first performance at the Variétés:[3] she had succeeded in acting at the same theatre as Brindeau, and she was earning twelve hundred francs a year.

Perhaps she already had other plans. Perhaps, like other *filles de joie*, she really sought public applause, and felt that this was the natural place to seek it. Certainly she appeared in theatres where a pretty woman was more important than an accomplished actress. But whether she was content to act, or dreamed of being a courtesan, she had to choose a professional name. She adapted her mother's maiden name, and changed the clumsy Julie-Justine for the more musical Alice. Julie-Justine Pilloy became Alice Ozy.

When she first entered the theatre, Alice Ozy had been remarkably, quite delightfully naïve. Informed that a Gruyère cheese mine had been struck near Montmorency, and that it would give work to the poor, she clapped her hands with joy. And then, already showing her business sense, she asked where she should go to buy shares. She was both innocent and shrewd, romantic and sensible, and it was practical politics, quite as much as romance, which dictated the next episode in her life. King Louis-Philippe and Queen Marie-Amélie summoned the company from the Variétés to give a command performance of *Le Chevalier du Guet* in honour of their son, the Duc d'Aumale. The Duc was nineteen, handsome, and just back from the North African campaign, in which he had commanded a regiment. He saw Alice at the Tuileries, and fell in love at once. Alice left Brindeau, and became his mistress.

The liaison established her in the first rank of courtesans. It was carefully chronicled by her neighbour, Henri de Villemessant, the journalist.[4] He watched, amused, as she left her rooms over the Maison d'Or, and roamed the streets, arm-in-arm with her lover; she remained an actress at heart, for she dressed as a man, and she was often mistaken for Aumale's brother, the Duc de Montpensier. It could hardly be said that Alice wore her masculine disguise out of tact; she was proud to publicise her liaison. As for the Duc, he could not have proclaimed it with more ostentation. When Alice arrived, in her calèche, to watch his regiment march past at Courbevoie, the band struck up, on his orders, *Kradoujah, ma maîtresse*. It

Alice Ozy

Innocent and shrewd, romantic and sensible. This portrait by Vincent Vidal shows Alice Ozy in 1842, at about the time of her *liaison* with the young Duc d'Aumale.

Alice Ozy's châlet on the shores of Lake Enghien.
From an engraving of 1861.

Opposite
Top. La Maison d'Or, in the boulevard des Italiens.
Opened in 1841, the restaurant became one of the centres
of *la vie du boulevard* during the Second Empire. Alice
Ozy lived in rooms over the restaurant in the early 1840s.
Bottom. The Café des Algériennes: a Bohemian corner of
Paris in the late 1840s.

Top left. The Duc d'Aumale in 1840.
This portrait, by François-Xavier
Winterhalter, was painted just
before the Duc met Alice Ozy.
Left. Edmond About, the novelist
and journalist (1828–85). One of
Alice Ozy's last lovers, he made
her the heroine of his novel
Madelon.

Above. A Bohemian gathering in the 1840s: the kind of party frequented by Alice Ozy.
Right. Alice Ozy's last lover, Gustave Doré: book-illustrator, caricaturist, artist and sculptor (1832–83). Doré's statue of the Virgin and Child guards Alice Ozy's tomb at Père-Lachaise.

Right. Alice Ozy's dearest
lover : Théodore Chassériau
(1819–56). Engraved after
a self-portrait.
Below left. One of Alice's
admirers : Théophile
Gautier in 1849, from a
sketch by Chassériau.
Below right. Alice Ozy
in a gandoura. From a
pencil portrait by
Chassériau, 1849.

Above. Baigneuse endormie
by Théodore Chassériau,
1850. This picture, now
at the Musée Calvet,
Avignon, shows Alice
Ozy as she appeared to the
one man she seems to
have loved.
Right. Victor Hugo (right)
and his sons Charles-
Victor and Jean-François-
Victor. Alice Ozy refused
to grant her favours to
the poet, but she became
Charles-Victor's mistress
in 1847.

The prosperous bourgeoise: Madame Pilloy, the former Alice Ozy, in her middle sixties.

was a popular song, brought over from Algeria, where all the soldiers sang it, but the Duc had made it the hymn of his happiness.

One might expect that Mlle Ozy was content to remain with her royal lover; but the Duc d'Aumale had one disadvantage: he was not yet entitled to spend his fortune. And when, one evening, a twenty-thousand-franc carriage, complete with footmen with powdered hair, drew up at the stage door of the Variétés, as an initial gift from a suitor, Mlle Ozy could not resist the attraction. She allowed herself to be driven away to begin a new liaison, this time with the Comte de Perregaux, the son of the King's banker. 'I love you more than ever since you have ceased to love me,' wrote the Duc d'Aumale. 'Go for two years without seeing M. de Perregaux, let your heart regain its virginity, and then . . .'[5] But Mlle Ozy did not pause to take advice.

At about this time she came to know Théophile Gautier. On 21 September 1843, *Un Voyage en Espagne,* a three-act vaudeville by Gautier and Paul Siraudin, was first performed at the Variétés. Alice had a small part, and she was afraid that it would be taken from her. She was advised to see Gautier, and Gautier asked her to dinner. She was not ungenerous. That evening, it is said, she inspired the quatrain:

> Pentélique, Paros, marbres neigeux de Grèce,
> Dont Praxitèle a fait la chair de ses Vénus,
> Vos blancheurs suffisaient à des corps de déesse.
> Noircissez, car Alice a montré ses seins nus![6]

Henceforward it was Alice who sat in the critic's box – for Gautier earned his living as a critic – when she was not admired on the stage. The letters she sent him well suggest the forces at work behind the scenes. 'My dear Théo,' she complained, 'I was very vexed not to see an account of our play in your article. Let's have it on Monday. Don't damn our authors too hard, they're nice people, and if you don't like my acting say I look like a real marchioness and that I must be attractive to the Marquis. That will please me, and it costs you so little to lie.' Alice Ozy was well aware of Gautier's powers as a critic: she not only told him of her coming benefit performance, she drafted the advertisement he was to publish: '*You must hurry up,*' she wrote, 'and put it *in the middle* of your article.' In a third letter, sent from London, she made more extravagant demands, and implied a generous reward: 'I am very well, *say so in the Moniteur* . . . I will bring you some needles – and I will also give you something less sharp, but on one condition, get me a part for the Vaudeville. Work, you great lazybones, and I will refuse you nothing.' Alice later denied that she had been Gautier's mistress, but the denial was hardly convincing. In another coquettish note, she asked him, yet again, to use his influence:

Dear Théo—I am annoyed that you still haven't come to see me at my new apartment: 14 Boulevard Poissonnière. Don't forget, my dear, to put in your article that I was born on 6 August 1825 [she had in fact been born in 1820] and that I made my début in 1840 . . . Some impertinent fellow writes in his criticism Mlle Ozi whom we have seen for the past ten years; I look like a duenna. It's for you my excellent friend to make amends for the outrage, you can at the same time criticise the mania people have for making actresses older than they are . . . [7]

Alice Ozy's relationship with 'dear Théo', more or less amorous, lasted the rest of his life; and, after he died, she lamented: 'How sweet it would have been to ease his latter days! I should have loved him poor, infirm, so that I could care for him, regale him with everything, fill his house with books and flowers . . .' In 1880, she offered to pay for a monument to him in Paris, but the *Conseil municipal* refused to erect it. Gautier had been librarian to Princess Mathilde, the cousin of Napoleon III; now the Second Empire had fallen, and the Republic did not choose to remember him.[8]

Alice herself hardly needed a monument in the days of Louis-Philippe. Her witticisms were the talk of Paris. When she was asked if a certain courtesan was to take the veil: 'No doubt she is,' said Alice, 'she's just discovered that God took the form of a man.' When a pompous suitor declared that he loved her 'as the sun loves the rose', she answered: 'I hate you as the moon hates the sun: when you get up I go to rest, and when you rest I rise.'[9] (Mlle Ozy, someone said, only made comparisons between night and day.) She was more gracefully remembered by her style and beauty: her blue coupé was instantly recognised in the Bois de Boulogne, she introduced the fashion for dressing in a single colour: one day she would appear, clad entirely in pale blue, the next she would be a symphony in rose pink. Roger de Beauvoir, the writer and dandy, caricatured her as a bacchante, holding a glass of champagne in one hand and a cornucopia in the other. 'I don't know,' confessed Victor Koning, the journalist, 'if Mademoiselle Ozy has as many admirers as the miller's wife in Pomponne, who was so pretty and so cruel that her lovers' sighs were enough to turn the sails of her mill. I can only say that Mademoiselle Ozy is sought after by the pleasantest and liveliest society in Paris.'[10] Théodore de Banville declared that she was the friend of all the gifted men of her time. She left her rooms over the Maison d'Or for the aristocratic rue de Provence;[11] the child-sempstress of years ago now lived in enviable prosperity.

The Comte de Perregaux had abandoned her, for he had fallen in love with Marie Duplessis, the future *Dame aux camélias*. But Alice could now afford, in the fullest sense of the word, to choose her lovers; and not everyone reached the rosewood bed, enriched with Sèvres medallions of cupids, and draped in seductive, delicate swathes of lace. Early in 1847 she came to know Victor Hugo and his son Charles. Hugo himself was invited to see her *lit d'apparat*; he was mortified that she allowed no more. However, if she refused the father, she readily accepted the son. Every day, for six weeks, Charles Hugo wrote a poem for her, and copied it into an album; the volume, bound in black morocco, with a secret lock, expressed his lyrical devotion and gratitude. Victor Hugo remained a friend, called on her, and gave her occasional presents (among them was a sketch by Delacroix); but he could not forgive her completely for her rejection. In his recollections, *Choses Vues*, which appeared after his death, he described an intimate supper at which – he said – Alice Ozy had displayed her charms to him, and implied the grant of her favours, in the presence of her current lover. Hugo hardly troubled to disguise the names; and Alice was bitterly hurt, in her old age. For Hugo's Serio was Théodore Chassériau, the painter; Hugo had accused her of calculated cruelty to the only man she seems to have loved.[12]

Charles Hugo had known the pleasures of the rosewood bed for the summer of 1847; Chassériau became her lover in 1848, and he was to know them for two years. He was a plain man, but even his plainness had its originality, his voice was musical, and he had the reputation of a Don Juan. Introduced to Alice, very probably, by Gautier, he inspired a love which remained with her all her life. Alice Ozy, who was prepared to love princes for their panache, and bankers for their overwhelming fortunes, was prepared to love an artist for himself. While Vincent Vidal's sketch of her at the age of twenty caught her freshness and, somehow, her curious innocence, Chassériau perpetuated her powers of seduction. She gazes out of his pencil portrait, swathed in a gandoura, mature, and glowing with confidence; in his painting of the *Baigneuse endormie*, she shows an impeccable beauty which her career has somehow failed to tarnish. Her figure is classical, and, strangely, a symbol of purity.

During the two years of their liaison, she must often have used the secret door into the painter's studio in the avenue Frochot, at the foot of the Butte Montmartre. Here, in the quartier Bréda, not far from Madame Sabatier, among oriental furnishings, paintings, weapons, and a life-size cast of the Vénus de Milo, the liaison with Chassériau ran its course. It was broken because of a painting: a magisterial copy of El Greco's portrait of the Queen of Spain. Alice demanded to have it; Chassériau meant to keep it for his family. Alice insisted, and, at last, Chassériau submitted. On his next visit to her, he found it framed, and he was overcome by remorse for his weakness. He took a knife, slashed the canvas again and again, and strode out. Alice sent a servant to him with the picture and a note of dismissal.

A few years later, still in his thirties, Chassériau died. One day, as an old woman, Alice visited his nephew, and caught sight of the painting, now repaired. She fell on her knees before it, and wept. Then she asked if she might keep it. Baron Chassériau granted her request.[13]

In her youth, perhaps, she felt less deeply. She accepted the homage of Préault, the sculptor, who begged to kiss her classical feet.[14] She received a thousand notes expressing admiration and passion, from noblemen, working men, and even schoolboys.[15] She seemed irresistible: she had a brief affair with Gueymard, a tenor at the Opéra;[16] she seems to have had an affair with the Duc de Morny.[17] It was probably Morny whom Villemessant had in mind when he told the story of Alice Ozy at the Palais de l'Industrie. For there she met

a personage of very high rank giving his arm to a woman from the highest society. The situation was critical, and there was not a moment to lose; there had to be a quick decision to avert the head or acknowledge her. M. de *** did not hesitate for a second: he gave Mademoiselle Ozy the most polite and respectful of bows. Mademoiselle Ozy went home, and added the following codicil to her will: 'I bequeath M. de *** twenty thousand francs, for him to give to his charities, in gratitude for not being afraid to acknowledge me when he was escorting a very great lady.'[18]

Alice Ozy was urged by a friend to come to Russia, and try her powers on the Imperial court; but she was too Parisian to go so far afield. She went to London for a season at the St James's Theatre, where she ensnared a German prince, a Saxe-Weimar;[19] then she returned to Paris to join the company at the Vaudeville. It was the age of *féeries-revues*, and actresses were more and more décolletées; she was among the first fairies to wear flesh-coloured tights, with wings on her shoulders and a wand in her hand.[20]

She was still a radiant figure. In 1854, Banville saw her as a sign of spring:

Les lilas vont fleurir, et Ninon me querelle,
Et ce matin j'ai vu Mademoiselle Ozy
Près des Panoramas déployer son ombrelle:
C'est que le triste hiver est bien mort, songez-y![21]

And then, in 1855, at the age of thirty-five, Alice Ozy suddenly left the theatre for ever, and allowed herself her most surprising liaison: she was kept for twelve years by a rich man, a Monsieur Groening, who made no physical demands of her.[22]

This was fortunate, for in 1858 she had an affair, in Rome, with the brilliant young novelist and journalist, Edmond About.[23] He later made her the heroine of his novel, *Madelon*.

Madelon (for she it was) scanned her friend from head to foot, opening two grey-blue eyes, which were neither big nor small, but enchanting. The real merit of these eyes, their only originality, lay in something naïf and constantly astonished which is usually only found in the gaze of a child. She was not a beauty, this Madelon, so brilliant and so desired; she was less and more than that . . . The irregularity of her features was lost in the sweetest harmony. When you saw her, it was like smelling a bunch of heliotrope or tasting some delicious fruit, you felt something complete and superabundant which made your heart overflow . . . This strange creature, a mixture of unbelievable perfections and of still more charming faults, had the long, high-arched foot of Diana the huntress, a hand that was perhaps a shade too delicate and transparent, but so gentle that she exercised an irresistible attraction, and that she took possession of a man if she touched him with the tips of her fingers.[24]

Madelon, Alice Ozy, took a final lover: the prodigal, versatile artist, Gustave Doré.[25] It was a gentle, winter love. Then she simply became a prosperous bourgeoise. The actress had vanished, years ago, the romantic idol had gone, and the speculator came into her own. Long ago, as a naïve débutante in the theatre, Alice Ozy had asked how she should invest in the Gruyère cheese mines at Montmorency. In her heyday as a courtesan, she had shown her native prudence, and asked not for diamonds, but for railway shares.[26] Now, with a Midas touch (and, perhaps, making use of a fortune which had been left to her by a Polish lover), she invested money through the Bourse. 'My income is forty thousand livres,' she said in 1875. 'I am growing old with dignity.'[27] She amassed such wealth that she kept an apartment in the boulevard Haussmann, and – an hour away, by train – a châlet on the shores of Lake Enghien. (Villemessant observed what he called 'a characteristic detail: whenever she takes a train to the country, she always gets into the "Ladies only" compartment'.[28]) At Enghien, Alice Ozy was known for the splendour and variety of her roses;[29] and she would wander, in summer, from room to room, scattering rose petals, filling her châlet with the scent of flowers.

But time seemed to tick past more and more slowly, friends grew increasingly rare; only a few loyal admirers, like Gautier and Paul de Saint-Victor, the dramatic critic, still occasionally came to see her. Sad and lonely, seeing herself forgotten, she abandoned the name which had made her famous, and reverted to her real name, Madame Pilloy. She decided to retreat more completely to Enghien; and in April 1867, at the Hôtel Drouot, some of her possessions were sold: jewels, *objets d'art*, porcelain, delftware, furniture, bronzes and paintings. They would bring her some sixty thousand francs; but on the day of the sale she regretted that she had scattered so many mementoes. She withdrew some, and bought back others; later she tried hard to buy back the lost décor of her life.[30]

Age was unkind to her; at sixty-five she was photographed with a dog on her knees: dowdy, and fussily dressed. The camera revealed a décolletage which was now pitiably gross. She had no relatives, except nephews and nieces who, she felt, were just waiting for her fortune. She travelled from Saint-Malo to Rheims, from Nancy to Dieppe; she tried to forget the winter at Cannes, or at Amélie-les-Bains. She had long outlived her happiness, her solitude became overwhelming, and once she had to enter a home at Auteuil for a nervous breakdown. 'Dear, faithful friend,' she wrote to Arthur Chassériau, the painter's nephew, in 1889. 'You will be very glad to know that I am a little better. Death still refuses to have me: he is very wrong, I should be very happy to quit this sad existence.'[31]

'The man who had once spoken to her, heart to heart, remained hers all his life,' Edmond About had written in *Madelon*. 'And so people said that, in real danger, she would only have to beat a drum to reassemble an army.'[32] The truth was different. Some friends had forgotten her, and some had died. Few pleasures remained to the ageing Mme Pilloy, except the occasional visits of the Duc d'Aumale, who still felt some affection for his first mistress. And then there was her friendship with Baron Chassériau; he would talk to her about his uncle, show her the mementoes he was collecting. It was thanks to him that she could live with the damaged portrait of the Queen of Spain, the memory of her most loving liaison.[33]

Alice Ozy, who had loved Chassériau, died on 4 March 1893. She was seventy-two. Years ago she had adopted a child, the son of a Spanish woman, and promised to bring him up as an *honnête homme*. As an old woman, still loving children, she left all her fortune, two million, nine hundred thousand francs, to a theatrical charity, the Société des Artistes dramatiques, for the upbringing and education of the children of needy actors.[34] She is buried at Père-Lachaise, and a white marble statue of the Virgin and Child, by Doré, guards her tomb.

10

La Dame aux Camélias

Alphonsine Plessis, called Marie Duplessis,
later Mme la Comtesse de Perregaux (1824–47)

Early in the 1840s, Judith Bernat, the actress, Mme Judith of the Théâtre des
Variétés, was convalescing after a serious illness. Every day she received a
splendid bouquet. The flowers were brought, said her maid, by a beautiful
woman, apparently from the highest society, who refused to give her name
or to enter the house. As time went on, Madame Judith found the anonymity
intolerable, and at last she wrote a letter for her admirer, insisting that she
must make herself known. The mysterious woman answered:

Forgive me for hiding my name from you. I was afraid that, if you knew it,
you would refuse my flowers. And now I'm afraid that, when I reveal it, you'll
be sorry you received them.

Your devoted and unworthy admirer,
MARIE DUPLESSIS.

Mme Judith asked Marie Duplessis to call, and found her to be a young
girl of remarkable charm. 'She was very slim, one might almost call her
thin, but wonderfully delicate and slender; she had an angelic oval face,
black eyes caressing in their melancholy, a dazzling complexion and, above
all, splendid hair. Oh, that beautiful black silk hair!'[1]

The girl who had disarmed Mme Judith came from Lower Normandy.
She had been born in the village of Saint-Germain-de-Clairfeuille on 15
January 1824. She was the daughter of Marin Plessis, a travelling tinker, who
was himself the son of a prostitute and a country priest, Louis Descours. From
her father's side, Alphonsine (to give her her true name) may have inherited
her amorous nature; from her mother, of gentle descent, she may have
inherited her perfect manners. Her parents' marriage was unhappy; she was

their second daughter, and Marin was so disappointed that Alphonsine was not a boy, that he ill-treated his wife from the day of the child's birth, and Mme Plessis left home and became lady's maid to an Englishwoman in Paris.

She died, it is said, when Alphonsine was eight. The delicate little girl was entrusted to Mme Boisard, her mother's cousin, who had three young children of her own. At the age of twelve, Alphonsine was already roaming the fields, and meeting undesirable society. At last, it seems, she yielded to the entreaties of a farm-hand, and Mme Boisard sent her home to her father. Marin placed her as an apprentice with a laundress. One day (for he had always been a disreputable character) he took her to see a friend, a bachelor in his seventies by the name of Plantier, who lived in an out-of-the-way country house. He left her there. When she finally made her way back to the laundry, she was dismissed. She had no alternative: she returned to Plantier. She was then fourteen.

Eventually she escaped to an inn at Exmes, where she became a maid-of-all-work at sixty francs a month. It was nearly a year before Marin appeared, took her away, and put her with an umbrella manufacturer at Gacé. Two months later father and daughter set off together for Paris, where Alphonsine was left with some distant relations who kept a shop in the rue des Deux-Écus. Marin Plessis returned to Normandy, and died in the winter of 1839–1840. Alphonsine was employed by a laundress, and then by a milliner, until, in the summer of 1839, she happened to meet Monsieur Nollet, a restaurant proprietor in the Galerie Montpensier. He soon installed her in an apartment in the rue de l'Arcade.[2]

She hid her face [Mme Judith remembered] when she told me how she had taken up prostitution.

'Why did I sell myself? Because honest work would never have brought me the luxury I craved for, irresistibly. Whatever I may seem to be, I promise you I'm not covetous or debauched. I wanted to know the refinements and pleasures of artistic taste, the joy of living in elegant and cultivated society . . . I've always chosen my friends. And I've loved, oh, yes, I've really loved, but no one has ever responded to my love. That is the real horror of my life!'[3]

Nestor Roqueplan, the director of the Théâtre des Variétés, claimed to have met Alphonsine Plessis one evening on the Pont-Neuf; she was shabby, and gazing longingly at a fried potato stall. He bought her a cornet of *pommes frites*, which she ate avidly. About a year later, in the Ranelagh Gardens, the pleasure-gardens in Paris, he saw her with a young French nobleman. She was established.[4]

The nobleman was presumably the Duc de Guiche-Grammont, who spent ten thousand francs on Alphonsine in three months, and then disappeared.

La Dame Aux Camelias

Marie Duplessis, la Dame aux camélias, wearing her favourite flowers. From a miniature by an unknown artist.

Below. The *foyer de danse* at the Opéra in the 1840s. The Opéra was one of Marie Duplessis' favourite theatres.
Bottom. An arcade in the Palais Royal in the 1840s.

The Ranelagh Gardens in Paris in 1846. It was here that
Nestor Roqueplan, director of the Théâtre des Variétés, saw
Marie Duplessis with the Duc de Guiche-Grammont.

Alexandre Dumas *fils* (1824–95) made the story of
Marie Duplessis his own. His novel, *la Dame aux
camélias*, was published in 1848; in 1852 it was
dramatised and triumphantly performed at the
Vaudeville. Verdi's opera *la Traviata*, based on
the story, was heard for the first time in the
following year.

ALEXANDRE DUMAS FILS

LA DAME
AUX CAMÉLIAS

PRÉFACE DE JULES JANIN

ÉDITION ILLUSTRÉE
PAR GAVARNI

PROPRIÉTÉ DE MM. MICHEL LÉVY FRÈRES

PARIS
LIBRAIRIE MODERNE
BOULEVARD DE SÉBASTOPOL (RIVE GAUCHE) ET RUE DE LA HARPE
GUSTAVE HAVARD, ÉDITEUR
1858

Above. La Dame aux camélias:
title-page of the edition
of 1858, illustrated by
Gavarni.
Right. Gavarni's impressions
of Marguerite Gautier
and Armand Duval.

Left. Franz Liszt (1811–86), from the portrait by Lehmann. Liszt gave piano lessons to 'poor Mariette Duplessis' and said she was the first woman he had loved.

Top. Jules Janin, the dramatic critic (1804–74). He considered Marie Duplessis 'a woman of wit and taste and good sense'.

Centre. A box at the Théâtre des Italiens, in the days of la Dame aux camélias. From *l'Été à Paris* by Jules Janin, 1843.

Opposite. Marie Duplessis at the theatre, 1845. From a watercolour by Camille Roqueplan.

The old passage de l'Opéra in the rue Le Peletier. It was here that the
men-about-town waited for the dancers.

Years later, after her death, when Dumas *fils* had made her the heroine of *La Dame aux camélias*, some people claimed that the Duc was the model for Armand Duval, the hero of the novel and the play:

The late Duc de Grammont [wrote William Osgood Field] was, when Prince de Bidache, the prototype from which Dumas *fils* took his Armand Duval ... Of course, the original of Marguerite Gautier was Marie Duplessis, a famous demi-mondaine, who was madly in love with 'le beau Agénor' as the young Prince de Bidache was then called. All this was long before my time, but I had it from Dumas *fils* himself.[5]

At about the time that 'le beau Agénor' vanished from her life, Alphonsine had chosen to call herself Marie Duplessis: Marie, she said, because it was the name of the Virgin, and Duplessis, because she hoped some day to buy the Plessis estate at Nonant.[6]

In 1841, Marie was the mistress of a young vicomte attached to the Ministry of the Interior; that winter, she disappeared briefly from Paris, and went to Versailles, where she gave birth to his son. The vicomte (who became a prefect in Burgundy) placed the child with a nurse in the provinces, and later told Marie that it had died of pneumonia. It is hard to know if this was true. In 1869, a man of about twenty-seven called on Marie Duplessis's elder sister and asked to see the portrait of Marie. When he went away, he left a card: 'Judelet. Employé de Commerce, Tours.' His face was remarkably like the face in the picture.[7]

Marie herself, confirmed Gustave Claudin, in *Mes Souvenirs*, was a woman of exceptional beauty.

Her distinction, grace and charm were sure to make her a star in the world of gallantry ... Marie Duplessis was thin and pale, and had magnificent hair which came down to the ground. Her delicate beauty, her fine skin, marked by its little blue veins, indicated that she was consumptive, and would die young. She had a presentiment of this, and her bursts of nervous gaiety were always silenced by sudden moods of sadness. She was wayward, capricious and wild, adoring today what she had hated yesterday, and *vice versa*.

She possessed the art of elegance to the highest degree. You could certainly say of Marie Duplessis that she had *style*. No one tried to copy her inimitable originality. As long as the florists could provide them, she carried bouquets of white camellias.[8]

An old *ouvreuse* at the Opéra called her *la Dame aux camélias* long before Dumas *fils* wrote his novel.[9]

Early in 1842, she was living at 28, rue du Mont-Thabor, a little street parallel to the rue de Rivoli. Her way of life was regular. She generally rose at eleven, took her *petit déjeuner*, read the papers, practised the piano for fifteen minutes, dressed, and drove in the Bois, and walked, and then received her visitors. She ate a light dinner, went to the theatre, then she had supper (perhaps at the Café de Paris) and danced and gambled. Her greatest pleasure was the play, and her favourite theatres were the Théâtre-Français and the two Opéras. She never missed a first night, and the *régisseurs* always sent her, unasked, a ticket for a stage-box.[10] During the intervals she greeted her visitors; famous actors and actresses paid their respects, among them Marie Dorval, the star of Romantic drama, the heroine of Dumas's *Antony* and of Vigny's *Chatterton*.

Marie Duplessis was no common courtesan. She was also received at social functions which others of her kind would not have dreamed of attending.

She had a natural tact [recorded Albert Vandam, in *An Englishman in Paris*], and an instinctive refinement which no education could have enhanced. She never made grammatical mistakes, no coarse expression ever passed her lips. Lola Montès could not make friends; Alphonsine Plessis could not make enemies. She never became riotous like the others, not even boisterous; for amidst the most animated scenes she was haunted by the sure knowledge that she would die young, and life, but for that knowledge, would have been very sweet to her. Amidst these scenes, she would often sit and chat to me: she liked me, because I never paid her many compliments, although I was but six years older than the most courted woman of her time. The story of her being provided for by a foreign nobleman because she was so like his daughter, was not a piece of fiction on Dumas's part; it was a positive fact.[11]

It was at Spa, in the late autumn of 1844 or 1845, that Marie Duplessis met Baron de Stackelberg. He came of an ancient Polish family; he was old enough to be her father. Indeed, she reminded him strangely of his daughter, who had recently died. He tried to rescue her from her way of life. He asked her to abandon prostitution, and to name an income; he would give it to her in perpetuity.

Fatherlike, he installed her in the boulevard de la Madeleine; her apartment was almost facing the church of that name. It was almost 'as if she had sought protection from the saint who, before she devoted herself to God, had trafficked in her beauty'.[12]

She showed me her apartment [Mme Judith remembered]; it was all fragrant with flowers, for it is not true to say that she only liked the flowers that had no scent. She loved them all; it is Dumas's imagination which credited her with an exclusive liking for camellias.

The interior of her apartment was Louis XV in style . . . There were sofas covered in Beauvais tapestry, Clodion terracottas on rosewood stands, chased copper ornaments by Gonthière on divine chiffonniers by Riesener. It was furnished like a palace or a museum.

She told me about every piece with the passion of a *connaisseuse*. She laughed as she showed me a Sèvres biscuit statuette of a drunk bacchante teased by a faun . . .

'Are you happy?' I asked.

'Yes!' she answered . . . And then, suddenly growing grave: 'Oh, no, I'm not happy, but you wouldn't suspect it!'[13]

She might, as Albert Vandam explained, have led the most retired existence:

She might, like so many demi-mondaines have done since, have bought herself a country-house, re-entered 'the paths of respectability', have had a pew in the parish church, been in constant communication with the vicar, prolonged her life by several years, and died in the odour of sanctity: but, notwithstanding her desperate desire to live, her very nature revolted at such self-exile.[14]

For a while she lived in chastity, as she had promised the Baron, and hoped that a young man would marry her, that she could devote herself to him, and reform. But no young suitor claimed her hand, the Baron's fatherly visits grew less frequent, and, in despair, she returned to her life of sin.

She still could not be a common prostitute: she is said to have given some twenty thousand francs a year to charity. She was religious: she often heard Mass at the Madeleine, and, after her death, someone found, among her papers, an invoice from a local upholsterer for a prie-Dieu, covered in velvet, with gilt nails. If she confessed her lesser sins, her confession was disarming: she found it hard to speak the truth, but then, as she explained: 'I like telling lies because they keep the teeth white.'[15] There was something childlike about her minor pleasures: about the fact that her favourite sweets were *raisins glacés*. Her restaurant bills at the Maison d'Or show that on 30 August 1845 she dined off a dozen biscuits, a franc's worth of macaroons, and a glass of maraschino; on 17 September her lunch appears to have been twelve meringues glacées.[16] Perhaps it was her curious innocence, as well as her distinction of manner, her spirited conversation, that drew celebrities to her: she even entertained Lola Montès, a courtesan the antithesis of herself. Her beauty and natural sweetness attracted men of stature, and among them were Dumas *fils* and Franz Liszt.

It was, recalled Jules Janin, the dramatic critic, in about 1845, in the crowded foyer of some boulevard theatre, that he and Liszt had seen her for the first time.

Head held high, she made her way through the astonished throng, and we were surprised, Liszt and I, when she came and sat down familiarly on the bench beside us, for neither he nor I had ever spoken to her. She was a woman of wit and taste and good sense. She began by addressing herself to the great musician; she told him that she had recently heard him, and that he had made her dream . . . And so they talked throughout the third act of the melodrama . . .[17]

Janin saw her again, in a box at the Opéra, and again at a gala ball which was held in Brussels to inaugurate the Chemin de Fer du Nord. As for Liszt, who gave her piano lessons, he felt more than a music master's affection for her. 'Poor Mariette Duplessis,' he would write to Mme d'Agoult (who had been his mistress) after Marie's death. 'She was the first woman with whom I was in love.'[18]

Mariette, as he called her, lived intensely; she meant to make the most of her brief existence. It was at a masked ball at the Opéra that she excited the attention of Alice Ozy's lover, Comte Édouard de Perregaux, the son of the King's banker. She refused to disclose her identity, and when she was invited to supper at the Maison d'Or, she would not accept until she had seen the list of the guests. Only when she saw the name of Perregaux, whom she wanted to meet, did she agree to come and remove her mask. Henri de Pène, the journalist, who was present, remembered her first words to the Count: 'I often see you riding in the Bois de Boulogne, Monsieur, and your mount seems to delight in carrying such an accomplished cavalier.' This, according to de Pène, was the prelude to the liaison which inspired *La Dame aux camélias* and *La Traviata*. De Pène, unlike William Osgood Field, maintained that the real Armand Duval was Édouard de Perregaux (he even remembered that Marie had shrimps, prawns and lobster for supper that night, and champagne, which Perregaux uncorked himself). But whatever the origin of Dumas's novel and play, and of Verdi's opera, the Comte completely won Marie's heart. Alice Ozy was abandoned, and a new *grande passion* arose overnight.[19]

At first it seemed merely another famous, extravagant liaison: Marie went to the races with her lover, wearing a dress on which the lace was worth ten thousand francs.[20] But the relationship was deeper than many people suspected: on 21 February 1846, at Kensington Registry Office, Marie Duplessis became the Comtesse de Perregaux.[21] She had earned the outward sign of respectability.

Unfortunately the marriage soon foundered, and Édouard de Perregaux went hunting at Melton while his wife returned to the boulevard de la Madeleine. They saw little of each other; the Comte found himself in financial straits, and contributed nothing to her household expenses. She was already gravely ill. 'The last time I saw her,' remembered M. Des Hays, 'some months before her death, was on the day of the races at the Croix-de-Berny. I had gone to see the procession of carriages on the Esplanade des Invalides. I can see her still, pale and distressed, all dressed in white, in her faded green landau, borne along at full trot by four splendid white horses.'[22] To Liszt, who saw her again, about now, she said:

'I shall not live; I'm a strange woman, I shan't be able to cling to this life that I cannot live and cannot bear. Take me with you, take me away wherever you want; I shan't be in your way, I sleep all day, in the evening you'll let me go to the theatre, and at night you can do what you like with me!'

I've never told you [continued Liszt to Mme d'Agoult] how strangely attached I became to that charming creature during my last stay in Paris. I'd told her that I would take her to Constantinople, because it was really the only possible journey I could take with her . . .[23]

Marie Duplessis did not go to Constantinople; that summer she seems to have gone to Spa, and then to Baden. She returned to Paris, and led a wilder life than ever. On the first approach of winter she took to her bed. In November her doctors, Davaine and Chomel, prescribed ten grammes of Karabé syrup at night for her cough; if her cough grew worse, they said, she must inhale infusions of poppy flowers. She was only allowed to drink Eau de Bussang.[24]

Her friends fell away, her debts increased; towards the end of January 1847, in the final stages of consumption, she went to the Palais-Royal for the première of a frivolous vaudeville, *Les Pommes de terre malades*.

At about the third scene of Act I [recorded Alfred Delvau, in *Les Lions du Jour*], there appeared in a stage-box, in which two lackeys, gold-laced from head to foot, had set her down, a woman – or rather the shadow of a woman, white and diaphanous . . .

What was the shadow which attracted general attention by its consumptive pallor and a large bouquet of white camellias? Marie Duplessis was going to the theatre for the last time; for the last time she and her white camellias were presenting themselves to the public view . . . The two gold-laced lackeys who had borne her from her carriage to her box bore her back again from her box to her carriage as the actors were beginning the final song . . .

Marie Duplessis was dying, Marie Duplessis was dead.[25]

She died, in fact, at three o'clock on the morning of 3 February. She was just twenty-three. Liszt wrote that 'some unknown, mysterious chord from an antique elegy echoes in my heart when I recall her'.[26]

He recorded later that, even when she was dying, 'in that apartment in the boulevard de la Madeleine, there had been nothing but shameless pillage, and the bailiffs, sent by implacable creditors, were tearing away the very curtains of the bed on which she lay in her agony'.[27] John Forster, in his *Life of Dickens*, told another story of her last hours.

The disease of satiety [he wrote], which only less often than hunger passes for a broken heart, had killed her. 'What do you want?' asked the most famous of the Paris physicians, at a loss for her exact complaint. At last she answered: 'To see my mother [*sic*].' She was sent for: and there came a simple Breton peasant-woman clad in the quaint garb of her province, who prayed by her bed until she died.[28]

Marie's body was shrouded in lace, and laid in a coffin full of flowers. Her husband and Baron de Stackelberg attended her funeral at the Cimetière Montmartre.

She had the supreme good taste [remembered Jules Janin] to want to be buried at daybreak, in some obscure, lonely place, without fuss, without noise, just as some honest woman might go to rejoin her husband, her father, mother and children, and all she loved . . .
But it happened, in spite of her, that her death was a kind of event: people talked about it . . . And then, they opened the doors of her house . . .
The clock of olden days, which had struck the hour for Madame de Pompadour and Madame Dubarry, still struck the hour, as it had always done; the silver candelabra held the candles ready for the last evening conversation . . . Everything still spoke of her. The birds were singing in their gilded cage; in the cabinets, through the glass, one saw the rarest Sèvres, the most exquisite painted Dresden . . .
I heard the greatest ladies, the most fashionable women in Paris exclaiming at the beauty and rarity of the smallest accessories on her dressing-table. Her comb reached a ridiculous price; her hairbrush fetched its weight in gold . . . They sold some shoes which she had worn, and honest women fought as to who should wear Cinderella's slipper. Everything was sold, even her shabbiest shawl, which was already three years old; even her brilliant-feathered macaw, which repeated a rather sad little tune its mistress had taught it. They sold her portraits, they sold her love-letters, they sold some of her hair, everything was for sale, and her family, who averted their gaze when she passed in her crested carriage, rapidly carried along by her English horses, gorged themselves triumphantly with all the gold that her relics had produced.[29]

'Wonderful was the admiration and sympathy,' wrote Forster; 'and it culminated when Eugène Sue bought her prayer-book at the sale.' Forster's last talk with Dickens, who was then in Paris, 'was of the danger underlying all this'. Indeed, 'Dickens wished at one time to have pointed the moral of this life and death'.[30]
Happily for literature, it was the younger Dumas who made the subject

of Marie Duplessis his own. Someone observed that many women would probably have liked to earn Marie's jewels and dresses on the terms on which she had earned them. The observation caught the attention of Dumas *fils*; he conceived the idea of his novel, *La Dame aux camélias*.[31] It was published in 1848, some eighteen months after the death of Marie Duplessis. In 1852 it was dramatised and first performed at the Vaudeville. Dumas *fils*, snapped Arsène Houssaye, had made Marie Duplessis 'a saint twice over in the calendar of hussies'.[32]

Viel-Castel, the memoir-writer, the vigilant collector of contemporary scandal, professed himself to be shocked by Dumas's play.

La Dame aux camélias [he wrote] is an insult to everything that the censorship should make respected. This play is shameful for the epoch which allows it, the government which tolerates it, the public which applauds it. Every evening, the Vaudeville is packed full, the place de la Bourse is thick with carriages. Women from the highest society are not afraid to show themselves in the boxes. *La Dame aux camélias* is in fact a full-scale public scandal . . .

Such turpitude is not to be analysed, it is ignoble, but the spectacle presented by the audience itself is even worse.[33]

Viel-Castel was living in sin (and was later dismissed from his post at the Louvre for stealing some of its treasures). He was in no position to pass moral judgments. Nor in fact had he known Marie Duplessis. Against his comments should be set those of an Englishman living in Paris, Albert Vandam, who had often met her in the last years of her life.

The world at large, and especially the English [wrote Vandam], have always made very serious mistakes, both with regard to the heroine of the younger Dumas's novel and play, and the author himself. They have taxed him with having chosen an unworthy subject and, by idealising it, taught a lesson of vice instead of virtue; they have taken it for granted that Alphonsine Plessis was no better than her kind. She was much better than that . . . She was not the commonplace courtesan the goody-goody people have thought fit to proclaim her . . .

The sober fact is that Dumas *fils* did not idealize anything at all, and, least of all, Alphonsine Plessis's character. Though very young at the time of her death, he was then already much more of a philosopher than a poet.[34]

La Dame aux camélias, wrote Théophile Gautier in 1870, 'is perhaps the least perfect work of Alexandre, but it is certainly the most seductive . . . We are involved in the fate of Marguerite Gautier . . .; we feel that the poet loves her or has loved her, and that he keeps an affectionate memory of her.'[35]

Every writer, said Gustave Claudin, wanted to re-shape the play in his fashion; but it was with the play as it had been with Marie Duplessis herself.

169

It was impossible to imitate the one or the other. La Dame aux camélias would remain a type like Manon.[36]

The comparison had often occurred to Marie Duplessis herself. After her death, in the boulevard de la Madeleine, they found a copy of Prévost's *Manon Lescaut*. In the margins there were notes in her own hand.[37]

11

La Présidente

Aglaé-Joséphine Savatier, later Apollonie Sabatier (1822–89)

Many nineteenth-century courtesans were forgotten long before they died. Some lost their beauty, their means of livelihood, and awaited death in poverty. Some vanished into middle-class respectability, and some were proud to lose their notoriety, to find forgetfulness in marriages of remarkable distinction. But posterity, like death, is a great leveller, and the famous Salade-à-la-Russe has been forgotten with La Madone (who became Princess Soltikoff). Only those courtesans who left their mark on literature or music or the visual arts have earned their immortality; and in the whole turbulent demi-monde, the world of the courtesans, there seem to be only two who have earned both immortality and gratitude.

Marie Duplessis won them because her death led Dumas *fils* to write *La Dame aux camélias*, and Verdi to compose *La Traviata*. Aglaé-Apollonie Sabatier richly deserved them for her diverse, brilliant, lasting inspiration. She achieved more than Lola Montès, who held Bavaria and its king in fee; she achieved more than la Païva, for all her Aladdin wealth. La Présidente's triumph was to be loved for her goodness as well as her beauty: to be the understanding friend as well as the muse of some of the most notable men of her time. On Sunday evenings, round her table at 4, rue Frochot, she assembled a personal Court which the Emperor could not match, and even his cousin, Princess Mathilde, that admirable patron of the arts, must have envied. La Présidente was the most endearing, most respected of all the courtesans. Her influence was entirely benign, and it was directly responsible for some of the finest poems in the French language.

★

La Présidente, as Gautier christened her, and as posterity calls her, was born on 7 April 1822.[1] She was the daughter of the Vicomte Harmand d'Abancourt, Prefect of the Ardennes, and Léa-Marguerite Martin, a young sempstress. Through the good offices of the Prefect, Léa-Marguerite was married to André Savatier, a sergeant in the 47th Infantry Regiment; Sergeant Savatier agreed to recognise the child, and to give her his name. She was duly baptised as Aglaé-Joséphine Savatier; the name Apollonie had been given her (so she would always say), but the registrar of births refused to use it, as it did not appear among those of the saints. The moment she gained her independence, she adopted it, and changed her surname to the nobler Sabatier.

She spent her childhood in Mézières, Strasbourg and, finally, in Paris; when she was three, her nominal father left the army and the family settled in the quartier de la Monnaie and then in the rue des Dames, in the village of les Batignolles. André Savatier died in the autumn of 1832; Mme Savatier gave birth to a second daughter the following year.

Aglaé showed promise, already, of becoming a singer; and the principal of a nearby *pensionnat* was so impressed by her voice that she took her in at a special fee. It soon became clear that Aglaé was also endowed with quite uncommon beauty. When she was fifteen or sixteen, Auguste Blanchard and Charles Jalabert, two young pupils of Delaroche, collaborated in painting her portrait. She was wearing a black velvet bodice, a scarlet skirt, and a broad-brimmed hat draped in black lace. In this fancy dress, which she had worn at a carnival ball, she made her first appearance in the world of the arts.

She still seemed destined to be a singer; she had singing lessons from Mme Damoreau-Cinti, who had turned to teaching since she had retired from the stage. She also took piano lessons, and, no doubt, she might have been a concert artiste or sung in opera if, at a charity concert, she had not been introduced to one of the organisers. Alfred Mosselman determined her future.

No portrait of Mosselman can be found, but he was painted, in later life, by Dubufe. He was, it seems, smoking a fat cigar. He was fair-haired and bearded. One imagines a massive, sensual and prosperous man, and perhaps imagination is not wide of the mark. Mosselman came of a noble Belgian family, and he had come from Brussels to Paris, after the Revolution of 1830, with his brother-in-law, Comte Le Hon, whose famous wife was to be the mistress of the Duc de Morny. Le Hon was Belgian Minister to the Court of Louis-Philippe, and, for five years, Mosselman had been an attaché at the Belgian Legation. He had left the diplomatic service in

1837 to become an industrialist (his father was not only a banker, but the owner of the most prosperous coal-mines in Belgium). Since Mosselman was not a philistine, he also became a patron of the arts, and showed a taste for Romantic painting and for what was to be known as the Barbizon School.[2]

Aglaé Sabatier was dazzled by the prestige of an unknown world. Too excited – and, perhaps, too young – to consider her future, she became Mosselman's mistress. He installed her in an apartment at 4, rue Frochot.

★

The rue Frochot was in what was called the quartier Bréda – or, as the dandies called it, Breda Street; and, whatever her later distinction, Aglaé Sabatier was at first only a pretty girl who had found a rich lover and allowed him to set her up in the *quartier* of the kept woman.

However, since love and the arts are often found in the same place, the quartier Bréda was also the artistic quarter of Paris. On the slopes of the Butte Montmartre, it was sometimes called the New Athens. When Aglaé Sabatier was living in rue Frochot, her neighbours included Théodore Rousseau, the landscape painter, and Théodore Chassériau, who had just decorated the chapel of Sainte-Marie-l'Égyptienne, at the church of Saint-Merri. Delacroix lived nearby; so did Berlioz, Gérard de Nerval, and Théophile Gautier, Henri Monnier, the impersonator, and Henry Murger, the author of *Scènes de la vie de Bohème* (the work which would, years hence, inspire Puccini's opera).

Since Alfred Mosselman was married, he sometimes needed a confidant and go-between; he found one in Fernand Boissard, man of letters, musician, painter and art-collector. Boissard lived in the Île Saint-Louis, in one of the sumptuous apartments of the Hôtel Pimodan, 17, quai d'Anjou.

The Hôtel Pimodan, at this time, saw a number of Bohemian tenants. The first was Roger de Beauvoir, the dandy and minor Romantic writer,[3] who was soon obliged to sell his art collection and to leave his suite on the *piano nobile*. In a humble attic room, papered in black and red and hastily furnished, with a single window looking over the Seine, lived Baudelaire, the art critic, and the translator of Edgar Allan Poe, already writing the poems of *Les Fleurs du mal*. It was, however, Boissard's rooms, and especially his great salon decorated in the purest Louis XIV style, that have left their mark on literary history; for here the *club des haschichins* held their meetings, and Baudelaire, Balzac, and Gautier, the author of *Mademoiselle de Maupin* and *Giselle*, drifted into their frenetic hashish dreams. Indeed, it was in Boissard's salon, in the summer of 1843, that Gautier first met Baudelaire.

His appearance was striking. His jet black hair was close cropped, and, coming to regular points on his dazzling white forehead, it covered his head like a kind of Saracen helmet. His eyes, the colour of Spanish tobacco, had a deep, intelligent look, perhaps a little too searching; as for his mouth, . . . a slight silky moustache hid its contour, but allowed one to perceive the mobile, voluptuous, ironic curves like those of the mouths once painted by Leonardo da Vinci. His fine, delicate nose, slightly rounded, with quivering nostrils, seemed to scent some vague and far-off fragrance . . .

He was wearing a frock coat of some shiny black material, drab-coloured trousers, white socks and patent leather pumps, all of it meticulously clean and correct . . . One might say that he was a dandy who had strayed into Bohemia, but kept his rank and manners and that cult of self which is typical of the man imbued with the principles of Brummell.[4]

Baudelaire was not the only visitor to imprint himself, that day, on Gautier's receptive inward eye. In Boissard's salon, *le bon Théo* saw Aglaé Sabatier. She sat near the window, and, having cast off

her little black lace shawl, and the most delicious little green bonnet that Lucy Hocquet or Madame Baudrand had ever trimmed, she was shaking out her red-brown hair, which was still wet, because she had come from the École de Natation; and her whole person, draped in muslin, exhaled, like a naiad's, the freshness of the bathe. With glance and smile, she encouraged the verbal tourney, and from time to time threw in a word of her own, sometimes bantering, sometimes approving, and the battle raged harder than ever.[5]

In one swift impression, Gautier caught Apollonie – as he called her – with all the grace and freshness of her twenty-one years. In his sketch one seems to catch the essence of her nature: her ease, vitality, and radiant health. She is elegant, gay, assured, and already presiding over her brilliant Bohemia.

Mosselman, too, was determined to have her likeness in perpetuity. He asked Jean-Baptiste Clésinger, the sculptor, to make a cast of her body. The commission suggests a boastful owner, not a devoted lover or a civilised amateur of the arts, and at first Apollonie rejected the idea. One regrets that she agreed, at last, to the humiliation: that she countenanced Mosselman's vulgarity. But Clésinger made a single cast of her *Rêve d'Amour*.

However, since it failed to fulfil Mosselman's expectations, he asked Clésinger to sculpt a bust of Apollonie, and a marble statue, based on the cast. Long before the Salon opened, the statue was the talk of the Paris studios. In 1847, Clésinger's exhibits at the Salon included the bust of Mme A. S. and (No. 2047) *La Femme piquée par un serpent*. The crowds collected round the figure which – though it was marble – writhed in an ecstasy of pain on a bed of tinted flowers.

Gustave Planche, who was known for the acerbity of his criticism, condemned the statue dourly in the *Revue des Deux Mondes*:

To begin with, this woman stung by a serpent is not expressing pain in the least; the serpent is clearly an extra, it has quite obviously been added later. If one really had to define the expression on this face, if one had to say what it meant, what emotion it revealed, certainly no honest man endowed with commonsense would call it pain. It is impossible, in fact, to see anything there except the convulsions of pleasure.[6]

Delacroix dismissed the statue as 'a daguerrotype in sculpture';[7] Achille Devéria, the lithographer and book-illustrator, agreed that the statue appealed to sensuality rather than to taste, 'and this is a bad tendency which must not be encouraged'.[8] Gautier, a lover of the sensual, and already an admirer of Apollonie, praised the realism of the statue; in *Le Poème de la Femme: Marbre de Paros*, published two years later, he still dreamed of the living marble figure:

Sa tête penche et se renverse;
Haletante, dressant les seins,
Aux bras du rêve qui la berce,
Elle tombe sur ses coussins.

Ses paupières battent des ailes
Sur leurs globes d'argent bruni,
Et l'on voit monter ses prunelles
Dans la nacre de l'infini.

D'un linceul de point d'Angleterre
Que l'on recouvre sa beauté:
L'extase l'a prise à la terre;
Elle est morte de volupté![9]

Clésinger himself remained haunted by his statue. In the Salon of 1848, he showed a *Bacchante couchée* which was closely related to the *Femme au serpent*. It won him a medal and the Légion-d'honneur (though it only gained him an honourable mention at the Great Exhibition in London three years later). Copies were made of both statues: Émile de Girardin owned a small version of the *Femme au serpent* in Carrara marble. There were hundreds of counterfeit copies in plaster. As late as 1873, Clésinger made a new version; in 1878 he exhibited a terracotta reproduction. The original statue is now in the Louvre; it has the erotic charm of a Boucher painting. Yet the excessively ornate base, the coy addition of the serpent, and the choice of such a theme for marble, show, above all, the vulgarity of the sculptor and his patron. *La Femme piquée par un serpent* remains a likeness of a physically perfect woman; it is not a masterpiece of art.

★

One cannot deny that Apollonie Sabatier herself had a coarse streak in her nature. The moulding of the *Rêve d'Amour*, the sculpting of *La Femme piquée par un serpent*, were not alone in suggesting the permissive atmosphere of 4, rue Frochot. When the Goncourts defined Apollonie, years later, as 'une vivandière de faunes' – or, rather, as a sutler of satyrs – they implied the licence of her salon. One suspects that the licence was largely verbal: it is reflected, here and there, in the heavy gallantry of Flaubert's letters, the obscenities of Maxime du Camp's correspondence. It is seen, especially, in the famous letter which Gautier sent la Présidente from Rome, in the autumn of 1850.[10]

He wrote it, perhaps, to relieve his feelings, for he was on his way home from Venice, after a passionate interlude with his Corsican mistress, Marie Mattei.[11] But the fact that he sent la Présidente this enormity, 'this ribald letter, meant to replace the Sunday obscenities', is a comment on her character. Gautier's *Lettre à la Présidente* is not a Rabelaisian masterpiece; it is simply, as he intended, an outrageous essay in *grivoiserie*. It was a kind of essay which la Présidente enjoyed, for Gautier's published letters to her, which cover a decade, show the same extraordinary licence. They do not enhance the prestige of the writer or the recipient.

But one should not be too serious over the tone of conversation in the quartier Bréda. The woman who makes it her profession to please men can hardly be prudish; she may, indeed, welcome freedom of language as a sign that men feel happy and unembarrassed in her company. Verbal licence may, after all, be a tribute to her powers of attraction; and Princess Mathilde, the cousin of Napoleon III, who earned the name of Notre Dame des Arts, was not averse to frank conversation. Art, like love, demands emotional liberty. And the liberty which allowed Gautier to write his *Lettre à la Présidente* allowed him, also, to address her a delicately sensual poem in *Émaux et Camées*. *A une Robe rose* is his verbal tribute to a magnificently desirable woman. He presents Apollonie in perpetuity: her rose-pink dress revealing her superbly sculpted lines, and caressing her with all the warmth of his own unassuaged desires.

> Que tu me plais dans cette robe
> Qui te déshabille si bien,
> Faisant jaillir ta gorge en globe,
> Montrant tout nu ton bras païen!

Frêle comme une aile d'abeille,
Frais comme un cœur de rose-thé,
Son tissu, caresse vermeille,
Voltige autour de ta beauté.

De l'épiderme sur la soie
Glissent des frissons argentés,
Et l'étoffe à la chair renvoie
Ses éclairs roses reflétés.

D'où te vient cette robe étrange
Que semble faite de ta chair,
Trame vivante qui mélange
Avec ta peau son rose clair?

Est-ce à la rougeur de l'aurore,
A la coquille de Vénus,
Au bouton de sein près d'éclore,
Que sont pris ces tons inconnus?

Ou bien l'étoffe est-elle teinte
Dans les roses de ta pudeur?
Non; vingt fois modelée et peinte,
Ta forme connaît sa splendeur.

Jetant le voile qui te pèse,
Réalité que l'art rêva,
Comme la princesse Borghèse
Tu poserais pour Canova.

Et ces plis roses sont les lèvres
De mes désirs inapaisés,
Mettant au corps dont tu les sèvres
Une tunique de baisers.[12]

In another poem, *Apollonie*, in the same collection, Gautier recalls that la Présidente's Christian name makes her the sister of Apollo. It was a name which she alone, among the great courtesans of her epoch, richly deserved. While Gautier celebrated her physical attraction and statuesque beauty, Baudelaire had long worshipped her in secret.[13] He had met her first, it seems, at the Hôtel Pimodan; he had become a fairly frequent visitor at the rue Frochot. And while her abundant gaiety, her radiant health had sometimes made him bitter, in his jealous and resentful moods, he was enthralled by the goodness of her nature. With his mulatto mistress, Jeanne Duval, his *Vénus noire*, he had known all the torments, complexities and pleasures of physical love; but Apollonie was his *Vénus blanche*. She was more: she was *la Muse et la Madone*. She was an inaccessible woman: cut off from him by Mosselman, by her health and happiness, by the fact that she did not need him. She greeted him on a Sunday as she greeted any other visitor; and, moving in the same room, seated at the same table, she remained an unattainable ideal, a permanent, benign inspiration.

Baudelaire wrote her a cycle of poems; and he sent them to her with anonymous letters, written in a carefully disguised hand. The convention of secrecy made expression easier; perhaps, indeed, it made expression possible. But the convention was always empty. The poems clearly came from an intimate of the rue Frochot; and, among la Présidente's circle, only Baudelaire, profound and reticent, could have written them. Indeed, one day her young sister Adèle asked him directly if he was still addressing poems to her. But it was only in 1857, when *Les Fleurs du mal* were published, that Baudelaire discarded his transparent disguise of anonymity. On 18 August he sent la Présidente his book, and with it he sent his explanation.

For the first time in her life, Apollonie Sabatier found herself loved by a man who demanded nothing in return. She had known the largely physical love of Mosselman, the vulgarity of the Clésinger sculptures and of Gautier's *Lettre à la Présidente*; now she had inspired devotion of a quite different order. And, knowing that Baudelaire was timid, wanting to show her gratitude, she did what to her was most natural, and offered herself to him.

It seems that, for a single night, she became his mistress. She found herself, for the first time, to be in love. She had also destroyed, for ever, the image of *la Muse et la Madone*: the aura of the unattainable. Baudelaire had worshipped her as an ideal; now he saw that she was merely a woman. Perhaps *la Vénus blanche* proved to be unattractive, after *la Vénus noire*. She herself seems to have felt it, for on his drawing of Jeanne Duval she scribbled angrily: 'Son idéal!' Whatever the reason for the disaster, her night with Baudelaire destroyed his essential dream.

You see, my dear, my beauty [he wrote], that I have hateful prejudices about women. In fact, *I have no faith*; you have a fine soul, but, when all is said, it is the soul of a woman. Look how our situation has been utterly changed in a matter of days. In the first place, we are both afraid of hurting a good man who has the happiness of still loving you. And then we are both afraid of our own passion, because we know – at least I do – that there are bonds which are difficult to break. And then, and then . . . a few days ago you were a deity, which is so convenient, so noble, so inviolable. And now there you are, a woman. And suppose if, by some misfortune, I should acquire the right to be jealous! Oh, what torture even to think of it! But with someone like you, whose eyes are full of smiles and favours

Opposite: Ernest Meissonier, *A l'ombre des bosquets chante un jeune poète.*
Mme Sabatier, 'la très-bonne, la très-belle', is the standing figure.

for everyone, it would be martyrdom . . . I am rather a fatalist; but I do know that I have a horror of passion – because I have experienced it, with all its degradation . . .[14]

Most women would have been too hurt or too indignant to trouble any further about the relationship. It is a measure of Mme Sabatier's character that she used all her tact, her loving understanding, to play the part which she would not have chosen. She determined to be accepted as a friend.

Listen, dear [she answered], shall I tell you what I think? It is a cruel thought, and one which hurts me very much. I think you don't love me. That is why you have these fears, why you hesitate to contract a liaison – for in such conditions it would become a source of vexations for you and a continual torment for me. Do I not have the proof in a phrase in your letter? It is so explicit that it makes my blood turn cold. *In fact, I have no faith.* – You have no faith! But then you have no love. What can be the answer to that? Isn't it clarity itself? Oh my God! How I suffer at the thought, and how I want to weep on your breast! I feel that that would relieve me. Whatever has happened, I shall not change anything about our meeting tomorrow. I want to see you, even if it be only to practise my part as a friend. Oh! why did you try to see me again?[15]

It would be difficult to say why Baudelaire had done so. Perhaps he himself did not know the reason. Perhaps he did not dare to break a liaison with such brutality. Perhaps he wanted to be sure that he was right to break it. Apollonie could hardly understand him, for he seemed to seek and escape her, to love and hate her, to desire her and reject her. She wrote to him simply. Her letter showed a sensibility, a warmth of feeling, a comprehension of love which few, if any, courtesans could have matched.

What comedy or rather what drama are we performing? For I don't know what to think, and I must confess that I am deeply troubled. Your behaviour has been so strange, for the last few days, that I don't understand it at all, any more. It's too subtle for a dullard like me. Help me, my dear, I only want to know what mortal cold has blown on that fine flame. Is it just the effect of wise reflection? That's come a little late. Alas! is it not my own surpassing fault? I should have been grave and thoughtful when you came to see me. But what can one do? When my lips tremble and my heart beats, my sensible thoughts fly away . . .

Your letter has come. I don't need to tell you that I expected the message. So we shall just have the pleasure of seeing you for a few moments? Very well, then, as you like. I don't generally criticise my friends' behaviour. You seem to be terribly afraid of finding yourself alone with me. But that's what is really necessary! You do what you want about it. When this mood has passed, write to me or come. I am indulgent, and I shall forgive you for the hurt you do me.

I cannot refrain from saying a few words about our disagreement. I had determined to behave with absolute dignity – but less than a day has passed, and my heart is already weak and yet, Charles, my anger was quite justified! What must I think when I see you fly from my caresses, if not that you are thinking about *her*, whose soul and black face have just set themselves between us? In fact, I feel humiliated and abased. If it weren't for my self-respect, I should abuse you. I'd like to see you suffer. Because I'm burning with jealousy and one cannot possibly reason at times like these. Oh! dear friend, I hope that you will never suffer from it. What a night I've spent, and how I have cursed this cruel love!

I have waited for you all day . . . In case your caprice should urge you towards the house tomorrow, I must warn you that I shall only be in from one till three, or, in the evening, from eight until midnight.

Good morning, my Charles. How is whatever heart remains to you? Mine is calmer, now. I am reasoning hard with it so that I shall not bore you too much with its weaknesses. Have no fear, I shall manage to force it to come down to the temperature you dream of. I shall very certainly suffer, but, to please you, I shall resign myself to bear every possible pain. [16]

In the meantime, in April 1857, Baudelaire's stepfather had died; and Baudelaire was free to transfer his idealism to his mother. Once again he had found a woman whom he could love from a distance: a woman who embodied, for him, goodness and purity of love. His need was satisfied. *La Vénus blanche*, Apollonie Sabatier, could only now remain as a friend; and this she did, with gentle tact: asking after his health, encouraging him to write a drama, *L'Ivrogne*:

Are you in better spirits [she asked], is the drama taking shape? I am afraid, my dear one, that you're working very little and that would be a pity for the public and a misfortune for you, because I think I can see an element of success in the plan that you explained to me. I am sure that in less than a fortnight of reasonably hard work, you would finish it. But no, you won't do a thing about it. You would have to give up opium, all the fantasies which pass through your mind and catch hold of you at every step. I am wasting my time and trouble by preaching to you; but, after all, as you'll only do what you want about it, I don't feel too much remorse for my little sermon. That being so, I want you to know that when the fancy takes you to see me, you can come and bid me good morning. [17]

Baudelaire, who had abandoned the rue Frochot, gradually resumed the habit of dining there, and his relationship with Apollonie became solid, tranquil and affectionate.

She had not only been too gay for him, she had been too sane, too healthy and too beautiful for a man accustomed to Jeanne Duval. A few weeks before she died, when she was speaking of Baudelaire, she said: 'Perhaps I was the one who had no faith.' Perhaps, in fact, she was not enamoured of physical love. The faith that she lacked with Baudelaire, she lacked with all her lovers; she does not seem to have known any one great passion.

She tried to use her influence to help Baudelaire when *Les Fleurs du mal* came before the courts for immorality; but after she left the rue Frochot in 1862, she rarely saw him, except at Gautier's. Legend said that she sat at his bedside when he was dying, playing passages from *Tannhauser* on the piano. When Baudelaire lay dying she was, in fact, on the shores of Lake Como, immersed in a new liaison. She was not present when he died, or when he was buried.

★

While Baudelaire remained her chief claim to immortality, la Présidente also earned the devotion of Flaubert – le sire de Vaufrilard, as her circle called him. He adopted the tone of the rue Frochot, and addressed her some clumsy verbal obscenities; as his letters bear witness, he also showed her engaging humour and tenderness, and understanding in her moments of stress. She felt both admiration and affection for him. And if she was not, as some have suggested, the model for la Maréchale in Flaubert's *L'Éducation sentimentale*, she earned several mentions in the Goncourt *Journal* – though when the second volume appeared, with the brutal phrase *une vivandière de faunes*, she understandably threw it into the fire. Her dining-room was the cradle of the *Revue de Paris* of 1850: the magazine which was to publish, among much else, some of Baudelaire's poems, and Flaubert's *Madame Bovary*. Gautier, Du Camp, Houssaye, Louis de Cormenin: the four directors of the *Revue* were all Apollonie's guests.

So, too, was Ernest Feydeau, the novelist and literary climber, who found that his friends were slow to introduce him, and presented himself at the rue Frochot. Out of the goodness of her heart, la Présidente invited him to her dinners, where she did the honours 'with as much urbanity as kindness'.[18] Looking back, some twenty years later, Feydeau could only marvel at her tolerance and the freedom of speech round her table. He took a particular dislike to Baudelaire, 'who was constantly racking his brains to make himself quite unbearable, and succeeded in doing so'.[19] As Feydeau listened – perhaps with a secret envy – to the paradoxes of Gautier, Flaubert and Baudelaire, he could not resist making use of them; and 'the novel of mine which bears the title of *Sylvie* was', he recorded, pompously, 'born of the eccentricities which were retailed round la Présidente's table'.[20]

Sylvie was published in 1861, four years after *Les Fleurs du mal*, and Mme Sabatier's circle must have known of Baudelaire's love for her. Feydeau's novel ends with the marriage of the heroine, Sylvie, and the poet, Anselme Schanfara, but in this mediocre romance one may still discern the high romance of the rue Frochot. Anselme Schanfara is clearly Baudelaire as

181

Feydeau saw him. 'He used to let off real verbal fireworks,' wrote Feydeau,

where wit was not lacking, but moderation was too often absent. If one was speaking of Raphael, he would quote some entirely unknown artist . . . As for Molière, he said he only liked his *farces* . . . Just as some spoilt gourmets can no longer live on anything except truffles, caviar and red pepper, Anselme preferred China to France, Bohemia to society, . . . hashish to lemonade, . . . and women who traffick in their beauty to angelic young girls.[21]

Anselme, like Baudelaire, was 'as clean as a new twenty-franc piece'; his eyes were sad, his hair was dark, he was bearded (as Baudelaire had been), he had almond-white teeth and, like Baudelaire, fine hands. As Feydeau continued to write his novel, he became fascinated by the character he had once despised, he looked deeper into the nature he had found superficial; and, in this curious romance born in the rue Frochot, he made an unexpectedly touching analysis:

So it is [he wrote] that, in the middle of the nineteenth century, in the heart of Paris, the city of light, good manners and good style, a man had found the means of setting himself quite apart from other men . . . A little sombre, like people who have sought much but found very little, sarcastic like all passionate people who have been hurt by indifference, dreadfully timid and secretly adoring love even while he mocked it with his friends and relegated it to the ranks of chimeras, he had finally grown resigned to life and to himself, and he lived gently, peacefully in his own way, leading a wild and solitary existence in his corner, like a Chinese.[22]

If Anselme was modelled on Baudelaire, Sylvie bore a certain likeness to la Présidente. She had the sensual mouth that Gustave Ricard painted in his portrait of Mme Sabatier – a portrait which Feydeau admired – and she had the same exquisite hands, 'those hands, with long fingers, invented by Raphael'. When she became Anselme's mistress, she wore 'a splendid Venetian costume of the sixteenth century': so did la Présidente, in Richard's portrait. Sylvie had, above all, the quality observed by every visitor to the rue Frochot: *la bonté*.[23]

In his memoirs of Gautier, Feydeau said – and it was probably true – that Gautier's wit shone most radiantly at the rue Frochot: there he felt himself in the 'sphere of benevolence' that every artist needs for the full flowering of his genius. No one, continued Feydeau,

could have any idea of the wit that sparkled round that table on Sunday evenings . . . I have not asked the opinion of everyone who used to come, but I think I can say for certain that the happiest moments in all our lives were spent with la Présidente, and we owe this not only to the sterling, unfailing verve of Théophile Gautier, but to the sweet benevolence of that charming woman.[24]

As Gautier said, la Présidente was superior to other women because of her beauty, and, above all, because she did not demand that men paid court to her. She allowed the most serious and the most abstract conversations. She also contrived – it was, perhaps, a greater distinction – to show no particular sign of favour, to be equally affectionate to all her guests. There was no obligation to be gallant, no rivalry, no sense of constraint. She was one of those exceedingly rare women who can create an atmosphere of emotional and intellectual freedom.

She was also a woman who understood children; and she made the conquest of Gautier's elder daughter, Judith. Ernest Meissonier, the master of small-scale painting, had taught la Présidente how to paint miniatures, and the child used to come to the rue Frochot to sit for her portrait. Nearly half a century later, Judith Gautier recalled the sunlit rooms which so many famous men had known.

The hall, which was only a sort of corridor, seemed gay and cheerful. A big glass window, which overlooked some gardens, lit it up brightly, through some light blinds painted with flowering branches. In a birdcage, full of parakeets, bullfinches and bengalis, out-chattering, out-singing one another, the wings were fluttering in the light, and the mischievous barking of two little griffons, which had rushed up to the door, added to the happy din which greeted you on the threshold.

The dining-room was just opposite the front door, and this famous room, where wit and verve were so lavishly spent every week, was neither very vast nor very sumptuous. The walls were covered with dark red stuff, symmetrically hung with delftware and pictures. The massive, square oak table must have been drawn out to the walls for the Sunday feasts . . .

La Présidente arrived from the far end of the apartment, and announced herself with a trill, which turned into a silvery laugh.

Three graces radiated from her the moment you set eyes on her: beauty, goodness and happiness . . .

She had a clear, smooth complexion, and regular features, with something mischievous and witty about her expression, and a small, smiling mouth. Her air of triumph seemed to shed light and happiness around her.

Her clothes were full of imagination and taste. She hardly conformed to fashion, she created a quite special one of her own. Great artists, among her Sunday guests, gave her advice and designed dresses for her . . .[25]

The woman who had posed for Clésinger continued to draw the world of art about her: Delacroix would come to dinner, and Maxime du Camp remembered seeing him, one evening, taking the wools from la Présidente's workbox and, passionate colourist that he was, twining them, plaiting them into a brilliant, original spectrum of colours. Ernest Meissonier, whom

Apollonie had known since the days of the Hôtel Pimodan: Meissonier, who recalled in a hundred diligent, devoted paintings, the Grande Armée of Napoleon I, had painted Punch on a panel on one of her doors; and, eight times at least, she sat for him.

She was fascinated by fashion, and by original clothes. When she posed in 1853, she wore a bodice like a cuirass, with blue-and-white puffed sleeves, and a tobacco-coloured skirt. 'Her half-closed eyes have an expression of mischief and intelligence,' recorded the catalogue of Meissonier's pictures. 'She is just about to smile.'[26] A year later, in 1854, she wore a full, cream-coloured dress, and a bodice trimmed with blue ribbons. Meissonier never tired of painting her: he recorded her, in watercolours, wearing a small black hood; he sketched her in red chalk and gouache, and again in black-lead. He painted her in a low white dress, gaily beribboned with green, and again in a yellow silk dress of the time of Louis XIII. He painted her yet again: she was wearing a little hood wreathed with forget-me-nots.[27] He portrayed her in the early 1850s, when Baudelaire was loving her in secret: laughing, fresh, seductive and endearing.

Meissonier portrayed a woman whose likeness was already known to amateurs of art: in the Salon of 1850, Gustave Ricard, another of her admirers, had made his first appearance with a portrait of Madame Sabatier which glowed with his skill and her own superb good health and good nature. She wore a low Venetian dress, with cherry-coloured slashings in the sleeves. On her lap, held by her delicate hands, was a little Havanese lap-dog, possibly the dog that was given her by Maxime du Camp. 'Her lovely hair, brown in shadow, gold in sun, brushes lightly over her brow, as if it were caressed by an amorous wind; her eyes gaze, fine and frank, her pink nostrils breathe in ardent life, her crimson lips seem half open for a smile or a kiss . . .' So Gautier described the Apollonie of Ricard's portrait;[28] in 1855, the portrait was shown again at the Paris International Exhibition. 'It is one of those challenging works,' Edmond About wrote, 'which catch the eye and compel admiration. I remember when it was first exhibited, I was at the École Normale, and I escaped with some of my friends from M. Saint-Marc Girardin's lectures to go and see Mme Sabatier with her little dog on her lap. Then we rushed back as fast as we could to the great hall of the Sorbonne, happy to keep, in our mind's eye, the memory of such a radiant beauty.'[29]

Mme Sabatier, the artist's inspiration, still kept her early devotion to music. She appreciated Beethoven and Weber, Mozart and Berlioz; and Ernest Reyer, the music critic of *La Presse* and *La Revue de Paris*, brought Berlioz himself to the rue Frochot. Berlioz was an old acquaintance: long ago, in 1839, after the first hearing of *Roméo et Juliette* at the Conservatoire, Apollonie had been so enchanted by the music that she had begged her teacher, Mme Damoreau-Cinti, to ask Berlioz to send her a copy of the song *Premiers transports que nul n'oublie*. Berlioz had gracefully transcribed the song for Apollonie, in his own hand. He had long since forgotten the incident, but it had been enough to make him her friend; and in 1855, on the evening of his great music festival at the Paris International Exhibition, Berlioz dined at the rue Frochot.

★

It was in the spring or summer of 1860 that, after a liaison of some fifteen years, Mosselman ceased to be Apollonie's lover. One reason for the break was, no doubt, his infidelity; another was very probably the financial ruin of his family. He still had enough, it is said, to offer la Présidente five hundred gold francs a month, but she refused them. She was thirty-eight, she still believed in her powers of attraction, and she decided to earn her living by repairing and painting miniatures. Indeed, she sent four portraits, in oils, to the Salon of 1861 (where Manet exhibited for the first time). Gautier loyally reviewed her:

Meissonier's pupil, or, rather, her own, Mme A. Sabatier has painted some charming portraits in oils which have all the delicacy of a miniature. In these little heads, as big as a fingernail, which one could set in brooches, there is a fineness of colour, a gentleness of contour, and a spirited touch which it would be hard, if not impossible, to obtain on ivory. The portraits of children . . . are adorable in their freshness and youthfulness of tone. The young woman dressed in black is charming, but even so we prefer the portrait of the artist: it shows us, in profile, a head that M. Ricard has shown us full-face in a painting that has become famous. [30]

However, it was impossible for Apollonie to earn her living by painting; and she resigned herself to selling some of her *objets d'art*. In December 1861, the *Bulletin de l'Amateur* announced:

A woman of much wit and grace, Mme Sabatier, has parted with a crowd of elegant *objets d'art* of the last century, all of them very well chosen: marquetry furniture, gilt bronzes, porcelain and terracottas. They still keep the distinction of being the nicest things one could choose for interior luxury. However, two modern works of art shine with great brilliance among them: *Monsieur Polichinelle*, a masterly painting by M. Meissonier, and the bust of Mme Sabatier by Clésinger.

The Clésinger bust was bought for the Louvre; the sale raised forty-three thousand francs.

In 1362, effacing the memory of Mosselman, Apollonie moved to a new apartment.

She accepted this new situation with charming pluck [wrote Judith Gautier, in *Le Collier des Jours*]. In her defeat, she still had an air of triumph . . . With the remnants of her past luxury, she arranged a little ground-floor apartment (10, rue de la Faisanderie) which was still a delightful nest. She did her own cooking, and sang as she did it, with turquoises on her beautiful hands, cocking her little finger . . . I much admired her courage and strength of character. She was still 'la très-chère, la très-belle', and 'la très-bonne', she to whom the author of *Les Fleurs du mal* had vowed so secret, so ideal a love, she who lives again in immortal poems and will outlive herself because, to her glory, she was once the ideal of a great poet.[31]

★

It has been suggested that if Apollonie refused financial help from Mosselman, she may already have accepted it from another lover. By the end of 1861, she seems to have been engaged in a new liaison, and preparing to go abroad. Her protector was, in all probability, Richard Wallace, the natural son of the Marquis of Hertford. She went with him, at one time, to England, and in 1867 she was living with him on the shores of Lake Como. He promised her that if ever he became rich, he would remember her; and in 1870 he inherited a fortune from his father: sixty million, the château of Bagatelle, and all the art collections in Lord Hertford's *hôtel* in the boulevard des Italiens. Two days before the Siege of Paris began, Richard Wallace settled a handsome sum on la Présidente (Flaubert said it was fifty thousand livres), and every month henceforth she received her income. After the Franco-Prussian War, she moved to the avenue de l'Impératrice, and decided to resume the Sunday dinners, to re-create the brilliance of the rue Frochot.

But some conjunctions of the stars do not repeat themselves; and time had changed both Apollonie and her friends. Baudelaire was dead, and Gautier had not long to live; Flaubert drifted out of her existence. She herself, as the photographs show, had long ago lost her physical perfection: only her hands were still beautiful, and since she had adopted the habit of taking a daily drive in her landaulet in the Bois de Boulogne, she had begun to grow stout – though she admitted that her love of food may have had its effect. In 1874 she moved to a house in the avenue d'Eylau where, in the dining-room, hung with Beauvais tapestries, Madeleine Brohan, the actress, came to dine with Worms, the actor from the Comédie-Française. But the dinners in Passy were pale reflections of the dinners in the quartier Bréda, and no doubt Apollonie regretted the past. When, in 1880, her old friend Maxime du Camp was elected to the Académie Française, she wrote

La Présidente

Madame Sabatier. The bust by Jean-Baptiste Clésinger
which was shown at the Salon of 1847.

La Bohème romantique: a vignette
from Arsène Houssaye's *Confessions*.
It suggests an ebullient gathering
at the Hôtel Pimodan.

Interior of the Hôtel Pimodan.
It was here that Gautier first saw
Madame Sabatier.

Opposite. The Hôtel Pimodan on
the Ile Saint-Louis, seen from the
quai.

Right. Ernest Meissonier (1815–91), was a friend of Madame Sabatier from the days of the Hôtel Pimodan. He painted her portrait at least eight times.
Below left. One of la Présidente's circle: Hector Berlioz (1803–69).
Below right. Théophile Gautier, from a photograph taken in London in 1862. It was Gautier who bestowed the title of la Présidente on Apollonie Sabatier. His *Lettre à la Présidente* and two poems in *Emaux et Camées* were addressed to her. He was the most popular and constant visitor in her brilliant Bohemia.

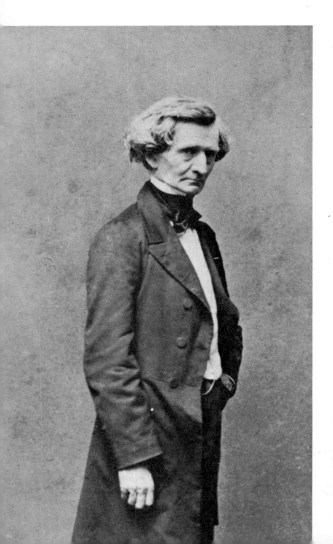

Right. Roger de Beauvoir
(1806–66): dandy, Romantic
writer, and sometime tenant of
the Hôtel Pimodan.
Below. Baudelaire. From a
photograph by Nadar, about 1861.

Left. Ernest Feydeau (1821–73). A
stockbroker turned novelist, Feydeau
invited himself·to the rue Frochot.
His *Sylvie* (1861) recalls the romance
between Madame Sabatier and Baudelaire.

Above. La Femme piquée par un serpent.
Madame Sabatier posed for this statue
by Clésinger, which created a sensation
at the Salon of 1847.
Left. Baudelaire, 1864. A detail from
Hommage à Delacroix by Fantin-Latour.

Top. Gustave Courbet, *l'Atelier du peintre* (1855). On the right of the picture are Madame
Sabatier, draped in a shawl, and Baudelaire, reading.
Below left. Madame Sabatier, by Gustave Ricard. This portrait was acclaimed at the Salon of 1850.
Edmond About escaped from his lectures at the Ecole Normale to see it, and Ernest Feydeau
recalled it when he wrote his novel *Sylvie*.
Below right. Madame Sabatier: one of Meissonier's portraits.

Left. Madame Sabatier in about 1862, when she was the mistress of Richard Wallace.
Below left. La Présidente in later life. From a photograph.
Below. Sir Richard Wallace (1818–90). A philanthropist and art collector, he was also the generous protector of Madame Sabatier.

to congratulate him, and he hastened to visit her. They talked a long while together; when he left her, greatly moved, she was weeping.

She spent her last years at Neuilly. In 1889 Augustin Thierry, then a pupil at the Lycée Louis-le-Grand, was taken by a schoolfriend to visit this remarkable relic of an age that seemed long past. At the age of sixty-seven, flaccid, lined, grey-haired, bereft of her fine complexion, at first she disillusioned him. But he went again to see her, and, talking of a recent article by Brunetière, a harsh criticism of *Les Fleurs du mal*, she came to talk, at last, about Baudelaire.

It was now more than thirty years since *la Vénus blanche* had ceased to be the poet's madonna. She was profoundly shocked by Brunetière's criticism. 'It isn't true,' she protested, 'poor Charles was a religious man. His blasphemies were only a pretence. But he worshipped beauty in all its forms. And then he was extremely proud, like all timid people – he was a dreamer, melancholy, perpetually troubled. I knew him very well, I think, better than this man who slanders him.' La Présidente broke off; and then, as if she had gone down into the depths of her past, she murmured: 'Perhaps it was I who had no faith.'

She died on 31 December 1889. She was buried in the old cemetery at Neuilly.

> A la très-chère, à la très-belle
> Qui remplit mon coeur de clarté,
> A l'ange, à l'idole immortelle,
> Salut en l'immortalité!
>
> Elle se répand dans ma vie
> Comme un air imprégné de sel,
> Et dans mon âme inassouvie
> Verse le goût de l'éternel.
>
> Sachet toujours frais qui parfume
> L'atmosphère d'un cher réduit,
> Encensoir oublié qui fume
> En secret à travers la nuit,
>
> Comment, amour incorruptible,
> T'exprimer avec vérité?
> Grain de musc qui gis, invisible,
> Au fond de mon éternité!
>
> A la très-bonne, à la très-belle
> Qui fait ma joie et ma santé,
> A l'ange, à l'idole immortelle,
> Salut en l'immortalité![32]

12

Mogador

Élisabeth-Céleste Vénard, later Mme la Comtesse de
Chabrillan (1824–1909)

The theme of the courtesan redeemed, the *fille de joie* transformed by the purifying love of an honest man, has long been a favourite theme in novels and on stage. Céleste Vénard, better known as Mogador, proved how this could happen in real life, and – if one seeks a moral – hers is among the few edifying histories of her kind.

Élisabeth-Céleste Vénard did not know her father; just before her birth, he joined the army, after which he disappeared completely. Her mother was Anne-Victoire Vénard, a woman of respectable family who had been thrown by her way of life out of her natural setting. Céleste, an illegitimate child, was born at 7, rue du Pont-aux-Choux, near the Boulevard du Temple in Paris, on 27 December 1824.

All her affection was naturally given to her mother; but as soon as she was old enough to notice, she became aware that her mother's life was dominated by the moods of a man. This lover (to whom Céleste would refer as G. in her memoirs) was a drunkard and a ruffian. One day he beat up Anne-Victoire so brutally that she had to be taken to the police station on a stretcher. He was arrested, and swore he would kill both his mistress and her daughter. The commissioner of police advised Anne-Victoire to leave Paris with her child, for safety's sake.

As soon as she recovered, they set off together for Lyons, where Anne-Victoire became cashier at a hatter's. A few months later, her lover discovered where she was, and followed her. He decided to use Céleste as a hostage. One winter afternoon, he found her alone in a street, and he kidnapped her, and carried her off to a brothel. One of the prostitutes, seeing that the child was ill with fear, put her to bed in her own room, locked her in for safety, and promised to send word to her mother. Next day, while the prostitutes kept the angry G. at bay, Anne-Victoire arrived, and escaped to safety with Céleste. However, the melodrama continued: G. discovered their new address, and promised to live quietly if Anne-Victoire would take him back again; she did so, but she soon discovered that he was in league with a gang of robbers. She must have been almost relieved when he was killed in some riots in Lyons, and she could return, without let or hindrance, to Paris. With financial aid from her father, she found lodgings for herself and her daughter near the Boulevard du Temple, the centre of the theatrical world. Every Sunday they went together to the theatre. Céleste determined that when she grew up she would be an actress.

However, she now received a shock which helped to determine her future. Anne-Victoire fell under the spell of Vincent, a blue-eyed, fair-haired mason of thirty-five, who lived on the floor above them. Vincent both resented and admired Céleste; and Céleste detested this rough and temperamental man who had once again stolen her mother's affection. One day in 1838, when Anne-Victoire was visiting her father at Fontainebleau, Vincent drunkenly attempted to rape the girl who had just reached the age of puberty. Céleste ran from the room, in horror, and spent the next four days wandering in the streets by day and sleeping in a hay-loft by night, waiting for her mother to return. A prostitute, Thérèse, found her weeping outside the Église Saint-Paul, and was brave enough to give her shelter. It was a courageous action, for any registered prostitute who was found in the company of a minor would probably be sentenced to six months' imprisonment for corruption; and no one would be likely to accept her protestations of innocence, the explanation that she had acted from charity. A day or two later, Céleste was seen with Thérèse in the street; she was taken away, for safety's sake, to the women's prison of Saint-Lazare.

Her mother's disturbed, irregular ménage, even the prostitute's room, were less corrupting than the institution in which the abandoned child was now confined. Its inmates included not only girls like herself, who were in need of care and protection, but others, the refuse of the slums, who had already begun a life of petty crime and prostitution, besides older women with long and vicious careers. Relationships were sometimes intense, example was corrupting; and Céleste, who had ardently fought off the advances of her mother's lover, now came under the influence of an older girl, Denise, who advised her that prostitution was her only means of independence. 'All the things she had just told me danced about in my mind,' Céleste would write in her memoirs. 'I saw myself rich, and covered with lace and jewels. I looked at myself in my little bit of mirror; I was really pretty . . .'[1] Denise gave her new friend an address, and assured her that one day they would meet there.

Anne-Victoire had been warned by Thérèse, the friendly prostitute, that her daughter was now at Saint-Lazare; and, after a month, she troubled to come and rescue her. But the *ménage à trois* with Vincent proved as intolerable as ever; Céleste received small affection or understanding from her mother, and she saw that she was unwanted. Pestered again by Vincent, jealous of his influence, and needing independence, a brave, luxurious new world, she registered herself as a prostitute. She was just sixteen, the lowest age at which she could legally enter the profession.

★

'When, after twelve years, I ask myself why I took the step which would be my downfall, the step for which I was to pay so dearly, I can,' she wrote in her memoirs, 'attest to this. The actual idea of depravity had nothing to do with my decision; what I remember most clearly among my confused emotions, were my jealousy of my mother, my hatred of Vincent, and, above all, a compulsive need to understand the fine world which was the dream and envy of the poor. I damned myself out of vanity. My body was purer than my soul, and I fell.'[2]

She went to the address which Denise, at Saint-Lazare, had given her. It was, of course, the address of a brothel: one of the most fashionable in Paris. Her youthfulness roused the jealousy of the older women. She knew, from the first, that she hated the brothel; it seemed like prison to her. Indeed, she might have condemned herself to imprisonment for life; Denise explained that the food and lodging, the jewels and scent and clothes provided by *madame* would keep the prostitutes so deeply in her debt that they would never be able to free themselves. 'Oh, my God! what lives we led!' Céleste would remember. 'What tortures we suffered! To have to laugh when you want to weep, to be dependent and humiliated when you pay so dearly for the little you possess! If someone killed the wretched creatures who expose themselves to this, they would do them a service, and none of them but would bless the hand that gave her death. Love takes a cruel revenge on the women who profane its image.'[3]

The only way to earn freedom from the brothel was to buy it; and happily Céleste was able to do so. One of the clients, a Monsieur L., a sympathetic young man, was distressed to see her ill and in such misery; and when she explained that she really wanted to become an actress, that she had been almost forced into prostitution, he paid her debts to *madame*, and gave her a room in his Paris apartment. Ten days later, a doctor diagnosed that Céleste had smallpox, and that she was too ill to be moved. She overheard the diagnosis, managed somehow to dress herself, and struggled downstairs to the street, where she found a cab. She asked to be driven to the Hôpital Saint-Louis.

When she recovered, one of the medical students, Adolphe, found her a room; he also invited her to visit him at Versailles, where he had been appointed house-surgeon at the hospital. Céleste very naturally fell in love with Adolphe; but her happiness was all too brief. One day he invited her to a party at Versailles, where she found a *lorette*: an elegant and more experienced prostitute, who was clearly her lover's favourite mistress. The older woman, Louisa Aumont, resenting a young girl, determined that she would break the rival liaison. She fulminated against Adolphe for daring to invite her in such company. Céleste was sixteen and a half. The experience at Versailles turned her from a girl into a woman. She determined that one day Louisa Aumont would regret her conduct; and, as she plodded on, alone, on the long walk back to Paris, which took all night, she decided not to be guided by her heart. Henceforward, she would always ask what benefits her lovers could give her.

One of the gayest, most popular dance-halls in Paris at the time was the Bal Mabille, in the Champs-Élysées. Its fountains, its open-air restaurant and its bosky gardens, the pavilion where the band played the latest polkas and waltzes, all glittered seductively under the gas-lamps. It was a natural setting for supper, dancing, and flirtations, for the beginning of casual liaisons. One evening, at the Bal Mabille, Céleste saw the famous dancer, la Reine Pomaré: a pale young girl, who polka'd like a demon with her demoniacal partner, a little man with windmill arms called Brididi. Céleste was spellbound by their performance. Every Thursday she went back to the Bal Mabille; and, as it happened, la Reine Pomaré was already suffering from consumption, and Brididi was looking for a girl whom he might establish as her rival. At last one day he noticed Céleste, and asked her to dance a quadrille. She must have danced it with special verve, because he asked her to supper; next day, for five hours, he taught her the polka. 'By the end, I knew it wonderfully well,' remembered Céleste. 'You went through hundreds of movements, it made you look like a performing dog: arms and legs and body and head, everything moved at once; it was like a world of telegraph signals and puppets. But it was new, and people thought it pretty.'[4] The following day she danced the polka at Mabille with Brididi. She caught sight of Louisa Aumont among the spectators, and she danced more furiously than ever. The crowds of pleasure-seekers decided that she was better than la Reine Pomaré. All the men fought to invite her to dance. 'It would be easier to defend Mogador than my partner!' cried Brididi. 'That's it! I shall call you Mogador!' The name Mogador was on everyone's lips, because it was the name of the fortress which had just been captured by French troops in Morocco. Henceforward, it was the name of Céleste Vénard.

One evening, her former lover, Adolphe, joined the crowd at Mabille to watch the rival queens of the polka. He was now in love with Céleste, the famous, and applauded Mogador. It was the moment of revenge for which she had been waiting. She refused to take him back unless he made Louisa Aumont apologise, in public, for her conduct. The apologies were duly made.

When the Bal Mabille closed down at the end of the summer, Mogador was engaged to dance at the Théâtre Beaumarchais. The theatre closed down, too, and she was in despair. One day, however, she called on a friend who kept a beauty parlour in the Faubourg du Temple; and there, by some happy chance, she met Laurent Franconi. He was one of the family who had founded the Cirque Olympique, the Cirque d'été and the Cirque d'hiver. He was the finest riding-master in Paris, and he was looking for equestriennes for his circus at the Hippodrome. He engaged Mogador for a year. On 4 July 1845, she appeared in the opening performance at the grand new Hippodrome. She took part in a race between five girl riders. All her theatrical temperament, all her ambitions, all her past unhappiness led her to ride like a fury. She won the race, and was given the bouquet.

Her fame at Franconi's brought her admirers and suitors by the score.

In Paris [she would write in her memoirs], the moment a woman is in the public eye, everyone presents himself as a candidate, unless she is protected by a reputation of unassailable virtue. There are young women who, out of kindness or stupidity, believe themselves obliged to respond to all the advances made to them. In a few months they are lost . . . Fortunately for me, I had understood from the first that a love-affair is like a war, and that tactics help you to win it. I also had two defects of character which helped me greatly in my self-defence. I have always been capricious and proud. Among the women who often feel disposed to say *yes*, no-one feels more pleasure than I do in saying *no*. And so the men who have gained most from me are the ones who have asked the least.[5]

It needed a princely liaison to establish a courtesan, and Mogador allowed the Duke of Ossuna, a rich young Italian, to instal her in an apartment in the Rue de l'Arcade, and hire her an impressive carriage in which she might parade along the boulevards. She was not in love with the Duke, or, indeed, with anyone; and when the Duke went abroad, she became the mistress of an Italian tenor.

Her career was determined when, in mid-July, she had a serious accident at Franconi's: she fell from her chariot, and a wheel went over her leg. She was intrepid: as soon as she could walk again, she insisted on returning to the Hippodrome, and she drove in another chariot race. But she could not stay the course; and, besides, Franconi refused to increase her salary. Mogador was at last obliged to leave.

At the time of her accident, her mother, Anne-Victoire, had suddenly come back into her life, and asked to live with her, and look after her. Now she suggested that they should open a dress-shop together, and the two of them moved to the rue Geoffroy-Marie. But the shop did not prosper, and Mogador was compelled to continue the life she detested. For she had always detested it. Whatever her physical promiscuity, she seems to have kept a strange purity of heart. She was haunted by the thought that her name remained ineffaceably recorded in the register of prostitutes. She would have liked to rub out her past, to be an honest woman. 'The thought that my name is inscribed in that infernal book,' she wrote, 'is a thought that never leaves me. I don't want it to stay there; I want it to be erased. How shall I achieve that? Who will give me the means? . . . I don't know, but I shall do it. And if, when I have made every effort, it proves to be impossible, I shall quit this life which I shall only have defiled.'[6]

But chance, as Mogador observed, is the most accomplished shifter of scenes. One evening, at the Café Anglais, when she had been insulted by some drunk *noceur*, when she wanted, more than ever, to change her way of life, a handsome, somewhat shy young man of about twenty-five, who happened to be in the party, took her side, and showed her sympathy. She asked him if he would see her home.

'Of course,' he answered, 'in a few minutes. But first, I should like to dance with you.' He held me close to him [she wrote], and I felt his heart-beats . . . I closed my eyes and let him lead me on. I felt a flash of happiness – it passed like lightning. but I feel it still. [7]

★

Gabriel-Paul-Josselin-Lionel de Chabrillan came of one of the oldest families in France. He was unmarried, he was heir to a fortune, and to a castle and estate near Châteauroux, in the province of Berry. He had – which a courtesan rarely found in men – a sense of poetry, and a large capacity for love. Mogador became his mistress. She soon discovered that it was hard to keep the resolutions she had made on her lonely walk back from Versailles. A courtesan must love for money; she had met a man whom she loved, quite certainly, for himself. As for Lionel de Chabrillan, he was in love with Mogador. He was quite impossibly in love. The de Chabrillans expected him, very naturally, to make a suitable marriage.

The liaison was tempestuous; when he took Mogador to his rambling château, set in its broad estates and peopled by its throng of servants, she understood that a universe lay between them. She understood, too, that if her rich but improvident lover was to keep his property, he would need to marry a woman with a large dowry. Lionel de Chabrillan understood it himself: one day she found a draft of his proposal to a woman of suitable wealth and station.

The liaison broke, and Mogador took another lover. Richard – as he was called in her memoirs – was so in love with her that he offered to marry her. He repeated his proposal in writing, and since Lionel de Chabrillan was creating angry scenes, and she could no longer control her exasperation, Mogador informed him of the proposal. Lionel assumed that she had invented the story as a form of blackmail, and he urged her to accept the offer.

She went to London – for Richard was English, and planned to marry her there. He bought her a wedding outfit, a pearl-grey brocade dress, a black lace shawl, and a white hat. To Mogador it seemed like half-mourning. When their carriage reached the church where they were to be married, she implored him to tell the coachman to drive on, for she could not bear to go through the ceremony. Richard realised that he could not separate her from Lionel, and he left for California.

In the late spring of 1852, financially ruined, and disowned by his family, Lionel de Chabrillan sailed for Australia. The gold rush had just begun, and thousands of young men were hoping to retrieve from the soil the fortunes they had dissipated in Europe. From London, and from the clipper *Chusan* on which he sailed to Melbourne, he wrote devotedly to the woman who had been his mistress for four years; and it was partly due to the influence of his name, and partly to Prince Napoleon's affection for them both, that on 27 April 1852 the Fifth Bureau of the Paris Prefecture of Police recorded that 'Vénard, Élisabeth-Céleste, is not included in the present list of public prostitutes.' Mogador was free at last.

From London, from every port of call on his three-month journey, from Sydney and from Ballarat, Lionel de Chabrillan sent her letters. He also

Opposite: L'Orgie romaine, by Thomas Couture (1815–79).
Mogador is said to have posed for the central figure.

sent her his intermittent diary: his impressions of Australia in the early days of the gold rush; and she reprinted them verbatim in the memoirs she was writing.

It is not [she explained] from gaiety of heart that I have described a past full of griefs, regrets, miseries and shame. I wanted to destroy a hateful calumny for the person who was constantly pilloried at my side. His name was riveted to mine, he was exiled and unhappy, I defended him with heart and soul; I wanted to prove that the little I possessed was mine, since I had bought it with my moral suicide. I did not want to rehabilitate myself, you can never do that when you have fallen so low! But, I repeat, I was not attacking, I was defending myself. I did not want to excite poor creatures to copy me, to follow in my steps; I wanted to show them the perils of this kind of life, to prove to them that an honest girl, respected in her distress, is happier than these reprobates to whom nothing remains but scorn and destitution.[8]

In 1852, however, Mogador did not think of herself as a writer, but as an actress. She had at last achieved her ambition and gone into the theatre; she was enjoying a success at the Théâtre des Variétés. One evening, in the wings, she met the artist Thomas Couture, who asked her to sit for him; was one of the figures in his picture *L'Orgie romaine*, and he made a plaster cast of her hand. When her portrait was finished, she gave a party, and invited all the celebrities she knew.

Prosperity must have meant little to her; for three months she had not heard from Lionel de Chabrillan, and she had begun to have premonitions of disaster. But at last, one evening, when she was entertaining friends in her apartment, she learned that he had just arrived in Paris.

As she recorded in her memoirs, she dismissed her guests, and hurried to his hotel.

'Look what I've brought back for you,' he said.
And he uncovered some cages full of enchanting little birds of every colour.
'I've been looking after them for months so that I could give them to you,' he went on. 'I was cold at night so that I could keep them warm with my blanket.'
I began to cry, because he had not kissed me.
He took my hand and pressed it gently. 'My love would be unworthy,' he said, 'if it was material. It is your soul I love. I have told you already, Céleste, what I love in you is not Mogador; it is another woman who is struggling to escape from her.'[9]

Lionel de Chabrillan had lost all his possessions; he had nothing left, now, but his name. He offered it to Mogador, whom he called Céleste; he offered her a future as wife of the French consul-general in Melbourne.

On 9 November 1853 Mlle Anne-Victoire Vénard authorised the marriage of her natural daughter, Céleste, to Monsieur Gabriel-Paul-Josselin-Lionel de Chabrillan.

★

The de Chabrillans were so enraged by the thought of the *mésalliance* that Lionel determined to marry Céleste abroad. He left for London to arrange for the publication of the banns.

While he was away, she made a final, desperate attempt to retrieve her memoirs from the publishers. But, naturally enough, they knew that they were in possession of a best-seller, particularly as Mogador, the former prostitute, the former star of the Bal Mabille and the Hippodrome, would soon become the Comtesse de Chabrillan. Céleste appealed to her influential friends, Girardin and Dumas, to help her; but they could not save the situation. Nor could Prince Napoleon, who so admired her that he asked her to some of his weekly dinners at Voisin's, to meet his most distinguished intellectual acquaintances. Céleste could not bring herself to tell Lionel of the publication, and she would regret what she called her deceit for the rest of her life.

However, on 3 January 1854, with her little adopted daughter Solange (the illegitimate child of a former maid), with Marie, her peasant maid from Berry, and with two pet dogs, Céleste crossed the Channel. On 4 January, in London, she and Lionel de Chabrillan were married. There were three ceremonies to establish her legal status, to ensure her social acceptance. She and Lionel were married by registrar, and again in church, and yet again at the French Chancellery in London. No French judge would be able to question the validity of a marriage which had technically been solemnised on French soil.

On 5 January the de Chabrillans left for Southampton, and soon afterwards they sailed for Australia. Their ship, the *Croesus*, was so late in reaching Melbourne that rumour said she had gone down with all aboard, and the local press was publishing obituaries of the passengers. Among them was that of the new French consul-general, the husband of 'the notorious Céleste Mogador, the first two volumes of whose curious Memoirs have been published by the Librairie Nouvelle in Paris (they can also be purchased in Melbourne).'

Céleste de Chabrillan was not entirely accepted by Australian society; but she did what charity work she could, and she became a wife of the utmost respectability. Far from her friends, and married to a man who earned a hard and all too meagre living, she also decided to establish herself as a *femme de lettres*.

She had received no formal education, but her life at the end of the earth had given her material as rich as the Ballarat gold-mines, and she wrote a novel, *Les Voleurs d'or*. It was based on the heartrending stories she heard every day, the dramatic scenes she had diligently noted: on her observations of gold-diggers in Australia.

Alas! [she explained in her preface] I have written a book. The moment of publication approaches, and I am afraid.

I am afraid, because my book is about to enter a path that is bristling with obstacles, hedged in by prejudices against its author. I know that you'll smile and say to me: 'Why have you written it? Who asked you to? Are you impudent enough to believe you'll have any lasting fame?'

I began to write this book as a distraction. What was only a caprice came to be a passion. I didn't burn it, because I loved it; it was my companion in exile, the confidant of my troubles, the friend of my thoughts.

. . . However resolute you are, you cannot pass with impunity from sound to silence, from movement to immobility. The heart is not the pendulum of a clock which can be stopped by a touch of the finger. Mine was unmanageable; it beat fit to break at the thought of my native country, of France, which one never loves so much as when one has left it. I was so far away! And I wrote to console myself. That is my excuse, if I may be excused. Be indulgent, I am only a bird of passage; let me bear away to the end of the world the hope that I have not displeased you too much.[10]

After two years in Australia, Lionel de Chabrillan, who had speculated in flour to eke out his living, found himself involved in financial disaster; and in 1856 Céleste, who was ill and in need of a milder climate, returned to Europe with her adopted daughter. *Les Voleurs d'or* was acclaimed in Paris, and she was so encouraged that she wrote two more Australian novels, *Miss Pewell* and *The Emigrants*, and a novel with a French setting, *Sapho*, based on her own youthful experiences. In her ardour she overworked, and in the spring of 1858 she suffered a recurrence of the liver complaint which she had contracted in Australia. She was gravely ill.

Lionel de Chabrillan returned on leave to Paris, and she tried to conceal her ill-health from him, but finally she collapsed and the doctors advised a change of air. She and Lionel moved to her country house, Le Poinçonnet, near Châteauroux, and it was nearly six months before she began to recover. In January 1859, Lionel decided that she would not be well enough to return to Australia, and that he must try to find a post in Europe. But his *mésalliance* told against him; he was obliged to go back to Melbourne and wait for a vacancy. He left Le Poinçonnet on 12 July; he became ill on the voyage, and on 29 December, at the age of forty, he died.

★

Céleste was overwhelmed by the death of her husband. She wanted him to be buried in France, and she sold her jewels to pay to bring him home. The authorities refused to return his body. All she could do was to have his memorial designed and set up on his Australian grave. His family had always been intensely ashamed of her, and, now that she was a widow, they tried to persuade her to forego her title and her name. She naturally refused to abandon a title which she legally possessed, a noble name which had exorcised her past.

She struggled to make herself a career. She still felt her old passion for the stage, and she entered theatrical management. She obtained a lease of the Folies-Marigny (once known as the Bouffes-Parisiens), where Offenbach, Meilhac and Halévy had staged their famous operettas; it was now empty and dilapidated. On 19 April 1862 the refurbished theatre opened with three one-act plays. The most important was a comedy, *Bonheur aux Vaincus*: its author and leading performer used the transparent pseudonym of Madame Lionel. The first night was a triumph, and the audience included most of the famous demi-mondaines of the Second Empire. Adèle Page, Augustine Duverger, Clara FitzJames, la Païva, Marguerite Bellanger, Cora Pearl and Anna Deslions: all made their opulent appearance in support of their former colleague.

The triumph did not last for long. A series of spiteful articles appeared in the Press, resurrecting the past of Mogador. Céleste was told that she would be declared bankrupt. After the death of Lionel de Chabrillan, this was the worst blow she ever suffered. Indeed she grew so desperate that she tried to commit suicide; and, having made provision for her mother and her adopted daughter, she took sixty grammes of laudanum.

Her maid discovered her, and called a doctor, and Céleste was saved. On 24 May 1864, Dumas's version of *Les Voleurs d'or* was performed in the theatre in the working-class district of Belleville; it ran for several weeks, after which Céleste took it round the provinces, and to Belgium and Holland. She had at last achieved financial security. She decided to invest her capital in a small piece of land. Le Vésinet, near Paris, was being developed as a residential area. She bought a plot there, and built herself a country villa, in the Australian style, called the Châlet Lionel.

It was, again, Australia which inspired her to write *Crimes de la mer*: a melodrama about the adventures of a shipwrecked sailor. It was produced at the Belleville theatre on 8 May 1869, and it was almost as successful as *Les Voleurs d'or*. Céleste's dramatic triumphs continued: one of her plays, *Les Revers de l'amour*, ran for three months in 1870 at the Théâtre des Nouveautés; it was followed by *L'Américaine*, in which she took the title rôle.

On 19 July 1870 her management of the Nouveautés ended abruptly; the Franco-Prussian war was declared. In September, when the French were defeated at Sedan, she sent an impassioned plea to General Trochu, the Governor of Paris; she asked him to sanction the founding of a women's corps, 'to become the devoted servants of their country, to give it all their intelligence, courage and strength, so that our ramparts shall not be deprived of a single defender'. The Governor of Paris did not trouble to answer the letter. Céleste promptly sent it to the Press, signed *Une Parisienne*, and it brought many heartening replies. Émile de Girardin suggested that the women's corps should be called *les Sœurs de France*; and under this noble title it was officially founded on 15 September, four days before the Siege of Paris began.

Les Sœurs de France organised ambulance stations in empty houses on the outskirts of Paris; Céleste helped to nurse the wounded, and to raise funds for the work. But when the Prussians were about to enter the capital, she felt she could not bear the sight of their triumph; she disbanded *les Sœurs de France* and returned to Le Vésinet. She walked all the way there, only to find that the Prussians had ransacked her châlet, and she needed to raise money to rebuild it. She went on a lecture tour of Belgium, billed as Madame Lionel de Chabrillan. On 3 April 1872, she appeared in Brussels; and those who had expected a garish entertainment from Mogador received a lecture on Australia from a white-haired, middle-aged woman dressed in black, with white collar and cuffs.

Céleste would write, in all, twelve novels, twenty-six plays and seven operettas, not to mention poems and songs. Her *Mémoires* give her some claim to be remembered.

What is done is done [she had written in the preface]. I can do nothing about the past; isn't it already a great deal to have to answer for the future?
. . . I think I have proved that my will to do good was real and genuine. I have undertaken a long, hard task . . . I have tried to raise myself a little, I believed that great courage might obtain some indulgence. If I have been mistaken, it is an irreparable misfortune, and God grant that I alone will suffer for it.[11]

The misfortune was irreparable. Her domestic life with Lionel, her literary activities, her patriotism, her charity, should have earned her forgiveness for the past; but society still refused to forgive or forget it. She remembered her wretched days at the Saint-Lazare prison, and suggested that a home for war orphans from Alsace and Lorraine should be built on her own land. But she was not allowed, officially, to attend its inauguration on 22 August 1877. She was forced to watch from behind a tree as the little orphan girls presented bouquets to their wealthy patrons.

Poor woman [the *Figaro* wrote, years later], she has attempted the hardest thing on earth: rehabilitation. The public has a habit of classifying people. It rarely lets them change their original classification. The Comtesse Lionel de Chabrillan, widowed after five years of marriage, has been trying to kill Mogador for more than thirty years. She has never managed to do so.[12]

Her behaviour was exemplary: she had taken in and supported her aged mother, who had long ago driven her into her wretched career. Anne-Victoire died in 1874, and was buried in the family grave at Pré-Saint-Gervais, next to Vincent, the lover to whom she had always been strangely faithful. Céleste herself died at La Providence, an old people's home at Montmartre, on 18 February 1909, at the age of eighty-five. By some irony, she was buried beside her mother.

Epilogue

One day, towards the end of the nineteenth century, Henry de Pène was talking to Arsène Houssaye.

Do you remember? A hundred years ago, – or was it yesterday? – the promenade in the Bois was a fairytale. Crowds of eager spectators were massed along the paths on each side, from the Grande-Cascade to the middle of the Place de la Concorde. And in the thick of the coupés, the victorias, phaetons and landaus, . . . Mme Musard's eight-spring carriage with its powdered lackeys was passing the carriages from the Tuileries . . . in the sparkling crowd all flooded with purple light by the setting sun.

And then there were the Duchesse de Castiglione's discreet coupé, and Marguerite Bellanger's indiscreet barouche . . . [1]

It is in this rich, ever-changing procession, this splendid, opulent drive to the Bois de Boulogne, that the great courtesans finally present themselves to the mind's eye. Superb, sometimes vulgar, braving society as Esther Guimond had done in the days of Louis-Philippe, they symbolise much of the life of the Second Empire.[2]

La Joconde may have vanished with la Colombe and Salade-à-la-Russe. La Madone, who looked like a Virgin painted by a primitive artist, has long been Princess Soltikoff. But these belonged to an earlier generation. Here is the *haute bicherie parisienne* of the 1860s, the world within world of the Second Empire, the demi-monde which exists, like a small flash society, in the heart of the regular, legitimate world. Each of these women, these *expertes ès sciences galantes*, considers her beauty as her capital, and makes it pay breathtaking dividends. 'When I've been to your *hôtel*,' said

Alphonse de Rothschild to one of the *grandes cocottes*, 'my own *hôtel* seems like a hovel to me.' These are the patricians of gallantry: the women whom visiting princes consider it essential to see.

Here, in her superb yellow coupé, comes the baronne de Sternberg: the morganatic baroness, better known as Adèle Courtois; she will linger on into the early years of the twentieth century. She is now no longer in her first youth; but through her genius for dressing well, her gift for entertaining, her quasi-conjugal liaison with the immensely rich baron, she still sets the tone. The baron, says Alphonse Daudet, has given her ten thousand francs a month, and a hundred thousand for her *étrennes*; he has also given her permission to take a presentable young lover.[3]

Here is Constance Rezuche, who is one of two sisters dedicated to the profession.[4] Here is Juliette de la Canebière: Juliette Beau, the passionate Marseillaise. She has won the attention of connoisseurs by her air of innocence, and a rich foreign lover will marry her and bear her away from the demi-monde for ever.[5]

Here is Anna Deslions, sometimes known as Marie-Antoinette; her face is that of an adolescent of the *quattrocento* (some say it is the face of Cleopatra), her hair is black as night, and her velvet look is as moving as a caress. She was a humble officiant in a temple of love before she became a high priestess, a star of the Grand Seize, the inspiration of the succulent *pommes de terre Anna* at the Café Anglais, and the mistress of Prince Napoleon. When she grants a suitor her favours, she sends him her *toilette de nuit*, so that he may choose the colour for his night of love. This *toilette galante* costs from two thousand five hundred to three thousand francs, and it gives some idea of the price she demands for herself. Her *hôtel* is as sumptuous as her wardrobe, and the Goncourts shudder when they enter her bedroom, hung with red satin, and see a picture of labourers sweating in the fields: there is something appalling in the contrast between the honest, ill-rewarded toil and the destiny of the room. Anna Deslions has a passion for serious books: she has many handsome editions of *The Imitation of Jesus Christ*. In one of them a nameless admirer has written the comment: 'You never know what may happen.'[6]

Anna Deslions is followed by Adèle Rémy, dreaming of her mysterious love-affair at Saint-Firmin,[7] and by the great Soubise, still obstinately parading her faded charms, though it is said that yesterday she had to sell a dress in order to have horses today for her carriage. All the Jockey Club can recognise the carriages of *la garde*: Caroline Hassé's yellow barouche, drawn by two irreproachable half-bloods,[8] and la Barucci's big barouche, dark blue set off with red. Cora Pearl has decked out her servants in the

Mogador

Elisabeth-Céleste Mogador in male attire.

Above. The bandstand at the
Bal Mabille. It was in
these pleasure-gardens that
Céleste danced the polka
with Brididi, and earned
celebrity as Mogador.
Right. The *promenoir* at the
Bal Mabille, a sketch by
Constantin Guys.

Opposite
Top. The boulevard du
Temple, centre of theatrical
Paris in the early nineteenth
century. Céleste Vénard,
the future Mogador,
was born near here in 1824.
Bottom. Saint-Lazare, the
women's prison. It was here
that Céleste Vénard was
taken, at the age of
thirteen, for 'protection'.

Les Reines de Mabille: an audacious song sheet, evidence of Mogador's fame in the early 1840s.

'A pale young girl, who polka'd like a demon': la Reine Pomaré dancing at the Bal Mabille.

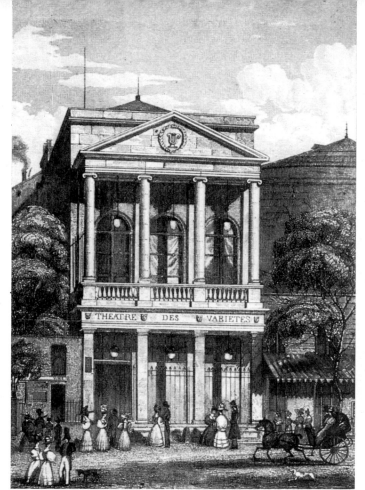

Above. The Théâtre des Variétés, where Mogador delighted her Paris public.

Top right. Mogador, the actress, at the Théâtre des Variétés: an impression of 1852.

Céleste Mogador and Adèle Page dancing the *Pas de l'Impériale* at the Théâtre des Variétés, 1852.

Above. Gabriel-Paul-Josselin-
Lionel, Comte de Morton de
Chabrillan, French consul-
general in Melbourne and
husband of Mogador.

Madame la Comtesse Lionel
de Chabrillan. Mogador at
the time of her marriage,
1854.

Above. The ruins of Paris, 1871: the Salle des Maréchaux, at the Palais des Tuileries, after it had been burnt by the Commune.
Left. The Comtesse de Chabrillan in later life. From a photograph, signed Mogador, which she gave to a friend in 1887.

'*La Cavalerie infernale.*'

bright yellow affected by Mme de Metternich, the wife of the Austrian Ambassador. Rosalie Léon, that famous 'lady of the evening', has lined her carriage with violet satin, and daringly equipped her lackeys and footmen with jackets of the same imperial hue.[9]

Today, a fine day in the 1860s, the Champs-Élysées – 'a Rotten Row flanked by palaces' – is one vast show of rare spring flowers: of 'gigantic lilies, geraniums of every colour, fuchsias of prodigious proportions . . . In the Bois,' observes an English journalist, 'there are the gardens where . . . strange animals are being acclimatized; and there is a new châlet on the island in the lake, to which gondolas, gay with coloured lamps, float the fine evening through . . .'[10] It is a fairy-like setting for fairy-tales; and some of the courtesans are indeed living lives that make the tales of Perrault seem pedestrian.

★

One of the most fantastic lives was that of Rosalie Léon, a humble girl from Guépavas, near Brest. She had made her début at sixteen, as a maid at the local inn, and a passing actor had carried her off to Paris. She had the air of a marquise, and an elegance all her own; she won the adoration of Prince Peter Wittgenstein: a general of division and aide-de-camp to the Emperor of Russia. The Prince was 'as handsome as a classical statue, and as rich as Croesus'. He offered her his hand and his forty-five million; he abandoned his diplomatic career and his highest ambitions for her. And then, inexplicably, in the flower of her youth, possessed of a situation beyond her dreams, she died from addiction to ether. The Prince 'went and shut himself up in the great château he had built for her in the heart of Brittany – that Brittany whence she had come, poor, humble and obscure – and, soon afterwards, he surrendered his soul to God'.[11]

There might be a book about Rosalie Léon, another about Skittles, the English courtesan who glowed on the Paris scene for two or three years and was recognised, towards the end of the century, in a railway refreshment room on the Canterbury line.[12] There might be yet another book about Lola Montès, the tempestuous Irish courtesan, who enslaved the King of Bavaria, and built herself a veritable palace at Beaujon. ('Madame,' said Arsène Houssaye, 'you should call it the Palace of the Thousand and One Nights.' 'Well, Monsieur,' she answered, 'I will give you the thousand and second night free of charge.')[13]

There would be a volume to write about women who were not courtesans, but were known for one or two resplendent love-affairs: Madame d'Agoult was the celebrated mistress of Liszt; Mme Le Hon, *l'ambassadrice aux cheveux d'or,* was the mistress of the Duc de Morny; Mme Musard owed her wealth to the King of the Netherlands; Miss Howard and la Castiglione in turn enslaved the Emperor. Many actresses, said Arsène Houssaye, believed that the theatre was a baptism which saved them from original sin, and Rachel and Sarah Bernhardt were two of the greatest lovers of the century.[14] Many an actress was a *femme carrossable* at heart.

Such women only confirm the theory that the century enjoyed its pleasures to the limit; it was an age for spectacular liaisons, and for women of unmistakable individuality. The great courtesans were not merely pretty women, they were not merely purveyors of physical pleasure. They were not even all of them beautiful. But they shared a belief in the pleasure of love, in the art of making love, in the joy of living; and most of them showed a spiritual energy and a shrewd and versatile intelligence which would have done much credit to honest women.

Many of them were overwhelmed by the fortunes they acquired, the fortunes they squandered wildly like the nouveaux-riches they were. Their dresses were over-elaborate, their jewels far too many, their food too rich and spiced and abundant; their *hôtels* and châteaux often proved that they were blessed with wealth, but devoid of all aesthetic sense. They behaved not only as if they had just come into a fortune – which in fact they had; they behaved like exhibitionist, petulant, pampered children. They would do anything for the *réclame.*

Most of them (but one must except Madame Sabatier) were entirely without morals. They lived for money, and for money alone; they would readily ruin men and, if need be, their wives and families, for the sake of increasing their fortune. They rarely loved a man for himself, they loved the material benefits he would bring to enhance their professional status, and to gratify their self-esteem. They strove to inspire the envy of their colleagues and *le grand monde*: of the honest, or more honest, women who would not accept them. Cora Pearl, who was one of the hardest of all courtesans, would readily abandon a lover when she had exhausted his fortune. She had made her conquest and bought her pleasure; his future did not concern her.

Human relationships hardly concern the woman who sells herself, but Esther Guimond was said to have built her fortune on blackmail, and to have caused at least one suicide. La Païva loved no living creature, man, woman, child or beast, and the whole of her long life, which reads like a romance by Rider Haggard, was designed to proclaim her triumph, to give her splendour and satisfaction. No speculator on the Bourse, no industrial magnate could have exploited men with such inhumanity, and with such effect.

*

The courtesan is a type as old as humanity itself; she will last as long as men are fascinated by the sexual arts, as long as women choose to exploit their powers. She will last as long as men want to love without responsibility, as long as they are ready to buy experience. Yet though the courtesan existed before the Second Empire, though she has existed since it fell, the Second Empire was her golden age. The courtesan is, by her nature, a woman in search of fortune; and this was the epoch of the fortune-seeker. Parvenus were on the make, in the reign of a parvenu; fortunes were being made and lost, fortunes were being spent. And if diamonds were made to glitter, as Cora Pearl observed, if golden louis were meant to change hands, she was quite entitled to enjoy them. The courtesan profited from passing millionaires, from mushroom fortunes; she profited from the *nouveaux riches*, and from the bourgeoisie. Sexual licence had always been a privilege of the aristocracy, an element in their education; but now it was claimed by the middle classes, who had risen to wealth and power. *Les mangeuses*, as the middle-class women called the courtesans, indulged their boundless appetites with the fortunes which the middle classes had patiently and laboriously acquired.

The courtesans of the Second Empire not only profited from the social revolution, they profited from political uncertainty. In the sixty or seventy years that had passed since 1789, France had known rapid changes of régime. The Directoire and the Consulate and the Empire had been followed by the Bourbon Restoration, the Hundred Days, by the second restoration of Louis XVIII. Charles X had been deposed, Louis-Philippe, the bourgeois king, had fled after eighteen years of monarchy; Louis-Napoleon had imposed himself on the country by a plebiscite and a *coup-d'état*. The Second Empire was itself far from secure: only the young Prince Imperial ensured that the widely-discredited Prince Napoleon would not succeed to the throne. Until the advent of the liberal Empire, in 1870, the Empire was a virtual dictatorship which harboured licence and corruption; and the rigorous censorship of the Press and the theatre suppressed, but did not destroy, any anti-imperial feeling. A correspondent of the *Athenaeum*, writing from Paris in 1862, remarked on the quantity of doubtful literature that was published. 'How is it,' he asked, 'that a Government which crushes the slightest expression of political feeling permits the publication of such literary filth as these books probably contain? Is it not to be explained by the fact that, so long as Parisians are amused, there is less probability of their thoughts dwelling on political slavery?'[15] The English journalist probably touched the heart of the matter; and what was true of books was also true of the Press. Indeed, since the Press was forbidden to publish political criticism, since religious questions could not be freely discussed, it naturally paid more attention to social life; and the courtesans enjoyed constant publicity. They had, as it were, their own Court circular; their dazzling daily round, their more outrageous behaviour, their theatrical triumphs and financial disasters, were chronicled as never before or since. The daily papers, the artistic periodicals and the more outspoken popular journals: all of them reflected the life of the courtesan, and kept the public constantly aware of her.

★

The régime which allowed her such publicity was also her most obvious supporter. The Emperor's own love-affairs were many and ostentatious. He enjoyed a woman, he said, as he might enjoy a good cigar after dinner; one commentator suggested that only two women at Court, among those who qualified by their beauty and easy virtue, had not in fact accorded him their favours. To be unfaithful with the Emperor was an honour, not a dishonour. He was the topmost tinsel star on the Christmas tree of Parisian gallantry. La Castiglione, sent by Cavour to make him pro-Italian in his politics, did not fail to seduce him; and Marguerite Bellanger had to be dismissed by the Empress. But the Imperial Court itself hardly set an example of morality. 'The example of bestial luxury came to us from above,' wrote Marguerite – or the author of her *Confessions* – of the Paris of 1863. 'Which of us had not seen in shop windows, between the portraits of the most famous courtesans, the most unbridled actresses, those of the great ladies-in-waiting, or, at least, those of the Empress's household?'

Prince Napoleon was as promiscuous as his cousin, the Emperor.

> He never shut the door [recorded Maxime du Camp, with indignation], and he hardly showed self-respect . . . Publicly, and with no more shame than a Bohemian, he lived with whores, with Anna Deslions, with Cora Pearl, with Caroline Letessier, with Constance and with masses of other creatures whose names I don't even know; he visited the little theatres in company with Mme Arnould-Plessy, a wreck from the Comédie-Française, and with la Détourbet, who had sold one of her lovers to Mirès as a son-in-law. He paraded himself, he compromised himself, he insulted himself. In the morning there was always some petticoat or other still trailing about in his private apartments . . .[16]

Morny, the Emperor's half-brother, was the lover of Cora Pearl, and had a long and public liaison with Mme Le Hon, the wife of the Belgian Ambassador. Prefects and generals, officers of the imperial household, men of the utmost distinction in public life, flaunted their mistresses with bravado.

> During the last few days [noted Viel-Castel, on 25 July 1857], M. Haussmann, the *honourable* Prefect of the Seine, Senator, grand cross of several orders, etc., etc., etc., was driving round in an open carriage at Enghien with Francine Cellier, a young reveller from the Opéra, ex-mistress of the young Fronsac Baroche.
> This example set by the first magistrate of a department has something consoling about it . . . for religion and morals.[17]

The very air of Paris seemed to encourage licence. Foreign celebrities passing through the capital hastened to pay their respects to the most notorious *filles en renom* (Hortense Schneider, the actress, was known as *le passage des princes*). A famous mistress, a wild way of life, became status symbols. The Duc de Grammont-Caderousse, so it was reported, lit his cigar on a racecourse with an English £1,000 note [sic], which he had won, because the crackling paper got on his nerves.[18] He gave Cora Pearl a silver bath-tub, filled it with magnums of champagne, and then climbed into it before the astounded company. 'We have fallen,' Viel-Castel ended his *Mémoires* in 1864, 'and those who were young about the Emperor are growing old, and those who were still not corrupted, four years ago, are now corrupted completely.'[19] Men of less distinction followed the fashions set by their social superiors. Aurélien Scholl, the wit and journalist, who collected *grandes cocottes*, was said to have been the lover of Cora Pearl, Léonide Leblanc, La Barucci and Marguerite Bellanger.[20]

Only a political revolution could change this way of life; and the revolution came with the fall of the Second Empire. After 1870, there was no Court, no aristocracy to confer distinction on the profession. It lost much of its social glamour in the Republic, when the men-about-town of the golden age had dispersed, the life of pleasure grew banal, and pornocracy became democratic, like everything else. The poets who had sung the praises of the courtesans had died, or had grown old and sober and conventional. The Romantic Age was out of fashion, the demi-monde was growing old with Dumas *fils*, and when Zola wrote of Nana, he was clinical rather than sympathetic.

★

Even under the Second Empire there had been those who lamented the general corruption: the immorality of Emperor, Court and nobility, of the middle classes and the poor. Those who were rich enough bought their pleasures, those who were poor enough sold them. Those who were not directly concerned in the traffic of sex were not averse to furnishing the décor of prostitution: the coachbuilder and the breeder of horses, the architect and the furniture dealer, the grocer and the butcher, the wine merchant and the restaurateur, enjoyed their prosperity.

So did the jeweller and the couturier. Rosalie Léon was one of the most elegant demi-mondaines, and given to an originality in dress which had Mme Worth, the couturier's wife, up in arms.

I remember [wrote Jean-Philippe Worth] that my mother once attended the races where Rosalie Léon appeared in a lemon coloured taffeta made entirely of tiny pleated flounces . . . About this yellow frock was tied a leaf green sash which was knotted at one side and its ends left floating. This combination of brilliant yellow and springlike green . . . created a sensation and scandalised my mother. When my father asked her upon her return if she had seen Madame Rosalie Léon's yellow and green dress, she snapped, 'I did. And I never saw anything so ridiculous. It looked just like an omelette aux fines herbes!'

The truth was that Madame Léon was very charming in her omelette dress and proceeded to set the fashion for wearing yellow trimmed with green, or vice versa. For by then people no longer shied at something new or different. My father had at last won the day, . . . and banished banality and sartorial unprogressiveness from Paris for ever.[21]

When a reception and dinner were given at the Maison d'Or, in honour of the visiting Prince of Orange, twelve of the smartest women in Paris were present, wearing white and orange dresses. Worth created a Louis XVI masterpiece for Rosalie Léon: a white tulle dress, trimmed with orange blossom and small oranges tied with orange ribbons. It was partly responsible for making her queen of the evening – though, as Worth's son observed, no Frenchman could see the combination of orange blossom and fruit without a smile.[22] It offended his sense of logic; besides, fertility symbols appeared a trifle misplaced on a *grande cocotte*.

Perhaps the strictly conservative presence of Mme Worth sometimes kept the great demi-mondaines out of the shop in the Rue de la Paix. But Rosalie Léon was not the only member of *la garde* who advertised the couturier's inspiration. Adèle Courtois, Constance Rezuche, Juliette Beau and Anna Deslions were among his clients. So were la Barucci (who used to wear fifteen strings of pearls at a time), and that grotesque woman, designed by Breughel: the Marquise de Païva. In 1867, Paris was laughing at the indignation of a princess who had found herself face to face at a fashion house with Léonide Leblanc. They were both waiting to be received by the great *habilleuse*.

Their turn came [said *La Vie parisienne*]; but Léonide Leblanc was received before the princess. *Inde irae*, fury, rage. But then why do people expose themselves to such misadventures? The tradesman only recognises equality of wealth – and he is right.[23]

Yet (as Arsène Houssaye observed in *Les Confessions*), the confusion between the *coquines* and the society women, between the marquises and the actresses, was a social revolution, and a much more serious revolution than people imagined. The creation of the demi-monde was the end of a world. In the days of Louis-Philippe, the courtesans did not appear in broad daylight; they did not have their civil status and their place in the sun. But during the Second Empire, the mondaines and demi-mondaines had begun to brush shoulders with each other at charity balls and races. At first sight, they were identical women, dressed by the same couturiers, with the subtle difference that the demi-mondaines had more *chic* than the mondaines (indeed, it was then that the word *chic* came into fashion among women).[24] By 1866, in *La Vie parisienne* by Meilhac and Halévy, the Baronne de Gondremarck could not distinguish the aristocrat from the *cocotte*:

Je regardai: mêmes frisures,
    Mêmes allures,
Mêmes regards impertinents,
Même hardiesse à tout dire,
    Même sourire
Allant aux mêmes jeunes gens.
Pour choisir, ne sachant que faire,
Je dis: la grande dame est là.
C'était justement le contraire;
Mais comment deviner cela?[25]

The social revolution was complete.

★

Henri Murger had presented the *grisette*, the Bohemian *fille de joie*, the Left Bank students' prostitute, in *Scènes de la vie de Bohème*. Dumas *fils* introduced – so it seemed – a new figure into literature. His novel, *La Dame aux camélias*, based on the life of Marie Duplessis, appeared in 1848, some eighteen months after her death; it caught the public imagination by the ring of truth. Four years later, in 1852, he dramatised the story, and la Dame aux camélias 'entered the French theatre for all time, and kept a place there which corresponded to the place she had so largely taken in public morals'.[26]

La Dame aux camélias perfectly suited the mood of the moment.

For some time [declared *L'Artiste* in 1852], all the *dames aux camélias* have put on sickly looks and played about like loving turtle-doves; but the serpent never wastes his time. There are eras when women play at being outrageous and scandalous. Today the game is not rewarding, so they are playing innocent.[27]

La Dame aux camélias was out-of-date even before the end of the Second Empire: in January 1868, when the play was revived, Barbey d'Aurevilly lamented its obsolescence:

We went to the revival of *La Dame aux camélias*. A revival . . . which hasn't revived. It was an evening of great sadness. Where are the days, dear God, when those camellias were in flower? . . . If you remember, all Paris, even the Paris of honest women, went to set their imagination on fire with this drama in which a rare *fille de joie* dies of love and grief. Oh, what a long time it is since our curiosity was so ardently, so shockingly excited! . . .

What is immensely striking, in fact, about this revival of *La Dame aux camélias* is the obsolescence, the sadness, the end of something which seemed for a moment to live so intensely . . . Compared with the courtesan of today and her monstrous corruption, squalor, language, slang and stupidity, the Marguerite Gautier of M. Dumas *fils*, who first interested everyone in courtesans, seems nothing but a faded engraving of some vague design . . .

It is this curious lowering of public morals, which has made us blasé, that we noticed more than ever at this revival . . .[28]

Twenty years later, in the 1880s, the Comte de Maugny found himself at his club, discussing women. He and his friends declared that Marguerite Gautier 'would only provoke a smile of incredulity among the *bons viveurs* of today'.[29]

But in 1852, on the threshold of the Second Empire, *La Dame aux camélias* was real and convincing; and some were incensed by Dumas *fils*' rehabilitation of the courtesan. It was *La Dame aux camélias* which led Théodore Barrière, the following year, to introduce the courtesan in her true colours. In May 1853 the Vaudeville first presented his drama, *Les Filles de marbre*.

Ah! if I had a family [said one character, in a famous passage], this is what I'd say to my son – an innocent, hardworking student. 'You see these ladies with diamonds, they're devils . . . they have horns . . . you don't notice them, but they've got them . . . those little pink nails are really talons; they ruin your purse and your heart . . .' That's what I should say to my son. It probably wouldn't stop him from making a fool of himself for the hell of it; but I should have a clear conscience about it . . . I should have said my say as an honest man . . . Hang it! it's gone on long enough. Off with you, ladies, into the shadows, keep your carriages in their proper place! Make way for the honest women who go on foot![30]

Opposite: Baigneuse endormie: detail from Chassériau's painting of Alice Ozy (1850).

Epilogue

The effect of Barrière's play was not what he intended. The courtesans arrived *en foule* to see themselves insulted. Indeed, one 'fast' actress, meeting the dramatist at the theatre, stopped and thanked him for giving her prosperity: she could now afford to keep two horses. The profit was not all on one side: Barrière replied that he had just bought a fine Arab horse himself.

Les Filles de marbre ran for a hundred and sixteen performances. The critics rightly questioned the dramatic merits of the work, but they welcomed Barrière's moral principles; they gave the drama an uncommon amount of space. The director of the Vaudeville shrewdly withdrew the play, revived *La Dame aux camélias* for four nights, and then continued *Les Filles de marbre* for a fortnight. In 1854 the dispute about the courtesans was so much in vogue that a character in a vaudeville protested: 'Now, gentlemen, please let us drop *les dames aux camélias* and *les filles de marbre*. I know that modern France is split into two camps about these poor sinners.' In 1855 Gautier suggested that 'perhaps it was time to leave these poor *filles de marbre* in peace on their pedestals. For over three years they have kept the theatre going almost single-handed.' But Barrière had prepared the way for the authors of *Le Mariage d'Olympe* and *Le Demi-Monde*. Both plays burst on the public this same year; and in *Le Demi-Monde* Dumas *fils* made his own reply to *La Dame aux camélias*. [31]

On 20 March 1855, when his play was first performed, he put a new word into international currency. 'The demi-monde,' he said, himself, 'does not represent the crowd of courtesans, but the class of declassed women . . . It is divided from that of honest women by public scandal, and divided from that of the courtesans by money.'[32] The word demi-monde came to have a much wider connotation than Dumas *fils* had intended. The Académie Française eventually defined it as 'the society of women of loose morals'. The definition came to include all those women known to be of easy virtue, of doubtful morality, who found themselves beyond the pale of society. No doubt the demi-monde had existed before Dumas *fils* defined it on the map; no doubt it exists today, and always will. But it was Dumas *fils* who discovered the brave new demi-monde; it remains Second Empire territory.

★

The courtesans, who left their impression on the theatre, the novel, and, above all, on poetry, also left their mark on the visual arts. Alice Ozy was painted by Chassériau, Blanche d'Antigny by Baudry. Apollonie Sabatier was painted by Meissonier and Ricard, and recorded in plaster and marble by Clésinger. The courtesans fostered the decorative arts by the extravagance with which they furnished their *hôtels* and country châteaux. They made their impact on fashion, for they spent hugely on dresses from Worth and Laferrière. They bought handsome carriages and impeccable horses. They paid unbelievable sums for food and drink. In fact, they largely encouraged the art of living.

At the end of the nineteenth century, there were those who regretted the sparkle which *les grandes horizontales* had given to life. There would never again be anything like the carriage procession in the Bois de Boulogne, where they dared to compete with, and often outshine, the Faubourg Saint-Germain. There would never be another decade like the 1860s, when *la garde* paraded their jewels and clothes and equipages at Longchamp, when they dazzled and infuriated the more decorous spectators at the Italiens; when, each September, they enthralled the inhabitants of Baden and Wiesbaden, of Homburg, Ems and Spa. Baden, with its clear hill air, had been the summer capital of Europe; it was Paris and its demi-monde (said *La Vie parisienne*), with a few foreigners to make it look respectable.[33] 'Nothing,' wrote Marie Colombier, one of the *filles de joie*, 'nothing can give any idea of the first fortnight in September at Baden-Baden . . . It was the fantasy, the irresponsible madness of the *kermesses* of olden times.'[34]

> Courses, concerts, théâtre, on trouve tout à Bade,
> On a le Vieux Château, on a la promenade
> Du Lichtenthal avec tous ses sentiers ombreux,
> Ses Autrichiens blancs et ses Prussiens bleus . . .[35]

Monte-Carlo would be the poorer when, in the 1880s, Cora Pearl was reduced to playing five-franc roulette.

Monte-Carlo would be the poorer; so would Paris itself. In 1888, in his *Mémoires d'un Parisien*, Albert Wolff recalled the career of Cora Pearl almost with regret.

Mme Cora Pearl was, so to speak, a glorious relic of imperial gallantry. One looked upon her, towards the end of her life, with the curiosity one would feel, for example, about the last survivor from the raft of the *Medusa* . . . Her predecessors and her contemporaries have alike disappeared. The former are dead; the latter run schools where little actresses are coached for their doctorate in gallantry. Cora Pearl is part of the Paris which has vanished . . .

We older men knew the time when a beautiful and intelligent woman, of easy virtue, could make her rooms a veritable salon, which no man of doubtful education ever entered; and we were happy to be admitted, because we showed, just by being present, that we were somebody in the streets of Paris. After this thoroughbred courtesan there came another of an inferior kind; since then, the profession has fallen a notch lower still. Today love in Paris is just a bazaar; it is like La Belle Jardinière, the multiple store of French gallantry, where, for a modest sum, you can buy a small kit for a man-about-town.[36]

I come, without transition, to the *cocodettes* [wrote the Comte de Maugny, recalling the Second Empire in *La Société parisienne*]. A whole epoch! And what an epoch! . . . Eighteen years of luxury, pleasure, recklessness and gaiety, of gallantry and incomparable elegance. It was for a time – alas, too short a time! – like an apparition of the dazzling splendours of the eighteenth century. Then a veil of mourning and sadness suddenly hid the décor; it all vanished again, into shadow and triviality. Who does not now regret them in his inmost heart, those poor years of corruption? Who can recall them and not repress a feeling of pleasure? Who can remember, without emotion, that swarm of pretty young women, each of them more charming and agreeable than the other, . . . happy to be alive, to flirt, and to be admired? You see, the mould for those women is broken. You will not find them again.[37]

As the nineteenth century drew to its close, Arsène Houssaye, who had known so many of the *dames galantes* of his age, recorded them in the six volumes of *Les Confessions*. The real Queens of France, as he rightly said, were the women who reigned by right of conquest, not by right of birth. Now they had gone:

I have seen it all pass: the gods, the kings, the beaux and the beautiful women, the whole menagerie . . . Here lies the carnival. I have seen the world of fashion pass at Longchamp. *Requiescat in pace*.[38]

Gustave Claudin, the journalist, in *Mes Souvenirs*, sadly remembered the boulevards of 1840 to 1870, the *jeunesse dorée*, the men-about-town who were now good husbands and fathers, and members of the general council for their *département*.[39] It was for them that Meilhac had written the rondeau in *La Vie parisienne* in which he described the orgies of the Grand Seize, and the aftermath of the nights of pleasure:

> On parle, on crie
> Tant qu'on peut crier;
> Quand on ne peut plus, il faut bien se taire;
> La gaîté s'en va petit à petit.
> L'un dort debout, l'autre dort par terre,
> Et voilà comment la fête finit . . .[40]

Early in the twentieth century, in *La Fête Impériale*, Frédéric Loliée still lamented the end of the orgy:

The *cocottes* of high rank, with their precise individuality, their personal influence, their name and originality, have well and truly vanished. With two or three exceptions, . . . there are now in that part of society only kept women and public mistresses, as there will always be to gratify and to endanger men.[41]

★

There had been some distinguished *filles de joie* in the reign of Louis-Philippe; but the *grandes cocottes* had been phenomena of the Second Empire. Certainly they had proclaimed its weaknesses: its avidity for money, its febrile quest for excitement – like Baudelaire, they had plunged *au fond du gouffre pour trouver du nouveau*. They had symbolised frivolity and irresponsibility, they had helped to undermine public morals, to make men lose their generous ambitions, their proper sense of values. When, in his massive study of Paris, Maxime du Camp came to write of prostitution, he blamed *les femmes interlopes*, as he called them, for corrupting the solid middle classes, and for making Sedan a possibility. It was, he said, the generation of *petits crevés* who had lost themselves in a life of pleasure, and therefore lost the Franco-Prussian War. They had changed the course of French history; for 'when France looked within herself for the men she needed, she saw emptiness, and she found no-one'.[42]

Today we look back on the great courtesans with some of the moral strictures, the political regrets of Maxime du Camp; we may speculate on the degeneration which the *grandes cocottes* inspired, and wonder how different history might have been. But we may also exchange our sombre speculation for fact, and look, beyond the romantic lives that these women led, to their lasting effect on the arts. Without Marie Duplessis we should not have known *La Dame aux camélias* or *La Traviata*; without la Païva we should not have the grim and astonishing *hôtel* in the Champs-Élysées, the architectural monument to the courtesan. Had it not been for Blanche d'Antigny, Nana might not have crystallised in the mind of Zola. Had it not been for la Présidente, posterity would have lost much of the splendour of *Les Fleurs du mal* – for Apollonie Sabatier, who loved Baudelaire, and was loved by him, inspired some of the greatest poems of the nineteenth or any century.

And finally, for all their vices, and for all their weaknesses, the *grandes cocottes* had given a diamanté sparkle to life, a kind of champagne zest to the art of living. In a sense they had been the incarnation of the Second Empire.

It was this thought which touched the heart of Marie Colombier, the actress-courtesan, when she was exiled from Paris during the Commune – and when, one evening, from the terrace of Saint-Germain, which overlooked the city, she saw Paris burning.

Sparks, borne by the wind, whirled overhead: they were the documents from the Cour des Comptes. Or, rather, they were the history of the Second Empire which was passing, page by page, in the smoke and flames. It was over, this Balzacian dream which had been realised in the romantic adventure of the time ... The great ladies who were really the d'Espards and the Maufrigneuses dreamed of by the creator of the *Comédie humaine*; the elegant careerists who incarnated Rubempré and Rastignac; the creatures of luxury and joy who had all the beauty of Esther, all the wit of Jenny Cadine, had only, now, to grow old and to die. Their reign was over for ever and ever; the ass's skin was worn out, all the goblets at the orgy had been drained. The quadrille from *Orphée aux Enfers* no longer made the brass roar under the chandeliers of the Opéra; there was nothing, now, but the saraband of the *pétroleuses* round the ruins. [43]

Notes

Blanche d'Antigny

1 The most complete account is Vauzat: *Blanche d'Antigny. Actrice et demi-mondaine* (1840–1874); see also Zed: *Le Demi-Monde sous le Second Empire*, 188–92. There are also details about Blanche d'Antigny in *Les Parisiennes* by Jacques Mardoche and Pierre Desgenais; *Les Lionnes du Second Empire* by Auriant; and in *Dictionnaire des Comédiens Français*, by Henri Lyonnet, I, 429–30.

2 Vauzat, op. cit., 27.

3 The painting is now in the museum at Nantes.

4 Arsène Houssaye: *Souvenirs de Jeunesse*, 162–3, quoted by Vauzat, op. cit., 29.

5 Tortoni's, in the boulevard des Italiens, was famous for its ice-creams, and renowned in the 1840s and later as a focal-point of boulevard life. In the first volume of his *Mémoires d'un Journaliste*, published in 1872, Henri de Villemessant observes (277 sqq.): 'Everyone who counted in Paris used to pass Tortoni's every day, at about five o'clock.' In the third volume of his *Mémoires*, published in 1873 (127 sqq.), Villemessant lists Bignon's among the principal restaurants of Paris, and gives details of the specialities at several of the restaurants.

6 The Maison d'Or, in the boulevard des Italiens, was opened in 1841. During the Empire, Charles Verdier made it one of the centres of *la vie du boulevard*; le Grand Six, at the Maison d'Or, was as famous as le Grand Seize at the Café Anglais, and it was particularly favoured by Cora Pearl and la Barucci. The restaurant closed down just before 1910.

7 Mardoche and Desgenais maintain, somewhat implausibly, that she took the name of her village as her pseudonym.

8 The Restaurant Dinochau (which allowed large credits) was patronised by journalists under the Empire; Dinochau himself was ruined by the Siege of Paris, and died in December 1871.

9 Mardoche and Desgenais, op. cit., 30 sqq.

10 W.O. Field: *Things I Shouldn't Tell*, 162.

11 Mardoche and Desgenais, op. cit., 28, 32; Field, op. cit., 162; see also Auriant: *La véritable Histoire de Nana*.

12 Field, op. cit., 162.

13 Charles Diguet: *Les Jolies Femmes de Paris*, 87–9.

14 *La Veilleuse*, 5 August 1868.

15 Raphaël Bischoffsheim, 1823–1906, was the naturalised son of a banker in Mainz; known as a *boulevardier*, he became deputy for Nice in 1881.

16 The first performance of *Le Château à Toto* took place on 3 July; the song is quoted by Auriant: *Les Lionnes du Second Empire*, 10–11.

17 Mardoche and Desgenais, op. cit., 31–2.
18 Théodore de Banville: *Critiques*, 288–90.
19 Mahalin: *Les Jolies Actrices de Paris*, 1re série, quoted by Vauzat, op cit., 127. For Blanche d'Antigny's *hôtel*, see Vauzat, 99–110, 115–6.
20 Vauzat, op. cit., 130.
21 Diguet, op. cit., 87–9; Gustave Claudin, in *Mes Souvenirs*, 170, recalled that the Muse took an interest in history, and read background literature when she was playing an historical part on stage.
22 From an article by Victor Koning, 26 February 1870, quoted by Vauzat, op. cit., 76–7.

23 Quoted by Auriant, op. cit., 36.
24 For Blanche d'Antigny's conduct during the War, see Vauzat, and Auriant, op. cit., 37–8.
25 E. Cresson: *Cent Jours du Siège à la Préfecture de Police*, 193–5.
26 Mardoche and Desgenais, op. cit., 32.
27 Auriant, op. cit., 43 sqq., 51–2; Claretie, *Souvenirs du Dîner Bixio*, 121. Vauzat, op. cit., 140, gives the date of Luce's death as 30 January 1873.
28 Vauzat, op. cit., 144.
29 Vauzat, op. cit.
30 Field, op. cit., 160.
31 Auriant, op. cit., 56.
32 Vauzat, op. cit.; Auriant, op. cit.
33 Claretie, op. cit., 121.
34 Quoted by Auriant, op. cit., 59–60.

La Barucci

1 I have only been able to presume the date of her birth from the statement that she was twenty-six at the time of the Calzado trial in 1863.
2 F. Loliée: *La Fête Impériale*, 253 sqq.
3 Zed: *Le Demi-monde sous le Second Empire*, 9 sqq.
4 Ibid; S. Kracauer: *Jacques Offenbach ou le Secret du Second Empire*, 240–2.
5 Goncourt *Journal*, VI, 146 sqq.; 8 November 1863; on 8 January 1864 (VI, 169), they record that Scholl has broken with la Barucci.
6 M. Colombier: *Mémoires. Fin d'Empire*, 308 sqq.
7 D. Bingham: *Recollections of Paris*, 70–1.
8 Ibid; and Loliée, op. cit.

9 Loliée, op. cit.; Zed: op. cit., 9 sqq.
10 Ibid.
11 Zed, op. cit., 27.
12 J.-P. Worth: *A Century of Fashion*, 107.
13 M. Colombier, op. cit.
14 W. O. Field: *Uncensored Recollections*, 58. The memoirs of Marie Colombier and Cora Pearl give some idea of the wild behaviour of the demi-monde, and the practical jokes they enjoyed.
15 M. Colombier, op. cit., 303 sqq.
16 According to Marie Colombier; Loliée, op. cit., maintains that she died 'after the sombre events of the war', while a note to the Goncourt *Journal* (XXII, 75) says that she died soon after the Siege of Paris. One cannot date her death more exactly than 1870–1.

Cora Pearl

1 The most complete account of Cora Pearl is given in W. H. Holden: *The Pearl from Plymouth*.

2 In his *Uncensored Recollections*, 55 sqq., W. O. Field, who knew Cora well, recorded that she had begun her career

'by running away from a convent school in Boulogne with a barber'.

3 E. E. Crouch: *Mémoires de Cora Pearl*, 299–300.
4 Ibid, 38–9.
5 M. Colombier, op. cit.
6 P. Audebrand: *Petits Mémoires d'une Stalle d'Orchestre*, 220 sqq.
7 A. Daudet: *La Doulou*, 127.
8 G. Claudin: *Mes Souvenirs*, 246 sqq.
9 D. Bingham, op. cit., I, 60–1.
10 *Mémoires*, 49.
11 *The Pretty Women of Paris*, 1883.
12 The Duc de Grammont-Caderousse was said to be the man in fashion about 1860; Aurélien Scholl, himself a *noceur*, described him as the most loyal friend and brilliant companion.
13 M. du Camp: *Souvenirs*, I, 165.
14 See Joanna Richardson: *Rachel*, 93–4, and *passim*.
15 *Mémoires*, 114–5.
16 Holden, op. cit., *passim*.
17 The *Petit Journal Pour Rire*, No. 9, has a cartoon by Nadar: *Les Caprices de la Lune Rousse: Un dessin . . . de saison*.
18 Holden, op. cit.
19 Ibid.
20 Audebrand, op. cit., 222–3.
21 Bingham, op. cit., 61.
22 Field, op. cit., 60.
23 P. Foucher: *Entre Cour et Jardin*, 429 sqq.
24 *Mémoires; La Vie parisienne* also records some of Cora's financial vicissitudes.
25 Field, op. cit., 58.
26 Ibid, 56.
27 *Mémoires*.
28 Ibid, 97; Dolph: *The Real Lady of the Camellias*, 147. *Le Pilori*, 9 May 1868,

gives an account of Cora Pearl beating a little girl of ten who had dared to laugh at her in public; Cora was heavily fined for the offence.
29 Holden, op. cit.
30 Ibid.
31 Ibid.
32 A. Wolff: *Mémoires d'un Parisien*, 256.
33 Field, op. cit., 58.
34 Zed, op. cit., 52 sqq.
35 *Mémoires*, 190–1.
36 Field, op. cit., 58.
37 Holden, op. cit.
38 Claudin, loc. cit.
39 Théodore de Banville: *Camées parisiens*, 272.
40 Worth, op. cit., 101 sqq.
41 Claudin, loc. cit.
42 *La Vie parisienne*, 20 January 1866; for further notes on Cora's fashions, see the same periodical for 1864 (132, 708); 1865 (598, 642, 685); 1866 (82, 252).
43 Dolph, op. cit., 139 sqq., gives some account of Cora Pearl and of the *affaire Duval*.
44 *Mémoires*, 241.
45 The *Gazette Anecdotique*, 31 May 1877, 311–2, gives details of the sale.
46 *Mémoires*, 178.
47 Houssaye, op. cit., VI, 38 sqq.
48 Ibid.
49 Julian Arnold: *Giants in Dressing Gowns*, 40–2.
50 For another reflective account of Cora Pearl, see *Les Femmes du Jour*, April 1886.
51 Loliée, op. cit., 308.
52 *Mémoires*, 299–300.
53 Wolff, op. cit., 251 sqq.
54 *Mémoires*, 355–6.

Esther Guimond

1 Loliée, op. cit., 275 sqq.
2 Maurice Talmeyr, 1850–1931.
3 M. Talmeyr: *Souvenirs d'avant le Déluge*, 1870–1914, 101.

4 Quoted in the *Gazette Anecdotique*, 31 August 1879, 112–4.

5 Goncourt *Journal*, V, 17; 3 November 1861.

6 For other harsh comments on Esther Guimond, see the Goncourt *Journal*, V, 153, and *passim*.

7 Colombier, op. cit., 152 sqq.

8 *Gazette Anecdotique*, 1881, 257 sqq.

9 Richardson, op. cit., 76.

10 *Le Pilori*, 18 July 1868.

11 Colombier, loc. cit.; M. Reclus: *Émile de Girardin. Le Créateur de la Presse moderne*, 127.

12 Richardson, op. cit., 75–6.

13 Reclus, loc. cit.; for Girardin's political life, see also Goncourt *Journal*, I, 107–8, note.

14 G. Claudin: *Mes Souvenirs*, 246–9; see also A. Vandam: *Undercurrents of the Second Empire*, 248–9.

15 Reclus, op. cit., 153, 171–2.

16 Goncourt *Journal*, I, 107.

17 Loliée, op. cit., 280.

18 Houssaye, op. cit., II, 326 sqq.

19 Ibid.

20 Ibid.

21 A. Vandam: *Men and Manners of the Third Republic*, 221.

22 Houssaye, loc. cit.

23 D. Bingham: *Recollections of Paris*, 55.

24 R. Christophe: *La Vie du Maréchal Bazaine*, 40; Loliée, loc. cit.; see also J. Claretie; *Souvenirs du Dîner Bixio*, 159.

25 Loliée, loc. cit.

26 Talmeyr, op. cit., 85 sqq.

27 Ibid, 89–90.

28 Ibid, 94 sqq.

29 Ibid.

30 Ibid, 99 sqq.

31 Goncourt *Journal*, XII, 11; 28 January 1879.

32 Colombier, loc. cit.; *Gazette Anecdotique*, 31 August 1879, 112–4.

33 Colombier, loc. cit.

34 Loliée, op. cit., 280.

35 Goncourt *Journal*, XII, 113; 3 May 1881.

36 Talmeyr, op. cit., 106.

37 Ibid, 106, 88–9.

La Païva

1 For Gautier and la Païva, see: Joanna Richardson: *Théophile Gautier: His Life and Times*, 202, 217.

2 Goncourt *Journal*, 27 September 1863.

3 Ibid, 3 January 1868.

4 *La Vie parisienne*, 9 July 1870, announces: 'En fait de modes, Mme Camille (3 rue Rougemont, au premier étage), a le sentiment de toutes les élégances et de toutes les coquetteries.'

5 Goncourt *Journal*, loc. cit.

6 Viel-Castel: *Mémoires sur le Règne de Napoléon III*: IV, 38 sqq. (2 April 1857).

7 F. Loliée: *La Païva*. This is the fullest account of her life, but it is badly written.

8 Viel-Castel, loc. cit.

9 Ibid. In *Souvenirs d'un Enfant de Paris*, II, 300–1, Émile Bergerat names Adolphe Gaiffe as the lover.

10 Houssaye, op. cit., V, 335 sqq.

11 Ibid.

12 Ibid.

13 Eugène Delacroix: *Journal*, III, 9.

14 Since Edouard Houssaye refers to 'last Wednesday' on 25 February, it seems that Delacroix had made a third, unrecorded visit – or, more probably, that Houssaye's article had been delayed.

15 Delacroix, op. cit., III, 20–1.

16 *Gazette Anecdotique*, 1882; II, 146–7.

17 Loliée, op. cit.

18 Ludcvic Halévy, *Carnets*, 77; 2 January 1866.
19 F. Loliée: *La Fête Impériale*, 150.
20 L. de Hegermann-Lindencrone: *In the Courts of Memory*, 37–8; the letter is dated 1863, presumably in error, but it is possible that the reference is to la Barucci's staircase.
21 *Gazette Anecdotique*, 31 May 1876.
22 Viel-Castel, op. cit., 16 May 1857.
23 Loliée, *La Païva*.
24 H. de Villemessant: *Mémoires d'un Journaliste*, 1re série, 127–9.
25 Worth, op. cit., 107 sqq.
26 A popular phrase in the last years of the Second Empire was: 'Quand la Païva va, tout va.' This hardly seems surprising. Bainville, 61 sqq.
27 A. D. Vandam: *Undercurrents of the Second Empire*, 228–9.
28 Bergerat, op. cit., 298.
29 Ibid, 300.
30 Goncourt *Journal*, 31 May 1867; see also *Journal*, 24 May 1867.
31 C. A. Dolph: *The Real Lady of the Camellias*, 82–3; see also Goncourt *Journal*, 14 February 1868, 24 October 1870.
32 Marquis de Roux: *Origines et fondation de la Troisième République*, 292 sqq.
33 See also Goncourt *Journal*, 21 November 1871.
34 Marquis de Roux, loc. cit.
35 Alexandre Dumas *fils*: *Théâtre Complet*, V, 210. *La Femme de Claude*. Introductory letter to M. Cuvillier-Fleury.
36 Worth, loc. cit.
37 Bergerat, op. cit., 295–303.
38 Marquis de Roux, op. cit., 295–6.
39 Ibid; and see Bainville: *La République de Bismarck*, 61 sqq.
40 Houssaye, loc. cit.
41 Ibid.
42 Loliée, op. cit.
43 The *Gazette Anecdotique*, 1884, I, 53–5, gives her age as 72.
44 Goncourt *Journal*, 1 June 1868.
45 Bergerat, op. cit., 295–6, 301–3.

Mademoiselle Maximum

1 Francisque Sarcey, in his *Comédiens et Comédiennes*, gives an account of Léonide Leblanc; he describes her father as 'un ingénieur des ponts et chaussées', and says that her godfather was 'un grand seigneur'. Sarcey offers some interesting details, but one suspects that he received them from Léonide herself, who was clearly a friend, and not averse to embroidering reality.
2 Jules Claretie: *La Vie à Paris*, 1907; 119.
3 V. Koning: *Les Coulisses parisiennes;* (1862) 6.
4 Sarcey, op. cit., 10.
5 Léonide Leblanc: *Les Petites Comédies de l'Amour*, iii sqq.; Sarcey, op. cit., 12, implies that she broke her contract with Montigny of the Gymnase, but Lemonnier says she broke with M. de Chilly, of the Ambigu.
6 Sarcey, op. cit., 12.
7 *La Vie parisienne*, 9 December 1865.
8 Leblanc, loc. cit.
9 *La Vie parisienne*, 20 January 1866.
10 Goncourt *Journal*, 10 March 1862.
11 F. Loliée: *La Fête Impériale*, 231 sqq.
12 Ibid, 236.
13 W. O. Field: *Uncensored Recollections*, 248–9.
14 Zed, op. cit., 155.
15 *La Vie parisienne*, 3 December 1864.
16 Ibid, 10 December 1864.
17 Jules Claretie: *La Vie à Paris*, 1908, 310–1
18 G. Claudin: *Mes Souvenirs*, 250 sqq.

19 M. du Camp: *Souvenirs*, I, 184–6; on 20 June 1868 *Le Pilori* recorded that she had just won sixty thousand francs at Homburg. 'A quel jeu?'

20 A. Lemonnier: *Les Femmes de Théâtre*, 50 sqq. There are some comments on Léonide Leblanc's literary career in *La Petite Revue*: 22 October 1864; 8 July, 9 September 1865; 17 February 1866.

21 Leblanc, loc. cit. Jules Claretie, in *La Vie à Paris*, 1906, 373, says that Léonide Leblanc wrote the book in collaboration with Lemonnier, 'aujourd'hui directeur à Bruxelles et rédacteur d'un journal très vivant, intitulé *Je dis tout*'.

22 Claretie, in *La Vie à Paris*, 1906, 76, records that there were some notable books at Léonide's sale.

23 Loliée, loc. cit.

24 W. O. Field, loc. cit.

25 W. O. Field: *More Uncensored Recollections*, 171–2

26 C. Diguet: *Les Jolies Femmes de Paris*, 23 sqq.

27 Sarcey, op. cit., 18–20.

28 Loliée, 237–8.

29 It is strange that she should be so described in 1883, for two years later she was still the mistress of the Duc d'Aumale (Goncourt *Journal*, XIII, 180, note).

30 W. O. Field: *Uncensored Recollections*, 56.

31 A. Mortier: *Les Soirées parisiennes de 1878*, 100–1.

32 Sarcey, op. cit., 22–3.

33 E. Daudet: *Les Coulisses de la Société parisienne*, 2e série, 4e édition, 28–9.

34 W. F. Lonergan: *Forty Years of Paris*, 187 sqq.

35 Daudet, op. cit., 21 sqq.

36 J. Claretie: *Souvenirs du Dîner Bixio*, 66.

Marguerite Bellanger

1 H. Fleischmann: *Napoléon III et les Femmes*, 269, dismisses the *Confessions* as 'cette spéculation de librairie qui hurle au faux'.

2 Henriette Celarié: *Marguerite Bellanger* (*les Œuvres libres*, mai 1955, 233 sqq).

3 *Ville de Paris. Bulletin de la Bibliothèque . . . VI* (1913).

4 A. Dansette: *Les Amours de Napoléon III*, 241 sqq.

5 Fleischmann gives the most authoritative account of Marguerite Bellanger; see also Loliée, op. cit., 291–4.

6 Fleischmann, op. cit., 260.

7 Dansette, loc. cit.

8 M. Bellanger: *Confessions*, 14–5.

9 Goncourt *Journal*, XXII, 79, note; Wilson was one of the most celebrated men-about-town during the Second Empire. See also Dansette, loc. cit.

10 Dansette, loc. cit.

11 Fleischmann, op. cit.

12 Bellanger: *Confessions*, 28.

13 Fleischmann, op. cit., 260.

14 *Recollections of Paris*, I, 49.

15 Dansette, loc. cit.

16 Ibid.

17 H. Kurtz: *The Empress Eugénie*, 183.

18 J. Claretie: *Souvenirs du Dîner Bixio*, 115.

19 Houssaye, op. cit., V, 213.

20 Kurtz, op. cit., 186.

21 Dansette, loc. cit.; Fleischmann, op, cit., 273–4.

22 Fleischmann, op. cit., 276.

23 Dansette, op. cit., 251–2; Fleischmann, op. cit., 278.

24 Fleischmann, op. cit.

25 H. Rochefort: *Les Aventures de ma vie* II, 329. Olivier Métra (1830–89), was a composer of waltzes.

26 Fleischmann, op. cit., 271.
27 Dansette, op. cit., 253–4.
28 F. M. Whitehurst: *My Private Diary during the Siege of Paris*, I, 145–6.
29 Dansette, op. cit., 253–4.
30 It has been suggested that she married an English naval officer, and that her married name was Lady Coulbach; the name hardly seems of British origin.

In *Le Demi-monde sous le Second Empire*, 39, Zed writes: 'I saw her again several years after the war, retired, married, forgotten, comfortably off though not rich, and I hardly thought, when I left her, that she would soon die and that I had spoken to her for the last time.'
31 Fleischmann, op. cit., 289.

Caroline Letessier

1 Colombier, op. cit., 66.
2 Zed, op. cit., 60–2.
3 Colombier, op. cit., 303 sqq.
4 Loliée, op. cit., 309–11.
5 H. Lyonnet: *Dictionnaire des Comédiens Français*, I, 361, notes that she was at the Théâtre du Palais-Royal, 1855–8, and at St Petersburg, 1859–1867.
6 Colombier, op. cit., 167 sqq.
7 Ibid.
8 Ibid.
9 W. O. Field: *Things I Shouldn't Tell*, 139–40.
10 *The Pretty Women of Paris*, 1883.
11 This story is told by Field in the book cited above, 124–7.
12 Holden, op. cit.
13 Loliée, loc. cit.
14 The directory does not mention Caroline Hassé, the second of *les deux Caro*; there is some account of her in Loliée, 283 sqq. and Zed, op. cit., 63–4.
15 Loliée, loc. cit.

Alice Ozy

1 The most complete account of Alice Ozy is in J.-L. Vaudoyer: *Alice Ozy ou l'Aspasie moderne*; but see also H. de Villemessant :*Mémoires d'un Journaliste* Ire serie, 134 sqq., etc.
2 The *Gazette Anecdotique*, 7e année [1882], tome I, gives an obituary of Brindeau.
3 For Alice Ozy as an actress, see H, Lyonnet: *Dictionnaire des Comédiens Français*, II, 499–501.
4 Villemessant, op. cit.; and see also Dolph: *The Real Lady of the Camellias*, 169 sqq.
5 For the ending of Alice Ozy's liaison with Perregaux, see Dolph, op. cit., 178–9.
6 Vaudoyer, op. cit., 29 sqq.; Richardson: *Théophile Gautier*, 52–3.
7 Richardson, op. cit., 304.
8 Ibid, 268, 279, 307.
9 *L'Artiste*, 5e série, tome XIII, 75.
10 Vaudoyer, op. cit., 39–40; V. Koning: *Les Coulisses Parisiennes*, 243.
11 Paul d'Ariste: *La Vie et le Monde des Boulevards* (1830–1870), 255–6, has an interesting comment on the *lorettes*, and their varying charges and perquisites, according to their *quartiers*.
12 Vaudoyer, op. cit., 43 sqq.; the Goncourt *Journal*, XIX, 196, gives a note on Alice Ozy and the two Hugos.
13 Vaudoyer, op. cit., 106–7.
14 Lorenzo Vendramin makes some

illuminating comments on Alice Ozy in *Mlle Ozy et ses Amis* (*Quo Vadis*, Nos. 65–70, 1954).

15 Vaudoyer, op. cit., 35 sqq.

16 Vaudoyer, op. cit.

17 Ibid.

18 H. de Villemessant, op. cit., 132–3.

19 Dolph, op. cit., 169 sqq.

20 Vaudoyer, op. cit., 34.

21 Théodore de Banville: *Odes Funambulesques*, 214–6. *Premier Soleil*. Dated April 1854.

22 Vaudoyer, op. cit.

23 Ibid, 85–7.

24 Edmond About: *Madelon*, 9 sqq.

25 Blanche Roosevelt, in her life of Doré, records that there were rumours that the artist might marry Alice Ozy; Doré was apparently too fond of his mother to distress her by any marriage.

26 Goncourt *Journal*, XIX, 87; 22 March 1893.

27 Ibid, XI, 52; 21 December 1875.

28 Villemessant, loc. cit.

29 In *Les Eaux illustrées. Enghien et ses Environs*, which was partly written by Emile de Girardin, and published in 1861, there is an engraving of Alice Ozy's châlet, 'cette délicieuse retraite, qui est le véritable jardin des roses d'Enghien'.

30 Vaudoyer, op. cit., 88–9.

31 Ibid, 108.

32 About, loc. cit.

33 Vaudoyer, op. cit., 106–7.

34 For Alice Ozy's adoption of the child, see *L'Artiste*, tome IX, 28 (15 August 1852); for her will, see Vaudoyer, 110–1.

La Dame aux Camélias

1 P. Gsell (editor): *Mémoires de Madame Judith . . .*, 221 sqq.

2 Dolph, op. cit., 19 sqq.; Vandam: *An Englishman in Paris*, I, 163–5, note; Gros: *Alexandre Dumas et Marie Duplessis*, 95.

3 Gsell, loc. cit.

4 Dolph, loc. cit.; Gros, op. cit., 109.

5 Field: *Uncensored Recollections*, 5–6.

6 Dolph, loc. cit.

7 Ibid.

8 G. Claudin: *Mes Souvenirs*, 39–42.

9 Dolph, loc. cit.

10 Ibid.

11 Vandam, op. cit., I, 159 sqq.

12 Gsell, loc. cit.

13 Ibid.

14 Vandam, loc. cit.

15 Claudin, loc. cit.

16 Lucien-Graux: *Les Factures de la Dame aux camélias*.

17 Preface to *La Dame aux camélias*, iii sqq.

18 D. Ollivier (ed.): *Correspondance de Liszt et de la Comtesse d'Agoult*, 379; letter of 1 May 1847.

19 Dolph, op. cit., 178–9.

20 Dolph, op. cit.

21 Ibid.

22 *Les Annales romantiques*, x, 380.

23 Ollivier, loc. cit.

24 Dolph, loc. cit.

25 A. Delvau: *Les Lions du jour*, 149 sqq.; see also Gsell, op. cit., 230–1.

26 Ollivier, loc. cit.

27 *Les Annales romantiques*, loc. cit.; Liszt to Dr Koreff, 12 February 1848.

28 John Forster: *The Life of Charles Dickens*, I, 474–5. The story is picturesque but I have not found it elsewhere, and it hardly tallies with the statement that Mme Plessis died when her daughter was a child. Moreover, Mme Plessis was said to

come from Normandy, while the mysterious visitor is wearing Breton costume.

29 Preface to *La Dame aux camélias*, xix sqq.

30 Forster, loc. cit.

31 Vandam, loc. cit.

32 Houssaye, op. cit.

33 Viel-Castel, op. cit., II, 34–5; 11 February 1852.

34 Vandam, loc. cit.

35 *Journal Officiel*, 27 August 1870.

36 Claudin, loc. cit.

37 Ibid.

La Présidente

1 The most complete account of Madame Sabatier is given by André Billy in *La Présidente et ses Amis*.

2 In *L'Artiste, Revue de Paris*, 15 December 1849, 62, we read: 'La saison des ventes s'est ouverte. Ces grandes assises . . . ont été inaugurées d'une manière assez brillante par la vente du curieux cabinet de M. Alfred Mosselmann [*sic*]. Voici quelques-uns des prix d'adjudication: *L'Allée des Châtaigniers*, de Th. Rousseau, a été payée 820 fr.; une *Etude de Cheval*, de Géricault, 750 fr.; . . . la *Descente des Bohémiens*, de Diaz, 3,000 fr.; . . . le *Corps-de-Garde* de Meissonnier, 8,800 fr.'

3 Roger de Beauvoir was the name adopted by Eugène-Auguste-Roger de Bully, 1806–66. His novel of mediaeval horrors *L'Ecolier de Cluny ou le Sophisme* (1832) is said to have given Dumas *père* the plot of *La Tour de Nesle*.

4 Article written by Gautier in 1868 for *Le Monde illustré*, reprinted in *Souvenirs romantiques*, 268 sqq.

5 Ibid, 276–7.

6 Quoted by Billy, op. cit., 65.

7 Ibid, 67.

8 Ibid, 59. *L'Artiste, Revue de Paris*, 25 April 1847, published a poem signed Henry Egmont: *Devant une statue du salon de 1847. A Madame ***. In the index the poem is called *Devant la femme piquée par un serpent*.

Lorsque je vis d'abord ce marbre palpitant
Dont un ciseau de feu fit battre les artères,
Sans m'avouer combien son aspect irritant
Attirerait sur lui de désirs adultères,
Je ne vis que la fleur de ses riches contours . . .
Je suivais, ébloui, le songe des amours . . .

Mais quand votre beauté, bien sûre d'elle-même,
Vint, devant moi, braver cette rivalité,
Si vous saviez alors de quel regret suprême,
Sous quels transports jaloux je frémis irrité!
Ce marbre me parut un miroir sacrilège
Livrant à tous les yeux les secrets de mon coeur,
Et je l'aurais brisé volontiers – sans la peur
Que votre sang jaillit de ses veines de neige.

9 *Emaux et Camées*, 7–10.

10 Théophile Gautier: *Œuvres Érotiques*, 95 sqq.; letter of 19 October 1850.

11 For Gautier and Marie Mattei, see Joanna Richardson: *Théophile Gautier, His Life and Times*, 89 sqq.

12 *Émaux et Camées*, 53–4.

13 For Baudelaire and Mme Sabatier, see Enid Starkie: *Baudelaire*, 253 sqq.
14 Baudelaire to Mme Sabatier, 31 August 1857.
15 Mme Sabatier to Baudelaire, quoted by Billy, op. cit., 132-3.
16 Mme Sabatier to Baudelaire, quoted by Billy, op. cit., 133-5.
17 Mme Sabatier to Baudelaire, quoted by Billy, op. cit., 136.
18 Ernest Feydeau: *Théophile Gautier. Souvenirs intimes*, 155.
19 Ibid.
20 Ibid, 164.
21 Ernest Feydeau: *Sylvie*, 21-2.
22 Ibid, 28-9.
23 Ibid, 38-40, 52, 77-8.
24 Feydeau: *Théophile Gautier*, 165.
25 Judith Gautier: *Le Collier des Jours. Le Second Rang du Collier*, 180 sqq.
26 Catalogue of the Meissonier sale, May 1893, quoted by Billy, op. cit., 149.
27 Billy, op. cit., 149-51.
28 *La Presse*, 8 April 1851, quoted by Richardson, op. cit., 87.
29 Billy, op. cit., 155.
30 Théophile Gautier: *Abécédaire du Salon de 1861*, 324.
31 Judith Gautier, op. cit., quoted by Billy, 210-11.
32 *Hymne. Les Fleurs du mal*, 156.

Mogador

1 *Mémoires de Céleste Mogador*, I, 173.
2 Ibid, I, 222-3.
3 Ibid, I, 240-1.
4 Ibid, I, 284-5.
5 Ibid, II, 37-8.
6 Ibid, I, 276.
7 Ibid, II, 236.
8 Ibid, *Préface*, I, i sqq.
9 Ibid, IV, 238-9.
10 Céleste de Chabrillan: *Les Voleurs d'or. Au lecteur*, i-ii.
11 *Mémoires: Préface*, I, iii-iv.
12 *Le Figaro*; quoted in *Gazette anecdotique*, 10e année [1885], II, 77-9. See also Jules Claretie: *Profils de Théâtre*, 208 sqq.

Epilogue

1 Houssaye, op. cit., V, 213.
2 The liveliest general picture of the *grandes cocottes* is given by Houssaye, loc. cit.; see also Loliée: *La Fête Impériale*, passim.
3 S. Kracauer: *Jacques Offenbach ou le secret du Second Empire*, 240-2; A. Daudet: *La Doulou*, 127-8; Loliée, op. cit., 265 sqq.
4 Loliée, op. cit., 283 sqq.
5 Kracauer, loc. cit.
6 Ibid; see also Claudin: *Mes Souvenirs*, 170, 246; Zed: *Le Demi-Monde sous le Second Empire*, 51-2; Loliée, op. cit.,
241 sqq. Anna Deslions's dates have been given as 1820[?]-73.
7 Loliée, op. cit., 269 sqq.
8 Ibid, 283 sqq.
9 Worth, op. cit., 101 sqq.
10 *The Athenaeum*, 22 June 1861, p. 831.
11 Loliée, op. cit., 306-7; Dolph, op. cit., 189 sqq.
12 Zed: *Le Demi-Monde sous le Second Empire*, has some account of Skittles.
13 See Houssaye, op. cit., I, 406 sqq., for Lola Montès and her colleagues.
14 Ibid; see also Joanna Richardson: *Rachel* and *Sarah Bernhardt*, passim.

15 *The Athenaeum*, 8 November 1862, 595.

16 Maxime du Camp: *Souvenirs d'un demi-siècle*, I, 184–6.

17 Viel-Castel, op. cit., IV, 121.

18 Ludovic, Duc de Grammont-Caderousse, 1833–65, was an habitué of the Café Anglais, and the lover of Mme de Persigny and Hortense Schneider.

19 Viel-Castel, op. cit., 27 August 1864.

20 Marcel Marter: *Aurélien Scholl et son Temps* (*Les Œuvres Libres*, 215 sqq).

21 Worth, op. cit., 101 sqq.

22 Ibid, 106.

23 *La Vie parisienne*, 21 December 1867, p. 916.

24 There were, of course, exceptions: *La Vie parisienne* reported on 29 May 1869 that Blanche d'Antigny had been seen driving in the Bois de Boulogne 'in clouds of lilac gauze . . . Her hair was of a shade that will soon make sky-blue or apple-green hair quite possible.'

25 H. Meilhac and L. Halévy: *La Vie parisienne*, IV, iv, p. 86.

26 Loliée, op. cit., 261.

27 *L'Artiste, Revue de Paris*, 15 February 1852, p. 29.

28 J. Barbey d'Aurevilly: *Dernière Série*.

Théâtre Contemporain, 1881–1883, 341 scq.

29 Zed: *Parisiens et Parisiennes en Déshabillé*, 229 sqq.

30 Théodore Barrière and Lambert Thiboust: *Les Filles de marbre*, IV, iv, 54.

31 E. C. Byam: *Théodore Barrière, Dramatist of the Second Empire*, 29 sqq.; Loliée, op. cit., 318–9.

32 The word invented by Dumas *fils* was defined as 'la société des femmes de mœurs légères' in the *Dictionnaire de l'Académie Française*, 1932.

33 *La Vie parisienne*, 1368, 723.

34 Marie Colombier: *Memoires. Fin d'Empire*, 158–9.

35 *La Vie parisienne*, 1363, p. 250.

36 A. Wolff: *Mémoires d'un Parisien*, 251 scq.

37 Zed: *La Société parisienne*, 94–5.

38 Houssaye, op. cit., I.

39 Claudin, op. cit., 249.

40 Meilhac and Halévy, op. cit., V, v, 110.

41 Loliée, op. cit., 323.

42 Maxime du Camp: *Paris. Ses Organes, ses Fonctions et Sa Vie dans la seconde moitié du XIXe siècle*. III, 453 sqq.

43 M. Colombier, op. cit., 318 sqq.

Selected Bibliography

French books have been published in Paris, English
books in London, unless otherwise stated.

About, Edmond, *Madelon* (Hachette 1863)

Allem, Maurice, *La Vie Quotidienne sous le Second Empire* (Hachette 1948)

Anon, *Les Courtisanes du Second Empire. Marguerite Bellanger* (Bruxelles. Office de Publicité 1871)

    Ville de Paris. Bulletin de la Bibliothèque et des Travaux historiques. VI (Imprimerie Nationale 1913)

    The Pretty Women of Paris (Privately Printed at the Press of the Préfecture de Police, by Subscription of the Members of the Principal Parisian Clubs 1883)

Ariste, Paul d', *La Vie et le Monde du Boulevard (1830–1870)*

    (*Un Dandy: Nestor Roqueplan*) (Editions Jules Tallandier 1930)

Arnold, Julian B., *Giants in Dressing Gowns* (Macdonald 1945)

Audebrand, Philibert, *Petits Mémoires d'une Stalle d'Orchestre* (Jules Lévy 1885)

Auriant, *La Véritable Histoire de 'Nana'* (Mercure de France 1942)

    Les Lionnes du Second Empire (Gallimard 1935)

Bainville, Jacques (tr.), *La République de Bismarck, ou origines allemandes de la troisième République par M. de Roux . . . suivi de la Correspondance secrète de Gambetta et de Bismarck, traduite . . . par Jacques Bainville* (Aux Bureaux de la 'Gazette de France' 1905)

Baldick, Robert (tr. and ed.) *Pages from the Goncourt Journal* (Oxford University Press 1962)

Banville, Théodore de, *Critiques* (Bibliothèque-Charpentier. Fasquelle 1917)

    La Lanterne Magique. Camées Parisiens. La Comédie-Française (Charpentier 1883)

    Odes Funambulesques (Poulet-Malassis et De Broise 1857)

Barbey D'Aurevilly, Jules, *Dernière Série. Théâtre Contemporain, 1881–1883* (P.-V. Stock 1896)

Barrière, Théodore, and Thiboust, Lambert, *Les Filles de Marbre* (Michel Lévy 1853)

Bellanger, Marguerite, *Confessions. Mémoires Anecdotiques* (Librairie Populaire 1882)

Bergerat, Émile, *Souvenirs d'un Enfant de Paris. II. La Phase critique de la Critique, 1872–1880* (Charpentier 1912)

Selected Bibliography

Billy, André, *La Présidente et ses Amis* (Flammarion 1945)

Bingham, D., *Recollections of Paris* (Chapman & Hall 1896)

Boulenger, Marcel, *La Païva* (La Galerie des Grandes Courtisanes. Editions M.-P. Trémois 1930)

Byam, Edward Colby, *Théodore Barrière, Dramatist of the Second Empire* (Baltimore, Maryland. The Johns Hopkins Press 1938)

Chabrillan, Céleste de, *Les Voleurs d'Or* (Michel Lévy 1857)

Christophe, Robert, *La Vie Tragique du Maréchal Bazaine* (Études et Documents d'Histoire Contemporaine. Editions Jacques Vautrain 1947)

Claretie, Jules, *La Vie à Paris, 1906* (Charpentier 1907)
  La Vie à Paris, 1907 (Charpentier 1908)
  La Vie à Paris, 1908 (Charpentier 1909)
  Paris Assiégé. Tableaux et Souvenirs. Septembre 1870–Janvier 1871 (Lemerre 1871)
  Profils de Théâtre (Gaultier-Magnier 1902)
  Souvenirs du Dîner Bixio (Charpentier 1924)

Claudin, Gustave, *Mes Souvenirs. Les Boulevards de 1840–1870* (Calmann-Lévy 1884)

Colombier, Marie, *Mémoires. Fin d'Empire. Préface par Armand Silvestre* (Flammarion 1898)

Cresson, E., *Cent Jours du Siège à la Préfecture de Police. 2 novembre 1870–11 février 1871* (Plon-Nourrit 1901)

Crouch, E. E., *Mémoires de Cora Pearl* (Jules Lévy 1886)

Dansette, Adrien, *Les Amours de Napoléon III* (Arthème Fayard 1938)

Daudet, Alphonse, *La Doulou. La Vie. Extraits des carnets intimes de l'auteur* (Fasquelle 1931)

Daudet, Ernest, *Les Coulisses de la Société Parisienne. 2e série. 4e édition* (Ollendorff 1895)

Delacroix, Eugène, *Journal 1823–1863* (Plon, Nourrit 1893–5)

Delvau, Alfred, *Les Lions du Jour. Physionomies Parisiennes* (Dentu 1867)

Diguet, Charles, *Les Jolies Femmes de Paris* (Librairie Internationale 1870)

Dolph, Charles A., *The Real Lady of the Camellias, and Other Women of Quality* (Werner Laurie 1927)

Du Camp, Maxime, *Paris. Ses Organes, ses Fonctions et sa Vie dans la seconde moitié du XIXe siècle* (Hachette 1869–76)
  Souvenirs d'un demi-siècle (Hachette 1949)

Dumas, Alexandre (*fils*), *La Dame aux camélias. Préface par M. Jules Janin. 4e édition* (Michel Lévy 1852)
  La Dame aux camélias. Préface de Jules Janin. Édition illustrée par Gavarni (Librairie Moderne. Gustave Havard 1858)
  Théâtre Complet. Tome V (Calmann-Lévy 1877)

Feydeau, Ernest, *Sylvie* (Dentu 1861)
  Théophile Gautier. Souvenirs Intimes (Plon 1874)

Field, William Osgood, *Uncensored Recollections* (Eveleigh Nash & Grayson 1924)
  More Uncensored Recollections (Eveleigh Nash & Grayson 1926)
  Things I Shouldn't Tell (Eveleigh Nash & Grayson 1924)

Fleischmann, Hector, *Napoléon III et les Femmes* (Bibliothèque des Curieux 1913)

Forster, John, *The Life of Charles Dickens* (Chapman & Hall 1911)

Foucher, Paul, *Entre Cour et Jardin. Études et Souvenirs du Théâtre* (Amyot 1867)

Gautier, Judith, *Le Collier des Jours. Le Second Rang du Collier. Souvenirs Littéraires* (Félix Juven 1909)

Gautier, Théophile, *Émaux et Camées. Introduction de Jean Pommier, Notes et Lexique de Georges Matoré* (Genève. Droz. 1947)

   Œuvres érotiques. Poésies libertines. Lettres à la Présidente (Arcanes 1953)

   Souvenirs de Théâtre (Charpentier 1883)

Girardin, Mme Émile de, *Le Vicomte de Launay. Lettres Parisiennes* (Michel Lévy 1857)

Goncourt, Edmond and Jules de, *Journal. Mémoires de la Vie Littéraire.* (Les Éditions de l'Imprimerie nationale de Monaco. 1956—)

Gros, Johannes, *Alexandre Dumas et Marie Duplessis. Documents inédits* (Conard 1923)

Gsell, Paul (rédacteur), *Mémoires de Madame Judith de la Comédie-Française et Souvenirs sur ses Contemporains* (Tallandier 1911)

Haldane, Charlotte, *Daughter of Paris. The Life Story of Céleste Mogador, Comtesse Lionel de Moreton de Chabrillan* (Hutchinson 1961)

Halévy, Ludovic, *Carnets* (Calmann-Lévy 1935)

Hegermann-Lindencrone, L. de, *In the Courts of Memory, 1858–1875* (Harper & Bros 1912)

Henriot, Émile, *D'Héloïse à Marie Bashkirtseff. Portraits de Femmes* (Plon 1935)

Holden, W. H., *The Pearl from Plymouth. Eliza Emma Crouch alias Cora Pearl. With notes on some of her celebrated contemporaries* (British Technical & General Press 1950)

Houssaye, Arsène, *Les Confessions. Souvenirs d'un demi-siècle, 1830–1890* (Dentu 1885–91)

   Souvenirs de Jeunesse, 1830–1850, 1850–1870 (Flammarion 1896)

Koning, Victor, *Les Coulisses parisiennes. Préface par M. Albéric Second* (Dentu 1864)

Kracauer, S., *Jacques Offenbach ou le secret du Second Empire* (Bernard Grasset 1937)

Kurtz, Harold, *The Empress Eugénie, 1826–1920* (Hamish Hamilton 1964)

Lano, Pierre de, *L'Amour à Paris sous le Second Empire* (H. Simonis Empis 1896)

Leblanc, Léonide, *Les Petites Comédies de l'Amour* (Librairie Centrale 1865)

Lemonnier, Alphonse, *Les Femmes de Théâtre. Avec une préface et un autographe de Mlle Léonide Leblanc* (Achille Faure 1865)

Loliée, Frédéric, *La Païva* (Tallandier 1920)

   Les Femmes du Second Empire. La Fête Impériale (Félix Juven 1907)

Lonergan, W. F., *Forty Years of Paris* (T. Fisher Unwin 1907)

Loviot, Louis, *Alice Ozy* (Les Bibliophiles fantaisistes 1910)

Lucien-Graux, Dr, *Les Factures de la Dame aux camélias* (Pour les Amis du Docteur Lucien-Graux 1934)

Lyonnet, Henri, *Dictionnaire des Comédiens Français (ceux d'hier)* (Jorel 1908–12)

Mardoche, Jacques, et Desgenais, Pierre, *Les Parisiennes* (Dentu 1882)

Meilhac, Henri, and Halévy, Ludovic, *La Vie parisienne* (Michel Lévy 1867)

Mirecourt, Eugène de, *Lola Montès* (Librairie des Contemporains 1870)

Mogador, Céleste, *Mémoires* (Librairie Nouvelle 1858–9)

Mortier, Arnold, *Les Soirées Parisiennes de 1877. Par un Monsieur de l'Orchestre* (Dentu 1878)

   Les Soirées Parisiennes de 1878. Par un Monsieur de l'Orchestre (Dentu 1879)

Moser, Françoise, *Vie et Aventures de Céleste Mogador. Fille publique, Femme de lettres et Comtesse (1824–1909)* (Albin-Michel 1935)

Ollivier, Daniel (ed.), *Correspondance de Liszt et de la Comtesse d'Agoult, 1840–1864* (Bernard Grasset 1934)

Pearl, Cora, *Mémoires* (Jules Lévy 1886)

Reclus, Maurice, *Émile de Girardin. Le Créateur de la Presse moderne* (Hachette 1934)

Richardson, Joanna, *Rachel* (Reinhardt 1956)
   Théophile Gautier. His Life and Times (Reinhardt 1958)
   Sarah Bernhardt (Reinhardt 1959)

Rochefort, Henri, *Les Aventures de ma Vie* (Dupont 1896–7)

Roqueplan, Nestor, *Parisine* (Hetzel 1868)

Rouff, Marcel, et Casevitz, Thérèse, *La Vie de Fête sous le Second Empire. Hortense Schneider* (Jules Tallandier 1931)

Roux, Marquis de, *Origines et fondation de la Troisième République* (Grasset 1933)

Sarcey, F., *Comédiens et Comédiennes. Théâtres divers* (Librairie des Bibliophiles 1884)

Saunders, Edith, *The Prodigal Father. Dumas Père and Fils and 'The Lady of the Camellias'* (Longmans 1951)

Séché, Léon (directeur), *Les Annales Romantiques.* Tome X (Bureau des Annales Romantiques 1913)

Starkie, Enid (ed.), *Les Fleurs du mal. Charles Baudelaire* (Oxford. Blackwell 1943)
   Baudelaire (Faber 1957)

Talmeyr, Maurice, *Souvenirs d'avant le Déluge, 1870–1914* (Perrin 1927)

Vandam, Albert, *An Englishman in Paris (Notes and Recollections)* (Chapman & Hall 1892)
   Men and Manners of the Third Republic (Chapman & Hall 1904)
   Undercurrents of the Second Empire. Notes and Recollections (Heinemann 1897)

Vaudoyer, J.-L., *Alice Ozy ou l'Aspasie moderne* (La Galerie des Grandes Courtisanes. Editions M.-P. Trémois 1930)

Vauzat, Guy, *Blanche d'Antigny. Actrice et demi-mondaine (1840–1874)* (Charles Bosse 1933)

Viel-Castel, Comte Horace de, *Mémoires sur le Règne de Napoléon III (1851–1864). Avec un préface par L. Léouzon Le Duc* (no publisher given 1883–4)

Vienne, Romain, *La Vérité sur la Dame aux camélias (Marie Duplessis)* (Ollendorff 1888)

Villemessant, H. de, *Mémoires d'un Journaliste.* 1re série. *Souvenirs de Jeunesse* (Dentu 1872). 3e série. *A travers le Figaro* (Dentu 1873)

Von Hutten, Bettina, *The Courtesan. The Life of Cora Pearl* (Peter Davies 1933)

Whitehurst, Felix M., *My Private Diary during the Siege of Paris* (Tinsley 1875)

Wolff, Albert, *Mémoires d'un Parisien. La Gloriole* (Victor-Havard 1888)

Worth, Jean-Philippe, *A Century of Fashion.* Translated by Ruth Scott Miller (Boston. Little, Brown 1928)

Zed, *La Société Parisienne* (Librairie Illustrée 1888)
   Le Demi-Monde sous le Second Empire. Souvenirs d'un Sybarite (Ernest Kolb 1892)
   Parisiens et Parisiennes en Déshabillé (Ernest Kolb 1889)

ARTICLES

Celarié, Henriette, *Alice Ozy. Dame de Beauté. Dame galante* (Les Œuvres Libres. Arthème Fayard. Juin 1953)
   Marguerite Bellanger (Les Œuvres Libres. Mai 1955)

Marter, Marcel, *Aurélien Scholl et son Temps* (Les Œuvres Libres. Arthème Fayard. Juillet 1936)

PERIODICALS CONSULTED

L'Artiste. Revue de Paris
The Athenaeum
Les Femmes du Jour
Gazette anecdotique
The Illustrated London News
La Petite Revue
Petit Journal pour Rire
Le Pilori
La Vie parisienne

Index

Index